Understanding Genesis

Understanding Genesis

NAHUM M. SARNA

SCHOCKEN BOOKS • NEW YORK

Understanding Genesis is Volume I of
The Melton Research Center series
The Heritage of Biblical Israel

First SCHOCKEN PAPERBACK edition 1970

10 9 8 7   81 82 83 84

Library of Congress
Catalog Card No. 66-23626

Manufactured in
the United States of America
ISBN 0-8052-0253-6

TO MY WIFE
MY FATHER
AND THE MEMORY OF MY MOTHER ז״ל

מצא אשה מצא טוב . . .
. . . ותפארת בנים אבותם
(משלי יח:כב;יז:ו)

Acknowledgments

I wish to take the opportunity to express my gratitude to Doctor Seymour Fox, Dean of the Teachers Institute-Seminary College of the Jewish Theological Seminary of America, to whom I owe the idea and inspiration for this book. Without his constant encouragement, gentle prodding and helpful criticism, it would never have seen the light of day. At the same time, I wish to acknowledge the vision and generosity of Mr. and Mrs. Samuel Mendel Melton, whose devotion to Jewish education created the Melton Research Center which originally sponsored this publication. I am also happy to record my indebtedness to Professor Simon Greenberg, who was kind enough to read through the manuscript and to make many valuable suggestions, and to Professor Joseph J. Schwab, whose guidance and advice saved me from numerous pitfalls. To Professor H. L. Ginsberg I stand greatly and gratefully beholden for the benefit of his penetrating observations and encyclopedic scholarship so freely dispensed at all times. Mr. Louis Newman and Doctor Azriel

Eisenberg are due a special note of thanks for many critical remarks and sage counsel.

I am greatly obliged to Mrs. Geraldine Rosenfield and to Miss Florence Pressman who contributed valuable editorial and technical assistance, and I wish to record my thanks to Miss Judith B. Ginsberg for compiling the bibliography and the indexes. The library staffs of the Jewish Theological Seminary and Union Theological Seminary, both of New York City, gave me unstinting and courteous service at all times. My sons David and Jonathan were of great help to me in numerous ways.

Of course, I take full and final responsibility for the contents of this book, and none of these worthy persons should be held accountable for any flaws, errors, opinions or interpretations to be found therein.

In quoting the Pentateuch, I am grateful to the Jewish Publication Society of America for the privilege of using their new translation. For citations from the Revised Standard Version, I am likewise indebted to the National Council of Churches in the U.S.A. To Princeton University Press, I am greatly beholden for kind permission to reproduce extracts from their *Ancient Near Eastern Texts Relating to the Old Testament*, ed. J. Pritchard, 2nd. ed. 1955. The publishers of *Midstream* kindly allowed me to reprint portions of my article that appeared in the 1961 Summer issue of that journal.

Finally, and foremost, I wish to record my deep gratitude to my wife for her unfailing encouragement, untiring helpfulness and infinite patience, beyond all praise.

NAHUM M. SARNA
Brandeis University

Contents

Foreword

This is the first volume to be published as a result of the activities for the past six years of the Melton Research Center of The Jewish Theological Seminary of America.

The Center, first of its kind in Jewish history, was made possible by the far-visioned generosity of Mr. and Mrs. Samuel M. Melton of Columbus, Ohio and the warm encouragement of Dr. Louis Finkelstein, Chancellor of the Seminary and the spiritual and intellectual leader of all its manifold activities. The Center has as its goal a thorough and creative examination of the curriculum of the Jewish religious schools of this country, with the hope of producing the kind of materials which will help teachers present the total Jewish spiritual heritage to their pupils so as to reveal effectively its urgent relevance to them as human beings, as Jews and as citizens of a democratic society.

While the Center's range of interest included all aspects of the Jewish religious educational process, its chief center of concern during these first years was the teaching of the Bible. The Bible is the core, the very heart and soul of the total Jewish spiritual heritage. It is, at the same time, the fountainhead of Christianity, the dominant religion of American civilization, and as such the chief source of the morals and ethics of the overwhelming majority of Americans. In his book Dr. Sarna has specified the historical, philosophical and sociological message which Genesis offers to modern man. It is a message which carries equal significance for Protestant, Catholic and Jew, and offers new insights about the way in which the religious precepts of the Bible may be taught to the young.

Precisely because the Bible has occupied so central a place in Jewish thought and life, it is the most difficult text to teach our children. Time and usage have bestowed upon many of the past generations' interpretations of the Bible a sanctity almost equal to that attached to the text itself. Moreover, the identification of the Book of Genesis in particular with stories told to six and seven year old children in both Christian and Jewish religious schools has left the widespread impression that this book was written primarily for the entertainment of youngsters. Since very few students continue their religious studies long enough to be exposed to a more mature understanding of what Genesis is seeking to tell us, it remains in their minds, even after they grow up, as a collection of mildly interesting fairy tales.

The Melton Research Center therefore set as its first task that of presenting the Book of Genesis on every level of instruction, not as a book of children's stories, but as a volume dealing with the ultimate, the profounder problems facing man—the problems of the nature of the universe, the nature of man, the presence of evil in the world, the nature of the good life and the role of the Jewish people in the salvation of mankind.

Since the Melton Research Center assumes that traditional Judaism has naught to fear from the strictures of philosophy and science and the discoveries of archeology, and since it assumes that the overwhelming majority of American Jews are or will be exposed to all of them, it seeks to present the Bible not only in terms of its past great interpreters, but also in terms of the authentic knowledge available to us but not to earlier generations.

This volume, written by a scholar deeply rooted in and personally loyal to traditional Judaism, and at home in all phases of modern biblical studies, is meant primarily for the teacher. In addition, detailed teaching units have been prepared by expert teachers who have been using this material these past three or four years, exploring the most effective methods of utilizing the scholarly information in this volume as an aid to enhancing the message of the Bible for the highly sophisticated youngsters of our generation. These teaching units are also available to the public.

Though this book was written primarily with the traditional Jewish religious school in mind, we believe that it can have great meaning for adults who want to understand what it is that the Book of Genesis seeks to tell us. This volume is not presented as having exhausted our understanding of Genesis. Far, far from it. It has only dipped into the boundless world of meaning which inheres in Genesis, and brought back a modest but precious cargo. Other excursions into that world will, we hope, be made by the Melton Research Center and others, for the treasures to be discovered and presented are inexhaustible. Man has urgent need of them today and will have need of them as far into the future as we can envisage.

SIMON GREENBERG
Vice-Chancellor
The Jewish Theological Seminary of America

Introduction

It is perfectly obvious that the twenty-four (or thirty-six) books that make up the Hebrew Bible cannot possibly represent the total literary productions of ancient Israel. The Scriptures, themselves, bear repeated testimony to the existence of an extensive literature, now lost. The Pentateuch refers to what must undoubtedly have been a well-known "Book of the Wars of the Lord," and both Joshua and Samuel cite the mysterious "Book of Jashar" as an easily accessible source. The writers of Kings and Chronicles constantly direct their readers' attention to external authorities that clearly had achieved a goodly measure of popular renown. All in all, over twenty works no longer extant are mentioned by name in the Hebrew Bible; who knows how many others failed to attract the interest of the biblical authors? In fact, the very concept of a Canon of Scripture, of a fixed corpus of sacred books, implies a long process of selection and rejection from among a host of candidates.

The quantitative disproportion between the literary productions and the literary remains of biblical Israel can be readily explained, and partakes of the common experience of the ancient world. The struggle for survival was always severe by the nature of things. In a predominantly illiterate society the circulation of the written word would of necessity have been strictly limited. Neither the demand for, nor the means of, commercial mass distribution existed. The very process of book production would tend to diminish life expectancy. The labor of hand copying on the part of the scribal specialist restricted the availability of the finished product and hence reduced its chances of attaining repute. More often than not, the writing materials used were highly perishable so that only for extraordinary reasons would a work be copied from generation to generation to defeat thereby the natural ravages of time.

As serious as were these problems generally throughout the ancient world, the prospects for survival in Israel were infinitely more uncertain than elsewhere. The strategically exposed nature of the land as a bridge between continents and as an arena of unceasing contention between the great powers, meant that it would be more frequently plundered and more thoroughly devastated than any other in the Near East. The meagre material and monumental remains of ancient Israel bear eloquent, if gloomy, testimony to this truth.

This situation is well illustrated through the writings of two early Jewish literati. The author of II Maccabees tells of the efforts of the victorious Judah to gather together the books that had been lost by reason of the recent wars, while the pseudepigraphical IV Esdras, in a passage written not long after the destruction of the Second Temple, laments the burning of the Law and the consequent widespread ignorance of God's will. No wonder then, that the volume of epigraphic finds in Palestine has been so slender. Inscriptions and books were simply destroyed in the wake of man's inhumanity to man.

Another factor, scarcely less destructive in its consequences, was the climate. The land of Israel was not blessed with the type of rich alluvial soil characteristic of Mesopotamia which yielded an inexhaustible supply of cheap, durable writing material in the form of baked clay. The Israelite scribe had to make use of far more expensive and highly perishable papyrus and animal skins. Unfortunately, the climatic conditions of Palestine, unlike those obtaining in Egypt, are thoroughly inhospitable to the preservation of such materials.

One final point in this connection. Until the Hellenization of the East, it is extremely unlikely that anyone in the ancient world, outside of the congregation of Israel, had the slightest interest in the Jewish people, its history and literature. Since, with very brief exceptions, Israel was neither an imperialist nor a mercantile power, there was little opportunity for the dissemination of its cultural productions beyond its own national frontiers. A copy of the Mesopotamian Gilgamesh epic can turn up at Megiddo in the territory of Israel, but it is unlikely in the extreme that any specimens of Israelite literature from biblical times will be unearthed in Egypt, Syria or Mesopotamia.

The wonder is that so much did, in fact, survive in defiance of such a combination of deleterious conditions; and no less remarkable is the fact that this relatively tiny collection of Israel's literature, known as the Hebrew Bible, ultimately succeeded in capturing the hearts, minds and loyalties of so many diverse peoples, totally removed racially, geographically and culturally, from its Israelite source. It is nothing short of miraculous that this literature, the product of a small people in a tiny segment of the ancient world that knew independence for but brief interludes, that possessed no political power and that generally encountered nothing but animosity, should not only have survived, but should have conquered, too.

There is one simple explanation. The books of the Hebrew Bible survived because men firmly and fervently believed them to be the inspired word of God, sacred literature. We can no longer know the criteria of selectivity adopted by those who fixed the Canon of Jewish Scriptures. Certainly, there must have been other books regarded by the people as being holy at one time or another, but why they did not enter the final Canon cannot be determined. Yet it is beyond doubt that it was not the stamp of canonization that affirmed the holiness of a book; rather the reverse. Sanctity antedated and preconditioned the final act of canonization. The latter was in most cases a formality that accorded finality to a situation long existing. Of course, the act of canonization in turn served to reinforce, intensify and perpetuate the attitude of reverence, veneration and piety with which men approached the Scriptures, and itself became the source of authority that generated their unquestioning acceptance as the divine word. Ultimately, it was this conviction that preserved the Bible and gave it irresistible power.

It is an undeniable fact that this attitude has undergone a revolutionary change in modern times. Ever since the break-up of the Middle Ages the impact of the Bible upon the lives of ordinary men and women has grown progressively weaker. In the long history of the Western world, to no other generation has the Bible been known so little and regarded as so spiritually obsolete as it is today. The "famine . . . of hearing the words of the Lord," has indeed materialized, but in the spiritual malaise and moral chaos that characterize the twentieth-century men do not look to what used to be known as "the Holy Scriptures" for light and guidance.

To be sure, any work of hoary antiquity is bound to prove difficult reading. Problems of text and language are unavoidable. The modes of literary expression will be strange to our ears. The categories of thought will undoubtedly differ from those of modern man. The socio-cultural milieu presupposed by narrative and law must be utterly alien to our fast-moving, complex, technological, megalopolitan society in the nuclear age. The historical allusions to events of local, national and international importance that lie behind the text require scholarly commentary to be made intelligible. Even to the religiously oriented, some of the religious concepts and values will hardly be palatable today.

This situation, however, is only part of the story. Strictly speaking, it is not wholly a product of modern times, for it existed as soon as the ancient Near Eastern world succumbed to the flood-tides of Hellenism. The old culture from which the Hebrew Bible had issued disintegrated and became radically transformed. Tradition had been breached and the Scriptures of the Jews could no longer be easily read; they could only be studied. Astonishingly, however, the discontinuity of tradition in no wise led to irrelevance and dissociation, for the sacredness of the Bible remained beyond challenge. On the contrary, the old text was recharged with new significance, and fresh meaning was constantly being extracted from it, or poured into it, in perennial renewal of its vitality, vigor, durability and sanctity. For nearly two millennia men found solace, guidance and inspiration in its words, and confidence and hope in its message. If the situation has changed today it is not solely due to the difficulties inherent in the understanding of the text. As a matter of fact, the modern student of the Bible has at his disposal a formidable array of primary and secondary tools, the fruits of a century of intensive scholarly endeavor. Excellent new translations into modern English, a deluge of popular works on archaeology, a plethora of encyclopedias, dictionaries, historical atlases, reliable non-technical commentaries of recent vintage, all deprive any literate person of the excuse of ignorance. Only the motivation is lacking; for the crux of the matter is that in the eyes of modern, secularized man, the Bible has very largely lost its sanctity and relevance.

It would not be profitable to trace here in any detail the rather complex pattern of events that has produced this unprecedented situation. It was probably an inevitable outgrowth of various intellectual movements which had long been gathering momentum and which converged in the nineteenth century. Already in 1670, Benedict Spinoza, in his *Theologico-Political Treatise,* had conceived of biblical studies as a science, and had formulated a methodology involving the use of rationalism and historical criticism. For this alone, and for his revolutionary conclusions, he must be regarded as the true founder of the modern scientific approach to the Bible. But he was not the primary inspiration for further studies in this direction. The new cosmology that had been gaining ground for three centuries and the later evolutionary theories were bound to lead to a questioning of the Genesis narrative. Moreover, the scope of the evolutionary thesis was sure to be broadened beyond the realms of geology and biology, so that it is not surprising that attempts were made to explain thereby the religious, cultural and social history of Israel. The revolt against intellectual and ecclesiastical authority that marked the rise of humanism, and the new concept of history that underplayed the supernatural and made the decisions of men predominant, could not but affect the approach to the theocentricity of the biblical narrative. But above all, biblical scholarship was touched decisively by the development and application of critical, historical and analytical methods used in the identification and isolation of literary sources and the determination of their dating. No longer could the Pentateuch be regarded as a unitary work, divinely dictated, word for word, to Moses. It became one of the finalities of scholarship that the narrative portions of the Pentateuch were thoroughly unreliable for any attempted reconstruction of the times about which they purported to relate. The devastating effect of all this upon faith, when faith was exclusively identified with a literalist approach to Scripture, is abundantly obvious. No wonder that the Bible became desanctified in the eyes of so many educated men.

Unfortunately, the response of the fundamentalists to the challenge of scientism served only to exacerbate the situation. They mistakenly regarded all critical biblical studies as a challenge to faith. There remained no room for the play of individual conscience; the validity of genuine intellectual doubt was refused recognition. By insisting dogmatically upon interpretations and doctrines that flagrantly contradicted the facts, the fundamentalist did not realize the self-exposure of an obvious insecurity that was more a reflection upon his own religious position than a judgment upon biblical scholarship. For it declared, in effect, that spiritual relevance can be maintained only at the expense of the intellect and the stifling of conscience.

The deadly effects of this approach can be easily measured by discussing the Bible with university students. It becomes immediately apparent that the literature of ancient Israel is not treated with the same seriousness and respect as that of ancient Greece. The childish image of the Scriptures, imparted at an early age, is well-nigh ineradicable. For this reason, the teaching of the Bible in the religious schools has, more often than not, become a self-defeating exercise in futility. Any intelligent child who studies mathematical logic in school, and most children now do, cannot but note the contrast in intellectual challenge between this and his biblical studies. He must, willy-nilly, conclude that the latter is inferior, an attitude hardly calculated to instil or encourage a feeling for the sanctity and relevance of Scripture. Why the elementary pedagogical absurdity of present-day Bible teaching in the religious schools is not obvious to those in control of curriculum and teacher training, is an utter mystery.

Of course, the fundamentalists frequently take refuge from modern scholarship by appealing to "tradition," by which they mean medieval authority. The illegitimacy of this position as an argument of faith is, however, easily demonstrable. The medieval scholars made the most of all the limited tools at their disposal. But they did not have access, naturally, to the modern sciences of literary and textual criticism and to the disciplines of sociology, anthropology, linguistics and comparative religion. We simply do not know how they would have reacted had all this material been available to them. To assume a blind disregard of evidence on their part is as unwarranted as it is unfair. Be this as it may, it is clear, at any rate, that "pietism," no less than its "scientific" opposition, bears a goodly measure of responsibility for the alienation of modern man from the sacred Scriptures.

This book, the first of a projected series, is designed to make the Bible of Israel intelligible, relevant and, hopefully, inspiring to a sophisticated generation, possessed of intellectual curiosity and ethical sensitivity. It recognizes the fact that the twentieth century has transformed our categories of thought and has provided us with new criteria for critical judgment. It is based on the belief that the study of the Book of Books must constitute a mature intellectual challenge, an exposure to the expanding universe of scientific biblical scholarship. It is predicated upon the profound conviction, born of personal experience, that the findings of modern biblical studies, in all their scholarly ramifications, provide the means to a keener understanding of the Hebrew Scriptures and may prove to be the key to a deeper appreciation of their religious message. Far from presenting a threat to faith, a challenge to the intellect may reinforce faith and purify it.

As a matter of fact, seldom have the times been more propitious for a revival of sympathetic interest and even involvement in the biblical word. The wealth of epigraphic material that has been unearthed in the Near East in recent years has revolutionized the scholarly approach to biblical studies. The Semitic lexicon has been greatly enlarged, completely new features of Hebrew grammar and syntax have been uncovered and, most important of all, biblical literature has been placed in its appropriate cultural setting. The net result has been an elucidation of the written word to an extent never hitherto possible. This, together with the manu-scripts found in the Dead Sea area and at Masada, has led in turn to a more positive re-evaluation of the general integrity and antiquity of our received Hebrew text. Furthermore, some sensational archaeological finds, coupled with new techniques of critical analysis, have abundantly demonstrated that the Pentateuchal narratives cannot be dismissed, as they were not so long ago, as late folkloristic legends, but must be treated with the utmost respect as historical documents.

Understanding Genesis naturally strives, first and foremost, to im-part to the general reader a body of essential knowledge, the distillation and integration of the results of specialized research in many varied dis-ciplines that shed light upon the biblical text. And it seeks to do this as comprehensively, as honestly and as objectively as possible, in non-technical language. If it rejects the literalist approach to Scripture, it is solely because that approach cannot stand the test of critical scholarly examination. Literalism involves a fundamental misconception of the mental processes of biblical man and ignorance of his modes of self-expression. It thus misrepresents the purport of the narrative, obscures the meaningful and enduring in it and destroys its relevancy. At the same time, literalism must of necessity become the victim of hopeless inconsist-ency. By what quirk of faith or logic has the science of astronomy finally merited indifference or even sympathy on the part of our fundamentalists, whereas the biological, geological and anthropological sciences still encounter hostility? A century after Darwin, some people still reject his theories as heresy, or else find it necessary to attempt some tortuous "reconciliation" between Scripture and evolution. Yet the heliocentric theories of Copernicus and Galileo effectuate no comparable stimulation of the sympathetic system. Phrases like the "rising" or "setting" of the sun occur scores of times in the Bible and were certainly meant and understood literally, in accordance with the prevailing cosmologies, until but a few hundred years ago. Today, no one would dream of citing these biblical phrases to discredit the science of astronomy. A metaphorical interpretation in these instances no longer causes an excessive secretion of adrenalin.

Another misapprehension, shared alike by the followers of "pietism" and "scientism," was that the recognition of the non-unitary origin of the Pentateuch must be destructive of faith and inimical to religion. But is it not to circumscribe the power of God in a most extraordinary manner to assume that the Divine can only work effectively through the medium of a single document, but not through four? Surely God can as well unfold His revelation in successive stages as in a single moment of time. The so-called "Higher Criticism" of the nineteenth century was guilty of many shortcomings. It exhibited an unmistakable bias against the people of Israel. It contained an enormous amount of unsupported or insufficiently supported conjecture. It made use of a substantial measure of *argumenta e silentio* and of a multitude of conclusions that were suspended only by a casuistic hair. Many of the "scientific" methods it claimed to have employed have not been validated by subsequent research, and the hypercritical process of source fragmentation into which it degenerated became self-defeating. Nevertheless, in its general outlines, the non-unitary origin of the Pentateuch has survived as one of the finalities of biblical scholarship. This is a fact that has to be reckoned with.

But source differentiation, as important as it is, is not the quintessence of wisdom. In fact, it alone is inadequate to the appreciation of the Bible as a religious document. For it cannot be overemphasized that it was only as such that the Bible survived the ravages of time to exert upon so large a segment of humanity, for so long a period, an influence so penetrating, so pervasive and so decisive. No study of biblical literature can possibly claim to do justice to the subject if it fails to take account of the world-view of the biblical writers, or if it ignores their ideas about God and man and pays no regard to their deep sense of human destiny. This imposes, however, both a limitation and an obligation upon the biblical scholar. He has to recognize the presence of a dimension not accessible to the ordinary norms of investigation. Truth is not exclusively coincident with scientific truth. After all the massive and imposing achievements of scientism have had their say, there must yet remain that elusive, indefinable, essence which lies beyond the scope and ken of the scientific method, and which is meaningful only to the ear that is receptive and attuned. Spiritual insight and sensitivity are as indispensable a scholarly ingredient as a faultless methodology. It is not unreasonable to demand, surely, that an awareness of the existential human predicament be an essential prerequisite for the understanding of the biblical message that addresses itself precisely to this predicament. Such a demand is no less scientific than to expect a musical critic not to be tone-deaf, even though he may be possessed of a prodigious and expert knowledge of the mechanics of production and conversion of sound waves, the theory and techniques of composition, the history of music and the biographies of the great composers.

In its enthusiasm for documentary analysis the critical school failed to take account of the fact that things in combination possess properties and produce qualities neither carried by, nor inherent in, any of the components in isolation. For this reason, the disentanglement of literary strands does not constitute the apotheosis of scholarship. This is not to decry the importance of source-criticism. On the contrary, only by isolation of the components can the new qualities and properties resulting from combination and harmonization be appreciated. But the inspired genius at work behind the interweaving of the originally disparate elements is ultimately of greater significance. This is a fact that often escapes recognition by both fundamentalist and "scientist" and constitutes a serious deficiency in their understanding of the Bible.

Mention has already been made of new developments in biblical research that have invalidated many of the postulates of nineteenth century criticism. One of the latter's basic flaws was its failure to distinguish between the date of the final editing of a work and the age of the material contained therein. This distinction is of vital importance, for the picture of the reconstructed history of the religion of Israel was based upon the dates assigned to the editing of the Pentateuchal documents. Archaeological finds have since necessitated a thorough-going but conservative revision of the dating of the sources and their chronological order. Much of the material is now recognized as being of very great antiquity. This discovery, however, has itself engendered fresh problems, for we now know that ancient Near Eastern civilization constituted, more or less, a cultural continuum with considerable cross-fertilization and interpenetration taking place over a wide area which included Palestine, Syria, the coast of Asia Minor, Cyprus, Crete and the Aegean, as well as Egypt and Mesopotamia. Innumerable parallels between the Scriptures and these several cultures are now well documented and have generated a vast secondary literature. While the frontiers of time have been pushed considerably backward for scriptural literature, cultural boundaries have simultaneously become far less distinct than they used to be. The lines of demarcation between Israel and her neighbors no longer seem to be as sharply drawn, and the comparative religionists have arrived at far-reaching conclusions casting doubt on the originality of Israel's heritage.

In actual fact, no advanced cultural or religious tradition has ever existed in a vacuum; it cannot therefore be studied in isolation. This is all the more true of the people of Israel, who strode upon the stage of history at a time when the great civilizations of antiquity had already passed their prime. By the testimony of its own traditions, this people came into contact with many cultures. The ancestors of Israel originated in Mesopotamia, wandered through Syria and Canaan, and settled for a prolonged stay in Egypt. In the course of their peregrinations they exchanged their Aramaic speech for the language of Canaan and enlarged their cultural estate. The Bible does not hesitate to record the mixed ethnic origins of Israel. "Abram the Hebrew" sends his servant to find a wife for his son among his very own kinsmen back in Aram-Naharaim, and the lady turns out to be an "Aramean." Jacob, the offspring of this union, had two Aramean wives as well as two concubines of unknown affiliations. If Mesopotamian documents are any guide, the latter two women were certainly of a different racial stock. At any rate, these four "foreign" wives mothered, by tradition, the fathers of the future tribes of Israel. Two of these, Ephraim and Manasseh, traced themselves back to the daughter of an Egyptian priest. Even the genealogy of the royal house of David led back to the union of Judah with a Canaanite woman. The prophet Ezekiel, in the Babylonian exile, clearly recognized Israel as the heir to a variety of cultures:

> Thus says the Lord God to Jerusalem: Your origin and your birth are of the land of Canaanites; your father was an Amorite and your mother a Hittite.
>
> (EZEK. 16 : 3; cf. v. 45).

To the testimony of biblical traditions about Israelite origins must be added the fact, already mentioned, that the land of Israel enjoyed a location of unique strategic importance as a corridor connecting Europe, Asia and Africa, as well as a window to the Mediterranean lands. Through it crossed the arteries of international communications, and into it flowed the powerful cultural and religious influences of surrounding civilizations. It is no wonder that the culture of Canaan was essentially a mixed one, for its geographic position perforce imparted to it a richly international character that impeded the maintenance of individuality and the development of cultural and religious independence. In view of all this, the discovery of numerous parallels between Israel and her neighbors should hardly occasion surprise and chagrin.

Understanding Genesis has taken full account of the numerous correspondences between the Hebrew Bible and the literature of Israel's earlier and contemporary civilizations in the Near East. But we have been mindful of the fact that it is not a difficult task to classify indiscriminately parallels between cultures or civilizations. Scholarly integrity demands that the conclusions drawn from the utilization of the comparative method be recognized for what they are—generalizations of limited value. One has to be sure that one is not dealing with mere superficial resemblances or with the independent development of analogical cultural features. Even having established the incontestability of the parallels, the problem of evaluation still exists. There always remains the possibility that we have touched upon purely external characteristics which may play an inconsequential role in one of the cultures compared, but which may occupy a highly significant position in the other. Further, we may have torn a motif right out of its cultural or living context and so have distorted the total picture. In other words, to ignore subtle differences is to present an unbalanced and untrue perspective and to pervert the scientific method.

Accordingly, we have constantly emphasized in this book the importance of difference, and have been at pains to delineate those areas in which Israel parted company with its neighbors. In so doing we hope we have brought out the essential religious concepts that underlie the Genesis narratives and which are characteristic of the Bible as a whole. On the one hand, there can be no doubt whatsoever that the cumulative effect of the parallels is to confirm that Israel shared the common cultural patrimony of the ancient Near Eastern world. On the other hand, it is equally incontrovertible that where indebtedness exists there has been a considerable amount of careful selectivity and adaptation. The old mythological motifs were not slavishly borrowed; there is no question here of uncreative imitation. Sometimes, in fact, these motifs seem to have been deliberately used in order to empty them of their polytheistic content and to fill them with totally new meaning, refined, dynamic and vibrant. At other times, they have been torn out of their life context to become mere literary devices, static and conventionalized.

In either case, it is in this sphere that the uniqueness of biblical literature becomes apparent. The Hebrew cosmology represents a revolutionary break with the contemporary world, a parting of the spiritual ways that involved the undermining of the entire prevailing mythological world-view. These new ideas of Israel transcended, by far, the range of the religious concepts of the ancient world. The presence of this or that biblical motif or institution in non-Israelite cultures in no wise detracts from its importance, originality and relevance. The germ of the monotheistic idea may, indeed, be found outside of Israel; but nowhere has monotheism ever been found historically as an outgrowth or development of polytheism. Nowhere else in the contemporary world did it become the regnant idea, obsessive and historically significant. Israel's monotheism constituted a new creation, a revolution in religion, a sudden transformation. The same observation applies to the phenomenon of apostolic prophecy, of the prophet on a mission, now known to have existed in the ancient town of Mari. Did the latter play any role in the reshaping of society? Did this episode, like Israelite prophecy, leave an indelible mark on human thinking, behavior and institutions? To raise these questions is to point up the extent to which the Near Eastern parallels project Israel's originality in ever sharper focus.

Moreover, in dealing with the problem of parallels there are other remarkable factors to be considered. First among these is the extraordinary consciousness of difference which characterized ancient Israel and which superimposed itself upon the awareness of a common background and the close and uninterrupted relationships with the other peoples of the Fertile Crescent. Israel saw its development and fate as unique. It felt itself to be

> "distinguished . . . from every
> people on the face of the earth,"
> (E X O D . 33 : 16)
> "set apart from other peoples,"
> (L E V . 20 : 24; cf. v. 26)

"a people that dwells apart,
not reckoned among the nations,"
(N U M . 23 : 9)

having a peculiar relationship with God, who had reserved for Israel a special role in history. That Israel, alone of the peoples of Near Eastern antiquity, arrived at such a concept is a phenomenon that cannot be ignored in the scientific study of the Bible.

Another factor, no less significant, is the relationship of Israel to its land. In the long history of Palestine never, apart from Israel's exceptional experience, has the fate of the country been tied exclusively, or primarily, to the fortunes of any one people. Topographical considerations proved to be a stumbling block to the achievement of unity. From Dan in the north to Beer-sheba in the south is only about one hundred and sixty miles, while from the Mediterranean coast to Rabboth Ammon in the east is only ninety miles. Yet within this small area can be experienced a most unusual combination of boundaries, a wide diversity of topography and extreme variations in climatic conditions, the like of which would be hard to duplicate in a much vaster area. The sea, the desert, and the snow-capped mountains circumscribe the limits of territorial expansion. In the narrow belt between the sea and the desert, the country is divided into no less than four parallel longitudinal zones, each itself undergoing considerable internal modification. The coastal plain gives way to the central mountain region which, in turn, yields abruptly to the Jordan valley, only to be succeeded by the Transjordan plateau. The extremes of altitude are astonishing. The mountains of Lebanon rise to a height of 8,300 feet above sea level, and the deepest point of the Dead Sea lies about 2,500 feet below the surface of the Mediterranean.

This geographic complexity has its counterpart in the climatic diversity. The intensity and direction of the winds and air movements, the seasonal rainfalls, the deposits of dew, the daily variations in temperatures—all are subject to wide-ranging regional fluctuations. It is as though the accidents of geography, topography and environmental conditions all conspired to produce irresistible centrifugal forces that could not but make for a maximum of ethnic diversity, for the intensification of the rivalry of political and strategic interests, and the interpenetration and interweaving of religions and cultures.

Miraculous it indeed is that in all of history, Israel alone, a foreigner in the land, managed to establish a nation on this soil, to convert it into a "holy land," and inextricably to bind up its own destiny with it forevermore. Israel, alone, was able to withstand and overcome the power-fully erosive and homogenizing forces of contemporary paganism to develop a unique religio-moral civilization of universal and eternal value. This was an accomplishment of stupendous proportions, rendered all the more astonishing because it came about in an area of the world in which the burden of tradition lay very heavily on men and in which other peoples always exhibited an amazing conservatism and an obstinate resistance to change.

Understanding Genesis

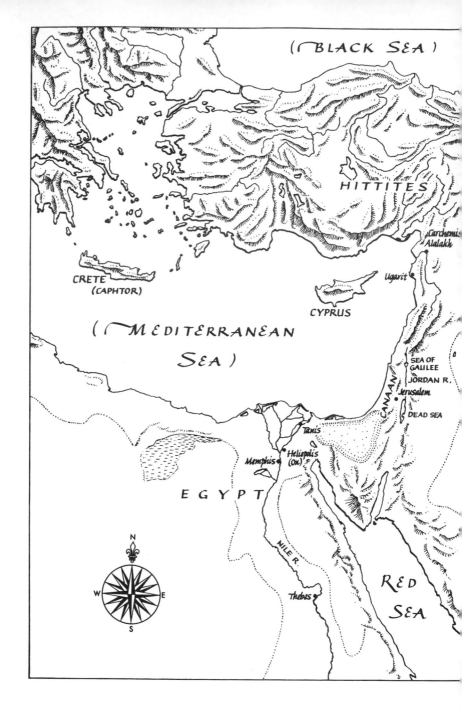

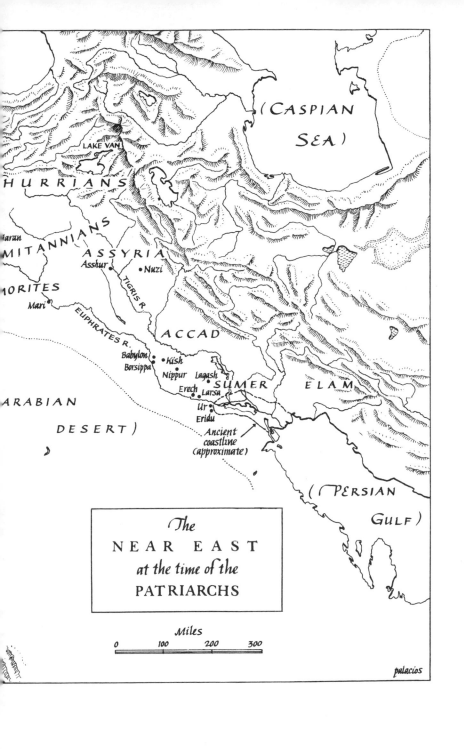

CASPIAN
SEA)

LAKE VAN

HURRIANS

Haran

MITANNIANS

ASSYRIA
Asshur • Nuzi

MORITES

Mari •

EUPHRATES R.

TIGRIS R.

ACCAD

Babylon • • Kish
Borsippa
Nippur • Lagash
Erech • • SUMER   ELAM
• Larsa
Ur •
Eridu •

ARABIAN

DESERT)

Ancient
coastline
(approximate)

(PERSIAN

GULF)

The
NEAR EAST
at the time of the
PATRIARCHS

Miles

0   100   200   300

palacios

CHAPTER I

Creation

GENESIS 1-4

The Bible does not constitute an ideological monolith. This fact is often overlooked. Ancient Israel encountered the world in many different ways and its varying responses to the stimuli of cosmic phenomena gave rise to several cosmologies or descriptions of the manner in which the world and its contents came into being.[1] Not all are equally prominent in biblical literature and some are merely fragmentary. Yet it is clear that the Bible reflects different notions current in Israel, some of which awaken memories of ancient Near Eastern mythologies.

The most famous is to be found in Genesis 1:1–2:4a.[2] It opens with the phrase, "when God began to create the heaven and the earth," and it closes with the formula, "such is the story of heaven and earth as they were created." Within this literary framework are described the divine activities within a seven-day period. The creative process is successively unfolded in the following stages: 1) light, 2) sky, 3) earth, seas and vegetation, 4) luminaries, 5) living creatures in the sea and the sky, 6) animal

1

life on earth and man "created in the image of God." The account
culminates in the Sabbath, or divine cessation from creation which, to
the Torah, is as much a part of the cosmic order as is the foregoing
creativity.

The second biblical account of Creation (2:4b–24) opens with the
formula, "When the Lord God made earth and heaven," and goes on to
tell how the entire surface of the earth was watered by a flow that would
well up from subterranean springs. But the main topic in this account is
the formation of man and his placement in the Garden of Eden. The narrative ends with the creation of woman because of divine recognition of
the human need for companionship.

From many scattered allusions in biblical literature—prophetic, poetic
and wise—it is certain that there were prevalent in Israel other notions
about the events connected with the creation of the world. Among these
is the popular belief that in days of old, prior to the onset of the cosmogonic process, the forces of watery chaos, variously designated Yam (Sea),
Nahar (River), Leviathan (Coiled One), Rahab (Arrogant One) and
Tannin (Dragon), were subdued by God.[3] There does not seem to be any
unanimity in these accounts about the ultimate fate of these creatures.
According to one version, they were utterly destroyed.[4] According to
another, the chaotic forces, personalized as monsters, were put under
restraint.[5] It must be remembered, however, that this combat myth, once
fully developed, appears in a very attenuated and fragmentary form in
the biblical sources and the several allusions have to be pieced together
into some kind of coherent unity. Nevertheless, there is ample witness
to the fact that the myths to which these allusions refer found literary
expression in ancient Israel and were sufficiently well known to be used
as reference points in literary compositions.[6]

Not science

It should be obvious that by the nature of things, none of these stories
can possibly be the product of human memory, nor in any modern sense
of the word scientific accounts of the origin and nature of the physical
world.

Biblical man, despite his undoubted intellectual and spiritual endow-
ments, did not base his views of the universe and its laws on the critical
use of empirical data. He had not, as yet, discovered the principles and

methods of disciplined inquiry, critical observation or analytical experimentation. Rather, his thinking was imaginative, and his expressions of thought were concrete, pictorial, emotional, and poetic.[7] Hence, it is a naive and futile exercise to attempt to reconcile the biblical accounts of creation with the findings of modern science. Any correspondence which can be discovered or ingeniously established between the two must surely be nothing more than mere coincidence. Even more serious than the inherent fundamental misconception of the psychology of biblical man is the unwholesome effect upon the understanding of the Bible itself. For the net result is self-defeating. The literalistic approach serves to direct attention to those aspects of the narrative that reflect the time and place of its composition, while it tends to obscure the elements that are meaningful and enduring, thus distorting the biblical message and destroying its relevancy.

The purpose of the narrative

Whether the Hebrew Genesis account was meant to be science or not, it was certainly meant to convey statements of faith. As will be shown, it is part of the biblical polemic against paganism and an introduction to the religious ideas characteristic of the whole of biblical literature. It tells us something about the nature of the one God who is the Creator and supreme sovereign of the world and whose will is absolute. It asserts that God is outside the realm of nature, which is wholly subservient to Him. He has no myth; that is, there are no stories about any events in His life. Magic plays no part in the worship of Him. The story also tells us something of the nature of man, a God-like creature, uniquely endowed with dignity, honor and infinite worth, into whose hands God has entrusted mastery over His creation. Finally, this narrative tells us something about the biblical concept of reality. It proclaims the essential goodness of life and assumes a universal moral order governing human society.

To be sure, these affirmations are not stated in modern philosophical terms. But, as we have already pointed out, the audience of the biblical writers had its own literary idiom. Therefore, to understand them properly we must not confuse the idiom with the idea, the metaphor with the reality behind it. The two have to be disentangled from each other and the idea conveyed must be translated into the idiom of our own day. If this is to be successfully accomplished, the biblical narrative has to be viewed against the background of the world out of which it grew and against which it reacted.[8]

A comparison with Near Eastern cosmogonies shows the degree of indebtedness of the Israelite version to literary precedent, even as Shakespeare was greatly obligated to his predecessors. Yet, at the same time, the materials used have been transformed so as to become the vehicle for the transmission of completely new ideas.

Enuma Elish

One of the most famous myths emanating from the ancient world is the Babylonian epic known by its opening words, *Enuma Elish* ("when on high"). For the purposes of our study this particular cosmology is the most important of all since it has been preserved more or less in its entirety, and because it belongs to the same ancient Near East of which ancient Israel was a part.[9]

The Babylonian creation epic tells how, before the formation of heaven and earth, nothing existed except water. This primal generative element was identified with Apsu, the male personification of the primeval sweet-water ocean, and with his female associate Tiamat, the primordial salt-water ocean, represented as a ferocious monster. From the commingling of the two waters were born the divine offspring. These, in turn, gave birth to a second generation of gods and the process was repeated successively. Then came a time when the young gods, through their unremitting and noisy revelry, disturbed the peace of Tiamat and Apsu. The latter decided to destroy the gods, but the evil design was thwarted by the quick action of the all-wise Ea, the earth-water god.

Tiamat now planned revenge and organized her forces for the attack on the gods. The latter, for their part, requested Marduk to lead them in battle. He acceded provided that he be granted sovereignty over the universe. To this condition the assembly of the gods readily agreed and Marduk, invested with the insignia of royalty, thereupon became their champion and took up the cudgels against Tiamat and her helpers. After a fierce battle in which he defeated the enemy forces and slew Tiamat, Marduk sliced the carcass of the monster in two and created of one half the firmament of heaven and of the other the foundation of the earth.

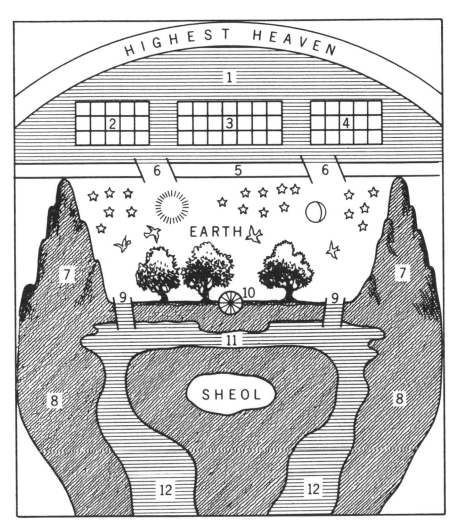

Biblical conception of the world: (1) waters above the firmament;
(2) storehouses of snows; (3) storehouses for hail; (4) chambers of
winds; (5) firmament; (6) sluice; (7) pillars of the sky; (8) pillars of the
earth; (9) fountain of the deep; (10) navel of the earth; (11) waters
under the earth; (12) rivers of the nether world.

The work of creation having thus begun, Marduk then established the heavenly luminaries, each in its place. This activity is described in the fifth tablet of the epic which, unfortunately, is fragmentary. However, from what follows it would appear that the gods complained to Marduk that, each having now been assigned his or her fixed place and function in the cosmos, there would be no relief from unending toil. Accordingly, Marduk decided to create man to free the gods from menial labor and this he proceeded to do, fashioning a human being out of the blood of Kingu, Tiamat's second husband and captain of her army. The gods showed their gratitude to Marduk by building for him a great shrine in the city of Babylon, "the gate of god." The epic ends with a description of a testimonial banquet tendered by the gods at which they recite an adulatory hymn of praise to Marduk that confirms his kingship for all eternity.

The meaning of myth

Before we proceed to analyze this epic, a word must be said explaining the meaning of myth and its function.[10]

The power of self-consciousness, the ability of the human mind both to contemplate itself and to apprehend the world outside itself, is what most distinguishes man from the beast. Since time immemorial man has used his faculty of detached thinking and his propensity to introspection to reflect upon the nature of the world about him, to wonder about the origin of things and to record in literary form his answers—be they mythical or speculative—to the mysteries of existence.

In the popular mind the word myth has come to be identified with fairy tale and associated with the imaginary and the fantastic. But to the Greeks, "mythos" meant originally nothing more than "the thing spoken," that is, a tale. More specifically, it came to be used in describing the deeds of the gods in their relations with one another, their associations with man and their roles in the cosmos. It is in this sense that "myth" is used throughout this book.

Myths, then, in the final analysis, have as their subjects the eternal problems of mankind communicated through the medium of highly imaginative language. A myth may be a vital cultural force. It can be a vehicle for the expression of ideas that activate human behavior, that reflect and validate the distinctive forms and qualities of a civilization, that signify a dynamic attitude to the universe and embody a vision of society.

This functional aspect of myth is well illustrated by its intimate association with ritual. Myth was "not merely a story told, but a reality lived . . . believed to have once happened in primeval times and continuing ever since to influence the world and human destinies."[11] Myth, therefore, in the ancient world was mimetically re-enacted in public festivals to the accompaniment of ritual. The whole complex constituted imitative magic, the effect of which was believed to be beneficial to the entire community. Through ritual drama, the primordial events recorded in the myth were reactivated. The enactment at the appropriate season of the creative deeds of the gods, and the recitation of the proper verbal formulae, it was believed, would effect the periodic renewal and revitalization of nature and so assure the prosperity of the community.

The function of Enuma Elish

The Babylonian epic we have summarized above is but one of many versions of cosmogony current in the ancient Near East. But its importance transcended all others, for it became the great national epic of Babylon. Recorded in seven tablets, it was solemnly recited and dramatically presented in the course of the festivities marking the Spring New Year, the focal point of the Babylonian religious calendar. It was, in effect, the myth that sustained Babylonian civilization, that buttressed its societal norms and its organizational structure.[12]

The epic performed several functions. First, it was theogonic. It described how the generations of the gods, whose names were so familiar to the people of Mesopotamia, came into being. Second, it was cosmological. It provided an explanation of cosmic phenomena and gave answers to human speculations about the origins of things. Both of these themes were naturally appropriate to the New Year festival. Still more important, the conception of the universe in *Enuma Elish* as a kind of cosmic state corresponded to the structural forms of Babylonian society. The position and function of man in the scheme of creation paralleled precisely the status of the slave in Mesopotamia, while the receipt of authority by Marduk and his consolidation of power by the exhibition of overwhelming force were symbolic of the Babylonian conception of the human rulership of the state.

At the same time, the epic served to validate Marduk's assumption of the divine government of the universe by explaining his ascendancy from relative obscurity as the city-god of Babylon to a supreme position in the Babylonian pantheon, "the king of all the gods." As a concomitant to this, it also reflected Babylonian imperialism and gave support to Babylon's claim to political pre-eminence in the ancient world.

Finally, and not least important, was the cultic-functional aspect of the *Enuma Elish*. The conflict between Tiamat and Marduk was expressive of the war between the forces of cosmic order and the forces of chaos. This struggle was believed to be repeated constantly in the annual life-cycle of the earth, particularly since the periodic and catastrophic upheavals of nature in Mesopotamia readily gave credence to such a belief. Hence, the mimetic New Year reenactment of the story was in reality ritual drama. At the critical time of the vernal equinox, when nature seemed to be suspended between inanimation and animation, between inertia and creativity, the ritual recitation served as an analogical repetition of the primordial victory of cosmic order. The participation of society in the struggle between the forces of death and those of revival portended and indeed, to the Babylonian mind actually effected, the renewal of communal life and its reinvigoration.[13]

The function of the Genesis narrative

If we have devoted so much space to a discussion of the role of *Enuma Elish* in Babylonian civilization, it is only because of the importance of the subject for the proper understanding of the biblical Genesis account and the perennial significance of its message.

It must be remembered that the Mesopotamian and Hebrew cosmogonies, each in its own way, express through their symbolism the world-views and values that animated the civilization each represents. The opening chapters of the Bible unveil the main pillars upon which the Israelite outlook rests. The characteristic trends of the religion of Israel assert themselves in Genesis as powerfully as does the rationale of Mesopotamian society and religion in *Enuma Elish*.

However, a vital and fundamental distinction must be made at once between Israel and Mesopotamia. The theme of creation, important as it is in the Bible, is nevertheless only introductory to what is its central motif, namely, the Exodus from Egypt. God's acts in history, rather than His role as Creator, are predominant in biblical thought.

The Bible opens with the account of Creation, not so much because its primary purpose is to describe the process of cosmogony, nor because its chief concern is with the nature of the physical world or the origin and constitution of matter. Genesis is but a prologue to the historical drama that unfolds itself in the ensuing pages of the Bible. It proclaims, loudly and unambiguously, the absolute subordination of all creation to the supreme Creator who thus can make use of the forces of nature to fulfill His mighty deeds in history. It asserts unequivocally that the basic truth of all history is that the world is under the undivided and inescapable sovereignty of God. In brief, unlike *Enuma Elish* in Babylon, the Genesis Creation narrative is primarily the record of the event which inaugurated this historical process, and which ensures that there is a divine purpose behind creation that works itself out on the human scene.

The biblical Creation account is non-political and non-cultic

This playing of the cosmological theme in a relatively minor key in biblical literature points up other basic distinctions between Genesis and *Enuma Elish*. The former has no political role. It contains no allusion to the people of Israel, Jerusalem or the Temple. It does not seek to validate national ideals or institutions. Moreover, it fulfills no cultic function. The inextricable tie between myth and ritual, the mimetic enactment of the cosmogony in the form of ritual drama, which is an essential characteristic of the pagan religions, finds no counterpart in the Israelite cult. In this respect too, the Genesis story represents a complete break with Near Eastern tradition.

The Creation account is non-mythological[14]

The reason for this detachment of cosmogony from the ritual is not hard to find. The supreme characteristic of the Mesopotamian cosmogony is that it is embedded in a mythological matrix. On the other hand, the outstanding peculiarity of the biblical account is the complete absence of mythology in the classical pagan sense of the term. The religion of Israel is essentially non-mythological, there being no suggestion of any theo-biography. The Scriptures themselves do not openly betray a true understanding of mythological paganism. In fact, as a result of their thorough-going monotheism the picture they paint of the religion of the contemporaries of Israel is really a distortion. The Bible shows no consciousness of any connection between the pagan gods and mythological motifs, no realization of the close relationship that existed between mythology and the cult. There is not a single biblical reference to the natural or mythological qualities of the pagan gods. There is not even a biblical term for "goddess." Actually, in its overt polemic with paganism Scripture never combats mythology. It frequently exposes the folly of idolatry, but never gives a hint of the true nature of the cult associated with it. A case in point is the not uncommon reference to the goddess Ishtar under the guise of "Ashtoret." [15] We may search the Bible in vain for any clear statement of her character. Who would know that in the Assyro-Babylonian literature she is the great goddess of love, fertility and productiveness, but also the cruel patroness of war? Who could guess from the scriptural sources that into this divine figure has been blended a rich and complex mythology, varied strains of thought and diverse religious concepts? Pagan representation of the gods by pictures and images, and its use of icons in worship, are conceived by the biblical writers to be nothing more than fetishism. In short, so remote are the biblical writers from the religious atmosphere of the pagan world that they are unable to present a true picture of it.

Nowhere is this non-mythological outlook better illustrated than in the Genesis narrative. The Hebrew account is matchless in its solemn and majestic simplicity. It has no notion of the birth of God and no biography of God. It does not even begin with a statement about the existence of God. Such speculation would have been unthinkable at this time.[16] To the Bible, God's existence is as self-evident as is life itself. The Hebrew concept of God is implicit in the narrative, not formulated abstractly and explicitly. The whole of biblical literature is really the attestation of the experiences of individuals and of a nation with the Divine. Genesis, therefore, begins immediately with an account of the creative activity of the pre-existent God.

Far different is the Mesopotamian account. Theogony is inextricably tied up with cosmogony. The gods themselves had to be created. Even Marduk, the head of the pantheon, is not pre-existent. The first supernal beings are demons and monsters, while the god of creation is only born at a fairly late stage in the theogonic process. Moreover, his creative activity is introduced almost casually and incidentally.

Mythology, magic and God's freedom

This absence or presence of the theogonic motif had profound consequences for the development of the religions of Israel and her Near
Eastern neighbors. The birth of the gods implies the existence of some
primordial, self-contained, realm from which the gods themselves derive.
The cosmos, too, is fashioned from this same element, personified in
Enuma Elish as the carcass of Tiamat. That is to say, both the divine
and the cosmic are animated by a common source. Moreover, the concept of the immanence of the gods in nature was one of the basic convic-
tions of the religions of the pagan world. It meant the existence of divine
powers, operative in nature, upon whom the well-being of man and
society depended. The periodic changes in nature were conceived as
episodes in the lives of the gods. Nature and man belonged to the same
realm. Hence, the goal of man on earth was to integrate himself harmoniously into the cosmic rhythm.[17]

This all-pervasive dependence upon the material explains the prominence in polytheistic religion of the tales of the personal lives of the gods,
their subjection to birth, growth, sex, hunger, disease, impotence,
senescence and even death.[18] Now, if there are many gods and these gods
are dependent upon physical existence, then they can have neither freedom nor omnipotence. Their immanence in nature limits their scope.
Their sovereign powers are circumscribed by the superior forces inherent
in the primordial substance of existence. Since, according to pagan concepts, man's destiny is controlled by two separate forces, the gods and
the powers beyond the gods, it was inevitable that magic became an
integral part of pagan religion. Man had to be able to devise the means
of activating those forces superior even to the gods. Religion, as a consequence, became increasingly concerned with the elaboration of ritual
designed to propitiate the numerous unpredictable powers that be.

Anyone who reads the Hebrew Bible, especially the Book of Psalms,
is aware that the ancient Israelite was as struck by the majesty of natural
phenomena as was any of his pagan neighbors. But unlike them, he did
not profess to see God within those phenomena. The clear line of
demarcation between God and His creation was never violated. Nowhere
is this brought out more forcefully than in the Hebrew Genesis account.
Here we find no physical link between the world of humanity and the
world of the divine. There is no natural connection between the Creator
and his handiwork. Hence, there is no room for magic in the religion of

the Bible. The God of Creation is eternally existent, removed from all corporeality, and independent of time and space. Creation comes about through the simple divine fiat: Let there be!

"Let there be!"

It has been maintained that this notion of the creative power of the word is known to us from elsewhere in the ancient Near East.[19] But the similarity is wholly superficial, for wherever it is found it has a magical content. The pronouncement of the right word, like the performance of the right magical actions, is able to, or rather, inevitably must, actualize the potentialities which are inherent in the inert matter. In other words, it implies a mystic bond uniting matter to its manipulator.

Worlds apart is the Genesis concept of creation by divine fiat. Notice how the Bible passes over in absolute silence the nature of the matter—if any—upon which the divine word acted creatively. Its presence or absence is of no importance, for there is no tie between it and God. "Let there be!" or, as the Psalmist echoed it, "He spoke and it was so," [20] refers not to the utterance of the magic word, but to the expression of the omnipotent, sovereign, unchallengeable will of the absolute, transcendent God to whom all nature is completely subservient. Such a concept of God and of the process of creation added a new dimension to human thought and marked a new stage in the history of religion. It emancipated the mind from the limitations of mythopoeic thinking, and it liberated religion from the baneful influence of magic.

"Male and female He created them"

This notion of creation by the divine will presents us with yet another radical departure from paganism. In polytheistic mythologies creation is always expressed in terms of procreation. Apparently, paganism was unable to conceive of any primal creative force other than in terms of sex. It will be remembered that in *Enuma Elish*, Apsu and Tiamat represent respectively the male and female powers which, through the "commingling of their waters" gave birth to the first generation of gods. The sex element existed before the cosmos came into being and all the gods were themselves creatures of sex.[21] On the other hand, the Creator in

Genesis is uniquely without any female counterpart and the very association of sex with God is utterly alien to the religion of the Bible. When,
in fact, Genesis (1:27; 5:2) informs us that "male and female He created
them," that God Himself created sexual differentiation, it is more than
likely that we are dealing with an intended protest against such pagan
notions.

The same may be said in regard to the place of the element of water in
the Hebrew cosmogony. The latter shares with *Enuma Elish* the idea of
the priority of water in time.[22] Just as Apsu and Tiamat, the two oceans,
exist before all things, so in Genesis the existence of water is taken for
granted. The darkness is over the surface of the deep; the wind,[23] or the
breath of God, sweeps over the waters and the primordial waters are
divided into two. Now this concept of the priority of water is fairly widespread among many unrelated mythologies. It most likely arose from the
fact that, being amorphous, water seems clearly to represent the state of
affairs before chaos was reduced to order and things achieved fixed form.
However, since in lower Mesopotamia the earth actually came into being
through the sinking of the water level and deposits of silt, it is more than
probable that we have in our Genesis account, which gives priority in
time to water and envisages the dry land as emerging from it, Babylonian
coloration. This is particularly so in view of the contrast between the rich
alluvial plains of the Euphrates-Tigris valley and the hilly, rocky soil of
Palestine, dependent for its fertility upon seasonal rainfall.[24]

However, the similarity ends here. For in pagan mythologies water is
the primal generative force—a notion utterly foreign to the Book of Genesis. Here God wills and the waters obey. At His command they divide.

> God said, "Let there be an expanse in the midst of the water,
> that it may separate water from water." . . . And it was so.
>
> (1 : 6–7)

In conformity with His will the waters gather into one area so that the
dry land may appear. If they spawn forth swarms of living creatures, it
is not due to any inherent, independent, generative powers they may
possess, but is solely in response to the divine command. For the first
time in history, therefore, we have a totally new conception of cosmogony
and one, strangely enough, that in its literary form has not hesitated to
make use of some of the symbols of its ideologically incompatible
predecessor. This is a characteristic of the Genesis narrative that we shall
encounter again and again.

Man the pinnacle of creation

Perhaps nowhere is the contrast between the mythological and the Israelite conceptions more striking and more illuminating than in their respective descriptions of the creation of man. Yet at first glance this statement may seem to be quite paradoxical, for the Hebrew story bears close resemblance to a Near Eastern mythic pattern.

In the opening chapter of Genesis we are told simply that God created man "in His image," (1:27) nothing being stated of the matter used in the act of creation. But in the subsequent narrative it is related how God "formed man from dust of the earth." [25] Now if we note that the word here translated "dust" is used quite often in biblical Hebrew as a synonym for clay,[26] we may recognize at once a theme frequently encountered in Scripture.[27] Here, again, we are confronted with a familiar motif, the shaping of man out of clay.[28] In *Enuma Elish* man is created from the blood of the rebellious Kingu.[29] But in the *Epic of Gilgamesh* of which we shall learn more in the next chapter, the goddess Aruru "washed her hands, nipped off clay" and fashioned it into Enkidu.[30] An Old Babylonian myth, paralleled in an Assyrian version, explicitly describes the creation of the first men from clay.[31] That this motif is of very great antiquity may be shown by its presence in a Sumerian composition of the third millennium B.C.E.[32] Conforming to the same conceptual pattern are the Egyptian paintings which depict the god Khnum sitting upon his throne before a potter's wheel busily fashioning men.[33]

Yet this very similarity between the Bible and Near Eastern mythology affords us an excellent example of the superficiality of parallels if a single feature is wrenched from its cultural moorings and treated independently.

The very fact that the creation of man in the Genesis description is an exception to the rule of creation by divine fiat, and that solely in the case of man is the material from which he is made explicitly mentioned, implies emphasis upon a unique position for man among created things and a special relationship to God. This, indeed, is reinforced in many and varied subtle ways. It is as though for the climactic performance the usual act of will was reinforced by an act of divine effort. Man, alone, has the breath of life blown into his nostrils by God Himself. Only by virtue of this direct animation did man become a living being, drawing directly from God his life source. The creation of nothing else in the cosmogonic process is preceded by a divine declaration of intention and purpose, "Let us make man" (Gen. 1:26). Man, in fact, is the pinnacle of creation and the entire story has a human-centered orientation.

This situation contrasts strongly with the story of the creation of man in *Enuma Elish*. There he is almost incidental, fashioned as a kind of afterthought as a menial of the gods to provide them with nourishment and generally to satisfy their physical needs. The Book of Genesis seems to be emphasizing the antithesis of this, for the very first communication of God to man—

> See, I give you every seed-bearing plant that is upon all the
> earth, and every tree that has seed-bearing fruit; they shall be
> yours for food . . .   (1 : 29f.)

> Of every tree of the garden you are free to eat.
>   (2 : 16)

—is an expression of divine concern for man's physical needs and well being.

So much does the Torah wish to signify the special status accorded man in the cosmos and to stress that the relationship between man and God is *sui generis*, that it employs certain unusual literary devices in the story. Three times in the course of a single verse it repeats the verb *bara'*, used in Hebrew exclusively to denote divine creativity. Furthermore, it reiterates the theme of man being actually created in the "image of God" (1:26–27; cf. 5:1; 9:6):

> And God created man in His image, in the image of God He
> created him; male and female He created them.   (1 : 27)

The phrase "in the image of God" is a difficult one and its origin and exact import have not been satisfactorily explained. [34] But it must be connected with the immediately following divine blessing:

> "Be fertile and increase, fill the earth and master it; and rule
> the fish of the sea, and birds of the sky, and all the living
> things that creep on earth."   (1 : 28)

This exclusive distinction endows man with power over the animal and vegetable worlds and confers upon him the right, nay the duty, to exploit the resources of nature for his own benefits. In this setting, the idea of man "in the image of God" must inevitably include within the scope of its meaning all those faculties and gifts of character that distinguish man from the beast and that are needed for the fulfillment of his task on earth, namely, intellect, free will, self-awareness, consciousness of the existence of others, conscience, responsibility and self-control. Moreover, being created "in the image of God" implies that human life is infinitely precious. Such, indeed, is the meaning given to the phrase in Genesis 9:6:

> Whoever sheds the blood of man, by man shall his blood be
> shed; for in the image of God was man created.

The Bible's concept of the divine image in man thus constitutes another revolutionary break with its contemporary world. The pagan bond between man and nature has been severed once and for all. No longer is man a creature of blind forces, helplessly at the mercy of the inexorable rhythms and cycles of nature. On the contrary, he is now a being possessed of dignity, purpose, freedom and tremendous power.

Yet the pre-eminence of man over beast is not the same as total independence. This is where the vivid picture of the clayey origin of man comes into play once again. The figure is suggestive of the activity of a potter molding the malleable raw material into the desired shape. The very verb used in the second account of the creation of man by God— *yaṣar* (2:7, 8)—is the same from which the Hebrew word for "potter" is drawn. Most significantly, the terms for "creator" and "potter" may be expressed in Hebrew by one and the same word *(yoṣer)*. This figure is a well-known biblical symbol evocative of the notion of God's absolute mastery over man,[35] so that through the ingenious employment of a common mythological motif, the Hebrew writer has subtly and effectively succeeded, not just in combatting mythological notions, but also in conveying, all at once, both a sense of man's glory and freedom and the feeling of his inescapable dependence upon God. Human sovereignty can never quite be absolute. It must always be subject to the demands of a higher law,the divinely ordained moral order of the universe.

The nature of God

This emphasis upon the uniqueness of man follows, of course, from the moral nature of God as conceived in the Bible. That God is moral is not accidental, for it is the fundamental difference between polytheism and monotheism. We are not dealing here simply with a matter of arithmetic; the cleavage between the two systems goes much deeper.

We shall soon take fuller note of the phenomenon of conflict inherent in the polytheistic system. Here we are concerned with the fact that the idea of many gods inevitably engendered a multiplicity of ethical values and moral standards. It is perfectly true that there were gods in the polytheistic pantheon who were guardians of justice and who demanded righteous conduct from man. However, their ethical quality was but one of many diverse and contradictory attributes and was neither inherent in the idea of the godhead nor absolute. Anyone who reads the *Enuma Elish* is struck by the moral indifference of the gods, and much the same is true of the Homeric epics. The pagan worshiper had no reason to believe that the decrees of his god must necessarily be just, any more than he could be convinced that society rested upon a universal order of justice. According to the pagan world-view the fate of man was not determined by human behavior. The gods were innately capricious, so that any absolute authority was impossible.[36]

This capriciousness of the gods is diametrically opposed to the biblical view. The God of Creation is not at all morally indifferent. On the contrary, morality and ethics constitute the very essence of His nature.[37] The Bible presumes that God operates by an order which man can comprehend, and that a universal moral law had been decreed for society. Thus, the idea embedded in Genesis of one universal Creator has profound ethical implications. It means that the same universal sovereign will that brought the world into existence continues to exert itself thereafter making absolute, not relative, demands upon man, expressed in categorical imperatives—"thou shalt," "thou shalt not."

It is not to be wondered at that Mesopotamian society suffered from a malaise which scholars have characterized as "overtones of anxiety." The nature of the gods could give no feeling of certainty and security in the cosmos. To make matters worse there were also environmental factors that had to be taken into account. Man always found himself confronted by the tremendous forces of nature, and nature, especially in Mesopotamia, showed itself to be cruel, indiscriminate, unpredictable. Since the gods were immanent in nature, they too shared these same harsh attributes. To aggravate the situation still further, there was always that inscrutable, primordial power beyond the realm of the gods to which man and gods were both subject. Evil, then, was a permanent necessity and there was nothing essentially good in the pagan universe. In such circumstances there could be no correlation between right conduct and individual or national well-being. The universe was purposeless and the deities could offer their votaries no guarantee that life had meaning and direction, no assurance that the end of human strivings was anything but vanity. History and time were but a repeating cycle of events in which man played a passive role, carried along relentlessly by the stream of existence to his ineluctable fate.[38]

Far different is the outlook of Genesis. One of its seemingly naive features is God's pleasure at His own artistry, the repeated declaration, after each completed act of creation, that God saw how good His work was (1:4 etc.). Following the creation of living things, we meet with the climactic observation that God saw all that He had made and found it to be "*very* good" (1:31). But this naiveté of idiom cloaks a profundity of thought that marks off the mood of Hebrew civilization from that of Mesopotamia in a most revolutionary manner. The concept of a single directing Mind behind the cosmic machine, with all its ethico-moral implications, emancipated Israel from thralldom to the vicious cycle of time. In place of a fortuitous concatenation of events, history has become purposeful and society has achieved direction. A strong streak of optimism has displaced the acute awareness of insecurity. The all-pervasive pagan consciousness of human impotence has given way to a profound sense of the significance of man and the powers he can employ. Contemplating the awesome majesty of cosmic phenomena, the Psalmist can yet extol the glory and dignity with which God has adorned man and the authority He has placed in his hands.[39]

This basic belief in the essential goodness of the universe was, of course, destined to exert a powerful influence upon the direction of the religion of Israel and to affect the outlook on life of the people. It found its expression in the concept of the covenant relationship between God and His people and ultimately achieved its most glorious manifestation in the notion of Messianism—two uniquely Israelite contributions to religion. The God of Israel, being a deity whose will is absolute and incontestable and whose word is eternal, was able to give assurances that human strivings were decidedly not in vain. Israelite society did not suffer from "overtones of anxiety."

The sabbath

This unshakable conviction in the essentially benign nature of divine activity, is reflected, too, in the description of the cessation from creativity. We are told God ceased on the seventh day from all the work which He had done. And God blessed the seventh day and declared it holy, because on it God ceased from all the work of creation which He had done. (2 : 2f.)

The institution of the sabbath will be discussed at greater length in a subsequent volume. Here, we can only address ourselves to the questions raised by this passage.

It will doubtless have been noted at once that the statement about God here cited contains no mention of the sabbath as a fixed, weekly institution. It refers only to the seventh day of Creation, to the divine cessation from creation, and to the blessing and sanctification of that day. But the name "sabbath" is not to be found, only the cognate verbal form *shabat*, meaning, "to desist from labor." Yet the connection between the weekly sabbath day and Creation is explicitly made both in the first version of the Ten Commandments:

For in six days the Lord made heaven and earth and sea, and all that is in them and He rested on the seventh day; therefore the Lord blessed the sabbath day and hallowed it. . . .

(EXOD. 20 : 11)

as well as in another passage emphasizing the sabbath as an external sign of the covenant between God and Israel.[40] In other words, while Genesis ignores the weekly sabbath-day, these texts understood this self-same passage as being the source of the institution.[41]

As a matter of fact, there are no biblical sources recounting the founding of the weekly sabbath-day. The antiquity of its existence is presupposed in all the legislation and even in the narratives. Just one month after the departure from Egypt, and before the Sinaitic revelation, the sabbath is assumed to be already established.[42] Moreover, the very formulations of both versions of the Decalogue—"Remember/observe the Sabbath day"—take for granted an existing institution.[43] There cannot be any doubt that the sabbath belongs to the most ancient of Israel's sacred days.[44]

The questions now assert themselves. What is the origin of the sabbath, and why does our Genesis text speak only of the seventh day of Creation, hinting at, without specifically mentioning, the sabbath institution? The answers to these questions involve us, once again, in the world of ancient Near Eastern belief and practice.

From very early times, a seven-day period as the basic unit of time calculation was current among West Semitic peoples.[45] In the Mesopotamian lunar calendar the seventh, fourteenth, twenty-first and twenty-eighth day of certain months, corresponding to the four phases of the moon, were all regarded as unlucky days. The nineteenth day, being the forty-ninth day ($=7 \times 7$) after the new-moon of the previous month, was called a "day of wrath."[46] These days were thought of as being controlled by evil spirits, and special fasts were prescribed. One ritual text forbids the king from eating cooked flesh, from changing his clothes, from offering sacrifice, from riding in a chariot, and from rendering legal decisions on these days. A seer may not give an oracle, nor may a physician attend to the sick. Curses uttered against enemies are ineffective.[47]

From all this one may learn that each seventh day of the lunar month possessed a special, if baneful, character. In addition, we also know that the day of the full-moon was known in Mesopotamia as the *shapattu*, described in the cuneiform texts as the "day of the quieting of the heart (of the god)." The meaning of this phrase has not been fully established, but it seems to indicate a day of good omen when certain rituals were performed, designed to appease the gods.

Many scholars see in the Mesopotamian calendar the origin of the biblical sabbath. They point to the significance attached to every seventh day of certain lunar months and to the similarity between the words *shapattu* and the Hebrew *shabbat*. It has to be remembered, however, that while the philological association is certainly feasible,[48] there is no evidence that the Mesopotamian *shapattu* was a day of cessation from labor. Nor was there any connection between the *shapattu*—the full-moon—and the four seventh days. These four special days are never designated *shapattu*. Moreover, the abstentions prescribed for these days did not apply to the entire population, but only to certain classes of people and there is no proof that any general curtailment of business activities was required. If, indeed, the biblical sabbath does owe anything to ancient Near Eastern culture, it is only to the basic concept of a seven-day unit of time.[49]

It is not at all unlikely, however, that our Genesis narrative telling of God's cessation from creation on the seventh day is, in its literary presentation, a reaction against the contemporary Near Eastern religious calendar. The careful avoidance of the use of the nominal form *shabbat* or of any reference to a fixed institution may well have been designed to exclude the possibility of confusion with the *shapattu* festival, while the use of the verbal form *"shabat"* was intended to hint at the connection with the later Israelite institution. The same tendency to dissociate the biblical sabbath from Near Eastern practice would perhaps be present in the threefold repetition of the phrase "seventh day." This seems to emphasize that the day derives its special character solely from God, and is to be completely divorced from, and independent of, any connection with the phases of the moon. The seventh day is what it is, because God chose to "bless it and declared it holy." Its blessed and sacred character is part of the divinely ordained cosmic order. It cannot, therefore, be abrogated by man, and its sanctity is a reality irrespective of human activity. Being part of the cosmic order, this day must, like all other divinely created things, be essentially good and beneficial to man. Hence, it is a "blessed" day, the very antithesis of the Mesopotamian notion of evil or ill-omened days. Finally, its connection with the drama of Creation makes the day universal in character. It is not to be wondered at that this combination of blessedness and universality soon expressed itself in the religion of Israel in socio-moral terms, so that the privileges of the sabbath rest were extended equally to all members of the family, to the slave and the stranger, to the beast of burden and to the cattle in the field.[50] Whatever its origins, the biblical sabbath was a unique institution, transformed beyond recognition from any Near Eastern antecedents it may have had.[51]

The cosmic battle

We have already stressed the fact that the notion of conflict was inherent in the pagan view of the cosmos. Implicit in the notion of a multiplicity of gods is a plurality of wills which, by human analogy, is bound, in turn, to engender strife. The internecine strife of the gods, the personified forces of nature, is an outstandingly characteristic feature of polytheistic cosmogonies. That is why polytheistic accounts of creation always begin with the predominance of the powers of nature, and invariably describe in detail a titanic struggle between two opposing forces. They inevitably regard the achievement of world order as the outgrowth of an overwhelming exhibition of power on the part of one god who, through a monopoly of violence, manages to impose his will upon all others.[52] This theme of the cosmic battle is the underlying motif of *Enuma Elish*. The existence in Israel of residual fragments of a popular version of this combat myth was pointed out earlier in this chapter.[53] The Book of Genesis itself has no direct reference to the notion of creation in terms of struggle. Indeed, the very idea is utterly alien to the whole atmosphere of the narrative. Yet one has the feeling that the narrator was not unaware of the place of the combat myth in pagan cosmogony, for he emphatically tells us that God created the "great sea monsters" (1:21), that these mythological beings, which elsewhere are counted among those who rebelled against God[54] were not at all pre-existent rivals of the one Supreme Creator, but His own creatures.

There is other evidence to indicate a knowledge of the Babylonian myth. We are told that when God began to create the heaven and the earth, darkness covered the surface of the deep (1:2). This latter word is the usual English translation of the Hebrew original *Tehom*, which is, in fact, the philological equivalent of Tiamat. This is the name, it will be remembered, of the female dragonesque personification of the primordial salt-water ocean in *Enuma Elish*. Note, moreover, that the Hebrew term *Tehom* is never used with the definite article, something which is characteristic of proper names. Although *Tehom* is not feminine by grammatical form, it is frequently employed with a feminine verb or adjective. Finally, several other biblical passages have preserved a reminiscence of the mythical origin of the term in such phrases as "*Tehom* that crouches below"[55] and "*Tehom* cried out" in panic at the angry approach of God.[56]

Another point of contact with the Babylonian myth may be found in the distinction made between the phenomenon of light, that was created on the first day, and the heavenly luminaries that did not come into being until the fourth day (1:14–19). This same situation is presupposed in *Enuma Elish*,[57] for Apsu there tells Tiamat that he finds neither relief by day nor repose by night from the noise of the gods, whereas the luminaries were set in the sky by Marduk only after his great victory over this same Tiamat.[58]

Despite the familiarity of the Hebrew account with some of the motifs of the cosmogonic myths of the ancient Near East, all notion of a connection between creation and cosmic battles was banished from Genesis with extreme care. The idea of strife and tension between God and nature is unthinkable. To emphasize the point, the words "and it was so" are repeated after each divine fiat.

Furthermore, it is highly significant that the biblical fragments of a cosmogonic combat myth have survived solely as picturesque metaphors exclusively in the language of poetry, something which strongly indicates a minimal impact upon the religious consciousness of Israel. Never once are these creatures accorded divine attributes, nor is there anywhere a suggestion that their struggle against God in any way challenged God's sovereign rule in the universe.

But the real qualitative difference between the pagan cosmogonic combat myth and the Israelite fragments is evidenced by the use to which the latter are put in biblical literature. They practically always appear as a literary device expressing the evil deeds and punishment of the human wicked in terms of the mythical conflict of God with the rebellious forces of primeval chaos. The plunderers and despoilers of Israel are compared to the noisy seas and the turbulent, mighty, chaotic waters which flee at the divine rebuke.[59] The sinful ones of the earth, the objects of divine wrath, are designated by the names of the mythological monsters,[60] while the defeat of the creature *Yam* in ancient times is cited as evidence of God's overwhelming power in dealing with the wicked.[61] Similarly, God's decisive overthrow of His mythical primeval enemies is invoked as an assurance of His mighty power for the redemption of Israel through a like victory over the present historical enemies of the nation.[62]

The gross polytheism of the combat myth, in all its implications for religion and society, was excluded from biblical literature. The motif itself underwent radical transformation. In Israelite hands, a backward-looking myth of the dim past re-enacted mimetically in the cult became a symbolic affirmation of the future triumph of divine righteousness in human affairs. Evil in the world is no longer apprehended metaphysically, but belongs on the moral plane. The events of pre-history have become in the Bible the pattern for history. The Lord of creation who wholly controls nature is by virtue of that fact an unfailing source of confidence that His word is eternal and His incursions into history effective; so that His absolute power over the forces of chaos carries with it the assurance of the historical triumph of righteousness over evil.[63]

The Garden of Eden

The biblical conviction of an essential principle of good in the world was diametrically opposed to the contemporary pagan concept of an inherent primordial evil. But so revolutionary a doctrine was not without its difficulties; for evil, after all, was seen to be a reality of life, and the contradiction between conviction and reality was far too serious to be ignored. The story of the Garden of Eden is the answer of Genesis to this problem. It wishes to indicate very simply that evil is a human product, that God created the world good but that man, through the free exercise of his will in rebellion against God, corrupts the good and puts evil in its place.

The allegory of the Garden of Eden which was chosen as the vehicle for these teachings is complicated by its rich symbolism expressed in fragmentary form, and by its being an interweaving of many and varied mythic strands. Several of these are redolent of well-known ancient Near Eastern motifs, while some appear to be distinctly Israelite.

There cannot be any doubt that some popular Hebrew story about a "Garden of God" existed in early times.[64] Frequently in the Bible this phrase is used in a purely metaphorical sense.[65] The prophet Ezekiel twice cites the legend, bringing a wealth of detail not to be found in Genesis and sometimes at variance with it.[66] Furthermore, the Genesis version itself still bears traces of an earlier edition. The language and style contain several classical features of rhythm, phraseology and parallelistic structure characteristic of Hebrew poetry. The use of the definite article with the first mention of "the tree of life," "the tree of knowledge" (2:9), "the cherubim and the fiery ever-turning sword" (3:24), indicates an allusion to something already well-known to the reader.

As a matter of fact, this situation should not really be surprising, since the notions of paradise and a garden of God are familiar themes in the literature of the biblical world. The Sumerians,[67] that highly gifted non-Semitic people of unknown origin who were already well settled in the lower Tigris-Euphrates Valley as early as the fourth millennium B.C.E., have left us the myth of Enki and Ninhursag.[68] This story tells of an idyllic island of Dilmun, a "pure," "clean" and "bright" land in which all nature is at peace and where the beasts of prey and the tame cattle live together in mutual amity. Sickness, old age and, apparently, death also, are unknown. It was to this place that Ziusudra, the hero of the Sumerian flood legend, came after being translated to the realm of the gods.

It is interesting that this paradise legend tells that only fresh water was wanting on the island of Dilmun and that the sun-god Utu brought it up from the earth to turn the place into a veritable garden of the gods. This notion of supernatural irrigation as the ideal state is familiar to readers of the Creation story, for before the advent of rain "a flow would well up from the ground and water the whole surface of the earth" (2:6).[69]

The Genesis version, however, has refined the entire "garden of God" motif. In the first place, it is highly significant that, unlike Ezekiel, and despite its metaphorical usage elsewhere, our Genesis writer never employs the phrase "garden of God." As if further to emphasize his rejection of the notion in its literal sense he observes that the garden was planted by God Himself for man, and only after the creation of man, that he might till it and tend it and not merely enjoy it. Moreover, in its description of the four rivers that branched off from Eden,[70] the narrative mentions the presence of gold, bdellium and lapis lazuli in the land of Havilah. If we look at the "garden of God" myth in Ezekiel[71] we find jewels, precious stones and metals as part of the landscape, while a glance at the Gilgamesh epic of Babylon shows mention of a magic, idyllic garden in which the trees bear jewels.[72] Genesis, through the seemingly irrelevant description of the land of Havilah, has quite clearly sought to naturalize a mythological aspect of the garden.

The two outstanding features of the Garden of Eden are the "tree of life" and the "tree of knowledge of good and evil." The former of the two, whether it be a tree or other plant, is a motif widespread throughout the ancient Near East that played an important role in Mesopotamian myth and ritual.[73] The biblical wisdom literature frequently uses the phrase in a metaphorical sense.[74] In Babylonian mythology the "plant of life" is closely connected with the "water of life," which constantly nourishes it. It is not unlikely that a reflex of this latter motif is to be found in the Genesis mention of the river that passed through Eden. Here again, it is significant that two of the branches of this river are the Tigris and Euphrates, so familiar to all biblical readers. The naturalizing tendencies of the writer are once more apparent.

The same is true, and even more so, in the treatment of the two trees. They possess no magical properties which operate independently of God. They are in no wise outside of the divine realm, and their mysterious powers do not exist apart from the will of God. The eating of the fruit of the "tree of knowledge" did not endow the man and his wife with any special supernatural powers. They were unable to hide from God or to conceal their sin. They made no effort to oppose the divine judgment, and the absolute sovereign will of God is never called into question. The magical element is entirely and conspicuously absent.

However, the most remarkable break of all with Near Eastern mythology lies in the subtle shift of emphasis. As far as is known, the "tree of knowledge" has no parallel outside of our biblical Garden of Eden story. Yet it is upon this tree, and not upon the well-known "tree of life," that the narrative focuses its main attention. The divine prohibition makes no mention of the "tree of life." The dialogue of the serpent and Eve likewise ignores it, as, too, does God's questioning of Adam after the latter had eaten from the forbidden fruit. It is mentioned again only at the end of the narrative in explaining the expulsion from Eden. All this cannot be accidental, particularly in view of the great prominence of the "tree of life" motif in Near Eastern religion and the absence of the "tree of knowledge" idea outside of the Bible. We shall shortly offer an explanation of this phenomenon, but first we must turn our attention to the symbolism of the serpent.

This reptile figures prominently in all the world's mythologies and cults.[75] In the Near East the serpent was a symbol of deity and fertility, and the images of serpent-goddesses have been found in the ruins of many Canaanite towns and temples.[76] This tradition probably explains why the serpent is introduced in our story as simply one of "the wild beasts that the Lord God had made" (3:1).[77] It is not an independent creature; it possesses no occult powers; it is not a demoniacal being; it is not even described as evil, merely as being extraordinarily shrewd. This reduction of the serpent to natural, insignificant, demythologized stature, is further pointed up in the difference between God's dialogues with Adam and Eve and his monologue to the serpent. God does not interrogate the serpent, and the voluble reptile utters not a sound in the presence of the Deity. The role of the creature is that of seducer, laying before the woman the enticing nature of evil and fanning her desire for it. The use of the serpent symbolism in this situation has most likely been conditioned by the place of the serpent in the old cosmic combat myth described earlier in this chapter. There, be it noted, the serpent is one of the epithets of Leviathan, one of the chief opponents of God and the representative of cosmic chaos.[78]

This brings us back to the shift of focus from the "tree of life" to the "tree of knowledge." The quest for immortality seems to have been an obsessive factor in ancient Near Eastern religion and literature. The preoccupation with death was the most characteristic feature of Egyptian civilization to the prominence of which the mighty pyramids still bear eloquent testimony.[79] The Gilgamesh legend of Mesopotamia, to name but one, is the best known literary expression of this recurring theme in that part of the world.[80] By relegating the "tree of life" to an insignificant, subordinate role in the Garden of Eden story, the Bible dissociates itself completely from this pre-occupation. Its concern is with the issues of living rather than with the question of death, with morality rather than mortality. Its problem is not the mythical pursuit of eternity, but the actual relationships between man and God, the tension between the plans of God and the free-will of man. Not magic, it proclaims, but human action is the key to a meaningful life.

The sin of Adam and Eve thus has implications far beyond the immediate context of the narrative. The conversation between the serpent and the woman shows that the most seductive attraction that the creature could offer was the potentiality of the forbidden fruit to make humans like God.

> "... as soon as you eat of it, your eyes will be opened and you
> will be like God. . . ." (3 : 5)

Now the imitation of God is indeed a biblical ideal. Man was fashioned in the divine image and "to walk in God's ways" is a recurring admonition of the biblical writings.[81] But true godliness is an expression of character, an attempt to imitate in human relationships those ethical attributes the Scriptures associate with God. The deceptive nature of the serpent's appeal lay in its interpretation of godliness which it equated with defiance of God's will, with power, rather than with strength of character.

Yet God Himself testifies that "man has become like one of us, knowing good and evil" (3:22).[82] In other words, man does possess the possibility of defying the divine word, and therein lies the secret of his freedom. The Garden of Eden incident is thus a landmark in the development of the understanding of the nature of man, his predicament and destiny. Man is a free moral agent and this freedom magnifies immeasurably his responsibility for his actions. Notice how each of the participants in the sin was individually punished. Freedom and responsibility are burdens so great for man to bear that he is in vital need of discipline. Significantly, the very first divine command to Adam pertains to the curbing of the appetite.[83] But man is free to disregard the moral law, should he wish to, though he must be prepared to suffer the consequences. In short, we are being told by the Garden of Eden story that evil is a product of human behavior, not a principle inherent in the cosmos.

Man's disobedience is the cause of the human predicament. Human freedom can be at one and the same time an omen of disaster and a challenge and opportunity.

Cain and Abel

This revolutionary principle, the endowment of man with moral autonomy and the stress upon the human aspect of evil, is illustrated, once again, in the story of Cain and Abel, the Bible's first naturally born human beings.

Cain was a tiller of the soil, Abel a shepherd. Both brought offerings to God from the products with which each dealt. Abel's animal sacrifice was acceptable, but to Cain's gift of fruit God paid no heed. It has been customary in modern times to interpret this narrative as reflecting the traditional rivalry between the nomad and the farmer, and to see in God's preference for Abel, the shepherd, the motif of the nomadic ideal in Israel.[84] This interpretation is untenable.

In the first place, the evidence for the existence of such an ideal in biblical literature is extremely flimsy.[85] Secondly, even if it could be shown to exist, it could hardly be present in our story. There is no hint of any disparagement of the occupation of tiller of the soil. On the contrary, it is regarded as the natural occupation of Adam in the Garden of Eden and after his expulsion.[86] There is also not the slightest suggestion of any comparative evaluation of the vocations of the two brothers, only of the offerings they brought. That Cain does not represent a type, either ethnic or occupational, which was regarded by Israel with enmity or distrust, is evidenced by the fact that the punishment is restricted to Cain himself, that his sons are not vagrants like him, that no discrimination is made between the offspring of Cain and those of his brother Seth, and that the three pillars of semi-nomadic culture—cattle-rearing, music and metal work—are actually said to have originated with the descendants of Cain.[87] The story, therefore, must be examined on its own terms, and not as the reflection of a historical situation.

As a story, however, it is tantalizingly incomplete. The narrative of events is extraordinarily terse and sketchy. No reason is explicitly given as to why Cain's offering was unacceptable, nor is it related how the brothers became aware of God's response. To what, or to whom, could

Cain have referred when he expressed the fear that anyone who met him might kill him? Alone in the world, supposedly, with his mother and father, Cain's fears could not possibly have been grounded in reality. Yet God took his words seriously enough to utter a curse upon a would-be avenger and to give Cain a protective mark "lest anyone who met him should kill him" (4:15). Where was the mysterious "land of Nod" in which Cain settled, and how did he find a wife (4:17)?

All these unanswered questions lead to one inescapable conclusion: the story of Cain and Abel must once have existed as an independent, full-bodied tale.[88] The gaps and inconsistencies now apparent arose when it was incorporated into the Torah literature and interwoven with the preceding narrative. But these literary problems were of minor significance, for the Bible's primary concern was to use the bare bones of the tale as a vehicle for the expression and inculcation of certain fundamental truths about some of life's most searching questions.

The story opens with a report ascribing sacrifice and offering to the first humans born of woman. We are not told that God demanded this of Cain and Abel or that some religious festival required it. This absence of motivation is instructive, for it assumes the willingness to sacrifice and worship to be innate in man, to be the utterly natural, instinctive and spontaneous expression of the spirit of religious devotion. But the story also tells us that man has it in his power to corrupt even the purest and noblest of emotions. God did not pay heed to Cain's offering. The descriptions of the brothers' gifts implicitly tell us why. Cain brought simply "from the fruit of the soil." Abel "brought the choicest of the firstlings of his flock." By contrasting the details the Bible is saying that Abel demonstrated a quality of the heart and mind that Cain did not have. Abel's act of worship was an inward experience, an ungrudging, open-hearted, concentrated devotion.[89] Cain's noble purpose was sullied by the intrusion of the self, a defect that blocked the spiritual channels with God. The Bible is thus, in its treatment of the very first recorded act of worship, formulating two basic concepts that characterize the religion of Israel.

The first is that the individual is the ultimate religious unit. In his relationship to God, man is a conscious personality who retains his distinctiveness within the community. Later on, the Bible is to add the new dimension of community to this religious individualism, so that society, too, is elevated to the status of a religious unit. But this principle can be operatively successful only because there must always be present an underlying tension, religiously speaking, between the individual and the collectivized mass.

The second concept postulated by the Cain and Abel story is the necessity of relating worship to piety. Throughout the Bible there is an acute awareness of the fact that human nature being what it is, the needs and demands of each may be in conflict. The prophets are to deal with this problem in its most extreme form and to formulate in clearest terms the application of the moral criterion as the only valid way of resolving the tension. Here, through our story, the Bible is expressing one of the most profound, if saddest, truths in the history of religions when it shows how an originally well-intentioned act of divine worship could become the cause of the first murder committed by man.

As to the crime itself, it will surely be noticed that the length of the dialogues between God and Cain contrasts strongly with the brevity of the narrative description. God gives a warning about the possible dangerous consequences of Cain's state of mind.

> "Why are you distressed,
> And why is your face fallen?
> Surely, if you do right,
> There is uplift.
> But if you do not do right
> Sin is the demon at the door,[90]
> Whose urge is toward you,
> Yet you can be his master."
>
> (4 : 6f.)

Despite the obscurity of some of the Hebrew original, the import of the divine declaration is beyond dispute. Man has been endowed with moral autonomy, with freedom of choice which enables him to subdue evil temptation through an act of will. This story thus reinforces the ideas expressed in the Garden of Eden legend about the nature of the human predicament.

One of the unusual stylistic features of our tale is the emphasis upon the fraternal relationship. No less than seven times the obvious fact is stressed that Abel was Cain's brother;[91] yet the very nature of the biblical Creation story automatically excludes any other possibility. The reason for this stress becomes clear when we recall Cain's response to the divine questioning.

The Lord said to Cain, "Where is your brother Abel?" And
he said—"I do not know. Am I my brother's keeper?"

(4 : 9)

The Bible wishes to establish emphatically the moral principle that man
is indeed his brother's keeper and that all homicide is at the same time
fratricide.

It is of interest that the culpability of Cain rests upon an unexpressed
assumption of the existence of a moral law operative from the beginning
of time.[92] That is why God intervened, for no man can hope to escape
His all-embracing sovereign rule. Again and again, the Bible returns to
this theme, unique to Israelite thinking. Cain had violated the God-
endowed sanctity of human life. His crime was an offense against society.
Hence, he was to be banished from society to become a "restless wan-
derer on earth" (4:14), a social pariah. But he had also sinned against
God, the source of all morality, in the biblical world-view. Hence, Cain
laments,

I must avoid your presence . . ." And Cain left the presence of
the Lord.   (4 : 14, 16)

A crime against man is a sin against God. Divine law had been disobeyed
and the spiritual ties uniting man with God severed.

Why did not Cain suffer the supreme penalty for his crime? It is not
just that God mitigated the effects of the punishment He imposed by
placing on Cain a protective mark. Why did he not have Cain killed in the
first place? It may be surmised that in the original, independent tale, the
circumstances of the homicide were more fully described. If our present
text is a guide, then there is no evidence that Cain's attack upon his
brother was premeditated. Furthermore, it must be remembered that
according to the biblical story no one alive had yet known the experience
of death, so that Cain had no way of determining that his blow against
Abel could extinguish his life. Cain's deed would, therefore, hardly fall
within the category of premeditated murder.

Finally, a brief word must be said about the notion expressed in
God's rebuke,

"Hark, your brother's blood cries out to Me from the
ground."   (4 : 10)

The Hebrew verb employed here is the same as that used on many another occasion when the cry of the oppressed comes before God.[93] The idea is that injustice sets in motion countervailing forces that must ultimately prevail because they are sustained by God. This is the confident assurance that the religion of Israel was able to offer as a direct concomitant of its concept of cosmogony.

NOTES TO CHAPTER I

1. See Gaster in *IDB*, I, p. 702ff.
2. Followers of the documentary hypothesis have assigned this section to the P source and the second account to the J source.
3. Cf. I S A . 27:1; 51:9–10; J O B 26:12–13. See below pp. 21ff. for a discussion of the "coomic battle."
4. See the biblical sources cited in the previous note.
5. Cf. P S . 104:9; P R O V . 8:27; J O B 26:10; 38:8–11.
6. See H. Gunkel, *Schöpfung u. Chaos;* U. Cassuto, *Knesseth,* VIII (1943–44) pp. 121–42; *Adam,* pp. 20–23, 30f.; *Exodus,* pp. 119–25.
7. For a comprehensive study of this subject, see J. Pedersen, *Israel.*
8. For a review of the speculative thought in ancient Egypt and Mesopotamia, see *Before Philosophy.*
9. For English translation of *Enuma Elish* and other Mesopotamian creation stories, see Heidel, *BG;* Speiser, *ANET,* pp. 60–72.
1 0. For recent thinking on this subject, see *Daedalus,* Spring, 1959.
1 1. B. Malinowsky, *Magic, Science and Religion,* p. 100.
1 2. For a detailed study of the Babylonian new year festival, see Pallis. Cf., also, Hooke,

BAR, pp. 48ff. and esp. pp. 101–123. For its role in Mesopotamian civilization, see T. Jacobsen in *Before Philosophy,* pp. 182–199.

1 3. See T. H. Gaster, *Thespis;* M. Eliade, *Cosmos and History.*

1 4. This is the central theme of Kaufmann's *Toldot,* abridged as *RI.* For a summary of his views and arguments on this particular problem, see his article in *JBL,* LXX (1951), pp. 179–197. See also on this subject, H. Gunkel, *The Legends of Genesis,* p. 15f.; B. S. Childs, *Myth and Reality in the O.T.*

1 5. Cf. I KINGS 11:5, 33; II KINGS 23:13.

1 6. On this subject in general, see A. B. Drachman, *Atheism in Pagan Antiquity.*

1 7. See E. Voegelin, *Order and History,* p. 41f.; Moscati, *FAO,* p. 78f.

1 8. Cf. E. O. James, *The Ancient Gods,* pp. 239, 260.

1 9. Kramer, *HBS,* p. 79f.

2 0. PSS. 33:9 (cf. v. 6); 148:5.

2 1. On the notion of the "sexualization of the world," see M. Eliade, *The Forge and the Crucible,* pp. 34–42; Jacobsen in *Before Philosophy,* pp. 158f., 170ff.; N. O. Brown, *Hesiod's Theogony,* pp. 8, 19.

2 2. See Jacobson in *Before Philosophy,* p. 159f.

2 3. GEN. 1:2, 6f. On the "wind from God," see H. M. Orlinsky, *JQR,* XLVIII (1957), pp. 174–182.

2 4. See L. Woolley, *PEQ,* LXXXVIII (1965), p. 15f.

2 5. For an explanation of the creation of woman out of Adam's rib, see Kramer, *HBS,* p. 146.

2 6. GEN. 11:3 (cf. LEV. 14:41f.); JOB 10:9; 27:16; 30:19.

2 7. JOB. 4:19; 10:9; 33:6; cf. ISA. 29:16; 45:9; 64:7.

2 8. For primitive, Near Eastern and classical parallels to this motif, see Frazer, *Folklore,* I, pp. 3–44.

2 9. *Enuma Elish,* VI:1–34.

3 0. Gilgamesh, I:II:34f.

3 1. *ANET,* p. 99f.

3 2. See Kramer, *HBS,* p. 108f.; *SM,* pp. 68–75; Jacobsen in *Before Philosophy,* p. 176.

3 3. *ANEP,* pp. 190, 318, No. 569.

3 4. See the remarks of H. H. Rowley, *The Unity of the Bible,* pp. 74f., 186, nn. 53, 55.

3 5. ISA. 29:16; 45:9ff.; JER. 18:21.

3 6. On this subject, see the remarks of M. I. Finley, *The World of Odysseus,* p. 150; Frankfort, *Kingship,* p. 277f.; J. J. Finkelstein, *Commentary,* Nov., 1958, p. 438f.; E. A. Speiser, *Centennial Review,* IV. 2 (1960), p. 219.

3 7. Cf. GEN. 18:25; ISA. 5:16.

3 8. Jacobsen in *Before Philosophy,* p. 137; H. Frankfort, *The Birth of Civilization,* pp. 54, 63.

3 9. Cf. PS. 8:4–9.

4 0. EXOD. 31:12–17.

4 1. See Cassuto, *Adam,* p. 39ff.

4 2. EXOD. 16:5, 22–30.

4 3. *Ibid.,* 20:8; DEUT. 5:12.

4 4. See N. M. Sarna, *JBL,* LXXXI (1962), p. 157, and the literature cited there in n. 11.

4 5. See H. and J. Lewy, *HUCA,* XVII (1942–43), pp. 1–152[c].

4 6. See Hooke, *BAR*, p. 53.
4 7. Cited by G. A. Barton, *Archaeology and the Bible*, p. 258f.
4 8. See de Vaux, *AI*, p. 475.
4 9. *Ibid.*, p. 476ff.
5 0. E X O D . 20:10f.; 23:12; D E U T . 5:14.
5 1. See Kaufman, *Toldot*, I, p. 579; II, p. 491.
5 2. See Jacobsen in *Before Philosophy*, pp. 139f., 153–7, 187–199; N. O. Brown, *op. cit.*, p. 40ff.
5 3. See above p. 2 and n. 6.
5 4. I S A . 27:1; 51:9.
5 5. G E N . 49:25; D E U T . 33:13.
5 6. H A B . 3:10.
5 7. *Enuma Elish* I:38.
5 8. *Ibid.* V:1ff.
5 9. I S A . 17:12–14.
6 0. I S A . 27:1.
6 1. J O B 38:4–15.
6 2. I S A . 51:9f.; H A B . 3:8–15; P S . 74:12–18.
6 3. See N. M. Sarna, *op. cit.*, p. 161f.
6 4. U. Cassuto in *Schorr*, pp. 248–258; *Adam*, 44ff.
6 5. G E N . 13:10; I S A . 51:3; E Z E K . 36:35; J O E L 2:3.
6 6. E Z E K . 28:11–19; 31:8–9, 16–18.
6 7. On the relationships between Sumerian culture and the Bible, see A. M. Van Dijk in *L'Ancien Testament*, pp. 5–28; S. N. Kramer, *SBO*, III (1959), pp. 185–204.
6 8. *ANET*, pp. 37–41; Kramer, *HBS*, pp. 144ff.; *SM*, 54ff.
6 9. E. A. Speiser, *BASOR*, 140 (1955), pp. 9–11; cf. Kramer, *HBS*, p. 145; *SM*, p. 56.
7 0. On the location and identification of the four rivers, see E. A. Speiser in *Festschrift Johannes Friedrich*, pp. 473–85.
7 1. E Z E K . 28:13; cf. G E N . 2:11f.
7 2. Gilgamesh, IX:V:47ff.; *ANET*, p. 89.
7 3. See G. Widengren, *The King and the Tree of Life*.
7 4. P R O V . 3:18; 11:30; 13:12; 15:4. On these passages, see R. Marcus, *JBL*, LXII (1943), pp. 117–120.
7 5. See J. Campbell, *The Masks of God*, pp. 9–41.
7 6. See W. G. Graham and H. G. May, *Culture and Conscience*, pp. 81–90. Cf. J. Finegan, *Light From the Ancient Past*, pp. 163f., 168, 171.
7 7. On this theme, see Childs, *op. cit.*, pp. 42–48.
7 8. I S A . 27:1; J O B 26:18.
7 9. See H. Frankfort, *Ancient Egyptian Religion*, chap. 4.
8 0. See A. Heidel, *The Gilgamesh Epic*, pp. 137–223.
8 1. G E N . 1:26f. Cf. L E V . 19:2; D E U T . 13:5; P S . 86:11.
8 2. On this passage, see R. Gordis, *JBL*, LXXVI (1957), pp. 123–138.
8 3. G E N . 2:16f.
8 4. On this theme, cf. *ANET*, p. 40; Jacobsen in *Before Philosophy*, pp. 180ff.; Kramer, *SM*, pp. 49ff., 53.
8 5. On the supposed nomadic ideal in Israel, see Kaufmann, *Toldot*, II, pp. 65, 625;

RI, p. 339, n. 13; de Vaux, *AI*, p. 13f.; H. L. Ginsberg, *JBL*, LXXX (1961), p. 346, n. 16.

8 6. GEN. 2:15; 3:19, 23.

8 7. *Ibid.*, 4:17ff.; 5:6ff.; 4:20ff.

8 8. See *GuG*, pp. 40–49; cf. *SkG*, p. 101; Cassuto, *Adam*, p. 118.

8 9. On the subject of devotion, see M. Kadushin, *Worship and Ethics*, p. 185.

9 0. For the justification of this translation, see *SpG*, p. 32. See also, Tur-Sinai, *LS*, II, pp. 199–203. G. R. Castellino, *VT*, X (1960), pp. 442–45; M. Naor in *Sefer Karl*, p. 78f.; M. Ben-Yashar, *Beth Mikra*, XVI (1963), pp. 117ff.

9 1. GEN. 4:2, 8–11.

9 2. See Kaufmann, *Toldot*, II, p. 69.

9 3. See *VRG*, p. 102.

CHAPTER II

The Flood

GENESIS 6:9–9:17

The biblical account

The Book of Genesis tells of a divine decision to wipe out mankind because of the corruption and injustice rife on earth. However, a righteous and blameless man named Noah was to be saved from the flood. God communicated His intentions to him and instructed him to build an ark, to provision it and to take aboard his family together with male and female representatives of the animals, birds and creeping things. When all was done, the Flood waters came upon the earth carrying the ark above the highest mountain peaks, so that all earthly existence was blotted out.

God's purposes having been accomplished, the rains ceased, the waters receded, and the ark came to rest upon a mountain top. After a wait of forty days, Noah sent out, first a raven, then a dove to reconnoiter the earth. On the third attempt the dove returned no more to the ark, and Noah knew that it was safe to disembark. This he did as soon as he received the divine order and he promptly offered sacrifices to God.

God, in turn, promised to restore the rhythm of nature and pledged never again to visit a universal inundation upon mankind. He further blessed Noah and his offspring and everything on earth, and set up the bow in the sky as an everlasting symbol of this promise.

History or legend?

Such, in brief, is the account of the biblical Flood. Was there indeed such a universal flood? Is the story historic or does it have another purpose and a different message?

In the first place, the science of geology offers no evidence in support of the notion that the earth's surface was at any time after the appearance of *homo sapiens* on earth submerged, wholly or in large part, by flood waters. Furthermore, we must take into account the great popularity and wide distribution of flood stories in the ancient world.[1] While many of these tell of purely local inundations, others describe floods overwhelming most or even all of civilization. Many of these stories conform to a basic pattern. Religious man saw in these upheavals of nature the activity of the divine and attributed their cause to man's angering of the gods. Most frequently, one man and his family, the favorite of the gods, survived the deluge to father a new human race.

The widespread popularity of flood stories, their prevalence among such a large variety of peoples living at different times as well as different places, argues against literary interdependence, a common source, or reference to a single historic event. Whatever historical foundations may possibly underlie such traditions, it is clear that popular imagination has been at work magnifying local disastrous floods into catastrophes of universal proportions. For this reason, the common features must be regarded as having developed independently, to be explained as common human psychological and religious reactions to a given set of circumstances finding expression in a literary stereotype.

The origins of the Hebrew account

If the evidence is against a straight-forward historical interpretation of the biblical narrative, how did the story of Noah arise and what is its relevance to twentieth-century man?

Modern scholarship has shown that the Torah made use of very ancient traditions which it adapted to its own special purposes. In order to focus clearly upon the objectives of the Bible we shall have to review those flood stories of the ancient world to which the Torah might have had access. Then we shall have to demonstrate the very close connection which exists between the biblical account and one, or perhaps a group, of such traditions. Finally, by careful comparison and contrast we shall better be able to appreciate the distinctiveness of the biblical account and the eternal verities it proclaims.

The Mesopotamian provenance of the biblical version

If we turn to the Noah episode in Genesis it will immediately strike us that the facts themselves argue for a Mesopotamian locale for the events and for a non-Canaanite origin of the tale. A flood of such cataclysmic dimensions could have taken place, or have been imagined, only in a land subject to inundations. The topography of Palestine, a very hilly country with a dry climate, makes such events extremely improbable. Furthermore, excavations at the site of ancient Jericho, in the sloping valley north of the Dead Sea, have revealed a walled town dating back nine thousand years. Examination of the ruins of the various levels of more-or-less continuous occupation throughout this period shows no accumulation of clay deposits, the tell-tale evidence of extensive flooding.

Further, the Hebrews were very little engaged in maritime enterprise and were not well practised in the arts of seafaring. The detailed and elaborate description of the ark building would be unlikely in a Hebrew prototype. Finally, if Canaan were the place of origin of the story of Noah, the ark coming to rest on Mt. Ararat in the Lake Van area in southeastern Turkey would be strange and inexplicable. None of these objections applies, however, to Mesopotamia. Bounded on either side by a mighty river, and being a flat alluvial plain, it would be the natural locale for a flood tradition. For this reason there exists a very strong *prima facie* case for supposing a Mesopotamian origin of the Hebrew flood story.

It is no longer possible to establish definitely the mode of transmission of the material from the Euphrates-Tigris valley to the biblical writers.[2] Hebrew traditions emphatically designate Mesopotamia as the land of Abraham's birth and the land with which the Hebrews continued to maintain close contact long after the migration to Canaan. The flood story might well have been part of the traditions which the forebears of the people of Israel carried with them in their wanderings from their Mesopotamian homeland. On the other hand, the widespread diffusion of Mesopotamian literature throughout the Near East meant that the flood story might have been available to the biblical writers through a Canaanite medium. At the present time, the evidence is weighted more heavily on the side of the first possibility.

The Mesopotamian flood stories[3]

The first Mesopotamian flood story known to the western world was a late one, that of Berossus. About the year 275 B.C.E. this priest of the god Marduk in Babylon wrote a three volume history of his country from creation to the conquest of Alexander. Unfortunately, only excerpts of his work survived in the quotations of later Greek historians. Enough remained of the flood episode, however, to show a distinct relationship to the biblical story of Noah. Yet the full significance of Berossus' account for biblical studies was not grasped until the nineteenth-century discovery of the Mesopotamian versions written in the cuneiform, or wedge-shaped syllabic script.[4]

At the present time, thanks to the archaeologist's spade we have at our disposal several versions of this flood story. It is evident that Berossus was able to draw upon very ancient literary materials that must have been available to him in his temple library. The name of the favored hero in Berossus' tale is Xisuthros, which is none other than a Grecized form of the name Ziusudra, the hero in the account of the Sumerians. This coincidence is amazing since the name is not found elsewhere. If it be remembered that at least fifteen hundred years separated Berossus from the earliest preserved Sumerian composition, the remarkable tenacity and popularity of the latter in the ancient world will be readily appreciated. Unfortunately, the Sumerian flood story has been preserved only on a very badly mutilated and unique clay tablet.

Another version of the deluge motif is to be found in what has come to be known as the Epic of Atra(m)hasis. Several fragments of this early Semitic work have been recovered, stemming from different times and places. An Old Babylonian recension that has survived was copied in 1692 B.C.E. from a still earlier text. Here the flood is one of many disasters visited upon man by the gods in punishment for human sins. Atrahasis is the name of the hero who survived the flood.

The Epic of Gilgamesh

The most famous, most detailed and most complete of all the Mesopotamian flood stories is that recounted as an incident in the eleventh tablet
of the *Epic of Gilgamesh*.[5] In the course of excavations conducted
between 1849 and 1854 at Nineveh, which in the seventh century served
the ancient Assyrian Empire as a capital, a copy of this epic was discovered in the library of King Asshurbanipal. This Gilgamesh epic, like
Berossus' flood story, goes back to Sumerian prototypes.[6] This could
have been guessed from the names of the gods and the heroes, even if the
Sumerian literary models of most of the episodes had not been recovered.
This flood story was originally quite independent of the Gilgamesh cycle
and was introduced into the epic only incidentally. For the real concern
of the writer is the inevitability of death and the folly of all human attempts to escape it.

The *Epic of Gilgamesh* constitutes one of the major literary achievements of the ancient world. In its final form as known to us, it is really a
fusion of several originally independent poems, all the most important
elements of which can, as we have pointed out, be traced back to Sumerian literature. In fact, the history of the epic takes us back as early as the
third millennium B.C.E.[7]

The widespread popularity which the epic achieved in the ancient
world is attested by the translations into foreign languages made in the
middle of the second millennium. Hittite and Hurrian renderings,
as well as the original Akkadian, have been found as far afield as
Boghazkoy in Anatolia. Other copies have been unearthed in Sultantepe
in southern Turkey, and an important fragment has turned up recently at
Megiddo in Israel.[8] There is no doubt that the influence of the *Epic of
Gilgamesh* penetrated beyond the confines of the ancient Near East into
the Greek sphere and beyond.

The story tells of Gilgamesh and Enkidu, two sworn friends who coop-
erated in many daring adventures. During one such, Enkidu died and the
grief-stricken Gilgamesh was suddenly brought to the realization that he,
too, was mortal. He became increasingly obsessed with death and was
seized with an overwhelming desire for immortality. Mindful of his
ancestor Utnapishtim who had once obtained the secret of eternal life, he
set out on the long journey to the island at the far end of the earth where
the old man resided. Standing at last before him, he begged for his secret.

Alas! Gilgamesh was to discover that Utnapishtim and his wife had
gained immortality, not by dint of esoteric wisdom, but by reason of

extraordinary and unrepeatable circumstances. They alone, of all mankind, had survived a great flood and the gods, by a special act of grace, had made the couple as one of them, removing them from the reaches of men.

Having heard the story of Utnapishtim, Gilgamesh, weary and exhausted, sank down into a deep sleep lasting six days and seven nights. At length, awakening from his stupor, the luckless hero prepared to start for home. That his travails and labors might not have been entirely in vain, Utnapishtim disclosed to Gilgamesh the secret of a magic plant to be found at the bottom of the sea. Its name was, "Man Becomes Young in Old Age." Eagerly he dived into the sea at the designated spot and indeed succeeded in finding it. He placed the precious plant of rejuvenation on the ground and went to bathe in a cool spring. But at that very moment a serpent snatched the prize away. Gilgamesh was left with nothing for all his exertions, except the realization of the utter futility of his quest. Resigned to his mortal fate, the hero turned his face homeward for the long trek back to his native city.

The origin of the Mesopotamian stories

As we have already pointed out, the flood episode, in the *Epic of Gilgamesh,* is but one of several Mesopotamian versions. But it is quite clear, despite differences of detail, that they are all closely related to each other. The question arises, as in the case of the biblical account, whether the Mesopotamian deluge story is the product of human memory and whether it is possible to identify the historic background, if any, that occasioned it.

Floods of considerable magnitude are frequent in the flat valley between the great Euphrates and Tigris rivers, and the area is subject to torrential rains and periodic cyclones. Excavations in lower Mesopotamia show notable flood-levels at Shurrupak, Kish, Uruk, and Ur. Layers of clay devoid of any remains of human activity often separate two different strata of occupation. However, the clay flood deposits vary in thickness from place to place, and belong to different stages of civilization in each city. Also, they do not always involve a cultural break. In this situation it is possible to say no more than that the Mesopotamian flood stories were originally inspired by one or another of the local devastating inundations that visited the lower Euphrates-Tigris valley in ancient times.[9]

The biblical-Mesopotamian parallels

If the Mesopotamian origin of our biblical Flood narrative is assured, to what particular cuneiform version is Scripture indebted? None of the versions now known served as the prototype, for the Genesis story differs in many details from all of them and has features found, now only in one, now only in another. It may perhaps go back to some independent version that has not survived or that has not yet been discovered. The difficulty is heightened by the fact that the Hebrew account in its present form is itself a fusion of traditions.[10]

There is evidence that the present Hebrew prose form of the story actually rests upon an earlier Israelite epic and that it was this poem that was indebted to a Mesopotamian source. Thus, it is still possible to sense the poetic substratum in Genesis 7:11,

> All the fountains of the great deep burst apart,
> And the flood-gates of the sky broke open.

This verse has retained the classic parallelism characteristic of biblical Hebrew poetry, and the phrases, "the great deep" and "the flood-gates of the sky" are obviously poetic expressions. Also, the Hebrew story contains words found nowhere else, or only once otherwise in biblical Hebrew. Thus, *gofer*, the wood from which the ark was made; *kinnim*, in the sense of "compartment"; *kofer*, meaning "pitch"; *ṣohar*, meaning an "opening for daylight"; *ṭaraf*, for "a plucked-off" (olive leaf); *mabbul* for "Flood"; and *yequm* as "existence" may all be poetic residue from a Hebrew epic version that preceded our present prose account. It would seem, moreover, that something of this poetic version was still known to the prophets Ezekiel and Deutero-Isaiah who refer to the story of Noah, but not in the language of the Pentateuch.[11]

Nevertheless, the ultimate Mesopotamian origin of the scriptural narrative is incontestable. It now remains to examine in detail those elements common to both traditions, although not all are of equal weight in deciding literary dependency. Some of the parallels are detailed and striking, while others might be otherwise explained. The cumulative effect is overwhelming.

The account of the Flood in the Bible concludes one era and opens a new one in human history. It occupies a central position between Creation and the advent of the people of Israel. The Book of Genesis expresses this notion through the genealogical catalogues which list ten generations from Adam to Noah and ten more from Noah to Abraham.[12]

This identical concept is to be found in Mesopotamian historiography. *The Sumerian King List,* which enumerates the rulers of Sumer in their different capitals, makes a clear distinction between the kings who reigned before "the flood swept over" the earth and those who came "after the flood had swept over (the earth), when kingship was again lowered from heaven."[13] To the Sumerian chronicler it is clear that the flood interposed between two distinct periods in the history of the world. Although he counts only eight antediluvian kings, it is significant that in the version of Berossus the hero Xisuthros is the tenth in royal line, just as Noah is the tenth generation from Adam.[14] Indeed, there are now excellent reasons for believing that the early Semitic version of the flood story was actually, like the biblical, an integral part of a larger history of mankind.[15]

The Bible emphasizes that the Flood was not a freak of nature, but the deliberate result of a divine decision. God said to Noah,

> "I have decided to put an end to all flesh. . .
> I am about to destroy them with the earth. . .
> I am about to bring the Flood. . .
> To destroy all flesh. . ."   (6 : 13, 17)

In a similar vein, Utnapishtim informed Gilgamesh that "the gods in their hearts were moved to let loose the deluge."[16] In the Sumerian story, the flood "is the decision, the word of the assembly of the gods."[17]

Once the divine decision has been taken, one individual is chosen to be saved, is informed in advance of the impending disaster and is told to build a vessel as the means of survival. Thus God said,

> "I will blot out from the earth the man whom I created. . . ."
> But Noah found favor with the Lord. . . . God said to
> Noah, . . . "Make yourself an ark. . . . I will establish my cove-
> nant with you."   (6 : 7, 8, 14, 18)

In the Sumerian version, Ziusudra, standing near a wall, heard the voice of a god informing him that "a flood will sweep over the cult-centers to destroy the seed of mankind."[18] In the *Epic of Gilgamesh,* the god Ea revealed indirectly the divine decision to Utnapishtim and advised him to "build a boat."[19] In the same way, the god Enki informed Atrahasis,[20] and Berossus had Cronos appearing to Xisuthros in a vision.[21]

In both biblical and Mesopotamian traditions exact specifications were given to the hero for the building of the vessel. Thus, God told Noah,

> "Make yourself an ark of gopher wood; make it an ark with compartments, and cover it inside and outside with pitch. This is how you shall make it: the length of the ark shall be three hundred cubits, its width fifty cubits, and its height thirty cubits. Make an opening for daylight in the ark, and terminate it within a cubit of the top. Put the entrance to the ark in its side; make it with bottom, second and third decks."
>
> (6 : 14–16)

Utnapishtim was told to build a vessel in the shape of a cube. It, too, was equipped with a hatch, a door and a covering. It had six decks, apart from the ground floor. Each deck was divided into nine compartments, making a total of sixty-three.[22]

Of special interest is the insulation of both vessels with pitch. The Hebrew word used, *kofer*,[23] is identical with that in the Akkadian account, *kupru*. This verbal correspondence is all the more remarkable in that this is the only place in the Bible in which the word *kofer* occurs.

Noah received from God special instructions as to who and what should be taken into the ark,

> ". . . and you shall enter the ark—you, your sons, your wife, and your sons' wives. And of all that lives, of all flesh, you shall take two of each into the ark to keep alive with you; they shall be male and female. From birds of every kind, cattle of every kind, every kind of creeping thing on earth, two of each shall come to you to stay alive. For your part, take care of everything that is eaten and store it away to serve as food for you and for them."
>
> (6 : 17–21)

In the Gilgamesh epic the hero was told by the god Ea to "take aboard the ship the seed of all living things."[24] In the Atrahasis version he was told, "into the ship which thou shalt make thou shalt take the beasts of the field, the fowl of the heaven."[25]

After boarding the vessel, specific mention is made of the closing of the door. In the case of Noah, "the Lord shut him in" (7:16). The god Shamash explicitly told Utnapishtim to "board the ship and batten up the entrance,"[26] and Atrahasis was likewise instructed to enter the ship and close the door.[27]

In both traditions, the flood exterminated man and beast.

> All flesh that stirred on earth perished—birds, cattle, beasts and all the things that swarmed the earth, and all mankind. All in whose nostrils was the merest breath of life, all that was on dry land, died. All existence on earth was blotted out— man, cattle, creeping things, and birds of the sky; they were blotted out from the earth.   (7 : 21–23)

Utnapishtim described the same state of affairs more concisely, reporting simply that there was silence everywhere and that "all mankind had returned to clay."[28]

The biblical narrative tells how the ark came to rest on the mountains of Ararat (8:4). Closest to this tradition is that of Berossus who reports that the vessel was driven to the side of a mountain in Armenia.[29] In the Gilgamesh story it is again a mountain on which the boat grounds, Mount Nisir.[30]

After the waters had begun to abate,

> Noah opened the window of the ark that he had made and sent out the raven; it went to and fro until the waters had dried up from the earth. Then he sent out the dove to see whether the waters had decreased from the surface of the ground. But the dove could not find a resting place for its foot, and returned to him to the ark, for there was water over all the earth. So putting out his hand, he took it into the ark with him. He waited another seven days, and again sent out the dove from the ark. The dove came back to him toward evening, and there in its bill was a plucked-off olive leaf! Then Noah knew that the waters had decreased on the earth. He waited still another seven days and sent the dove forth; and it did not return to him anymore.   (8 : 6–12)

Utnapishtim likewise sent out birds to reconnoiter the ground after his boat had come to rest. In his own words,

I sent forth and set free a dove.
The dove went forth, but came back;
Since no resting-place for it was visible, she turned round.
Then I sent forth and set free a swallow.
The swallow went forth, but came back;
Since no resting-place for it was visible, she turned round.
Then I sent forth and set free a raven.
The raven went forth and, seeing that the waters had
    diminished,
He eats, circles, caws, and turns not round.[31]

Berossus, too, records this theme.[32] Xisuthros sent out some birds from the vessel, and they too returned to him for they could not find food or resting place. He waited a few days and sent them forth again. This time they returned with their feet tinged with mud. The third time he sent out the birds they came back no more.

After he had emerged from the ark,

Noah built an altar to the Lord, and, taking of every clean animal and of every clean bird, he offered burnt offerings on the altar. The Lord smelled the pleasing odor.   (8 : 20f.)

This detail is strikingly paralleled in the Gilgamesh story.

Then I let out (all) to the four winds
    And offered a sacrifice.
I poured out a libation on the top of the mountain.
Seven and seven cult-vessels I set up,
Upon their pot-stands I heaped cane, cedarwood, and myrtle.
The gods smelled the savor,
The gods smelled the sweet savor,
The gods crowded like flies about the sacrificer.[33]

In the version of Berossus, Xisuthros, too, constructed an altar and offered sacrifices to the gods.[34]

Finally, just as "God blessed Noah" (9:1), after it was all over, so Enlil blessed Utnapishtim.[35]

The biblical-Mesopotamian contrasts

Despite the numerous and detailed points of contact between the
biblical and Mesopotamian traditions, the Hebrew version is not a mere
borrowing. Mesopotamian civilization was thoroughly polytheistic,
Israel's world-view was thoroughly monotheistic. Each version is consonant with its own terms of reference. In the Bible the old material has
been completely reworked and attuned to the spirit of the religion of
Israel. Just as this was true of the Creation story, so in the case of the
Flood tradition, a radically transformed narrative emerged. The real
meaning of the biblical message can be truly evaluated only in the context of contrast, rather than correspondence, and it is to the former that
we now turn our attention.

The omnipotence of God and the limitations of the gods

The limitations imposed upon the gods by the mythological polytheistic
system, their subservience to nature and their singular lack of freedom
are vividly illustrated in the Mesopotamian flood story.

The decision of Enlil to destroy all mankind was thwarted by the intervention of the god Ea who, by resorting to subterfuge, managed to reveal
the secret of the gods to man. Once the flood started, the gods were
terror-struck at the very forces they themselves had unleashed. They were
appalled at the consequences of their own actions, over which they no
longer had any control. The gods, we are told, "were frightened by the
deluge," they "cowered like dogs crouched against the outer wall;
Ishtar cried out like a woman in travail." After the deluge, there were
arguments, quarrels and mutual recriminations among the gods.[36]

In direct contrast is the absolute, transcendent character of God in the
biblical narrative. He is completely independent of nature and His will
is sovereign. The Bible has forcefully and artfully accentuated this
theme. Most effective is the almost complete lack of any human initiative
and the unbroken silence of Noah. The world had corrupted itself "before God." God decided to punish man. God resolved to save Noah
because Noah "walked with God." God openly revealed his intentions
to Noah and He commanded, not advised, Noah to build an ark. He gave
him precise and detailed, not generalized, instructions as to the manner
of its construction and the nature of the cargo to be taken aboard. The

writer was careful to point out that "Noah did so; just as God commanded him so he did." God predetermined the exact date for the commencement of the deluge and the extent of its duration. He told Noah when to board the ark and, after the flood was over, gave specific orders for disembarkation. It is God who shut Noah in the ark, whereas in the Mesopotamian versions this act is performed by the hero himself. The flood-waters do not cease of their own account, but only because,

> God remembered Noah and all the beasts and all the cattle
> that were with him in the ark, and God caused a wind to blow
> across the earth and the waters subsided. (8 : 1)

Highly significant is the fact that Utnapishtim built a ship and employed a boatman to navigate it. In contrast, the Bible speaks of an ark, a chest-like vessel having neither rudder, nor sail, nor any other navigational aid, and not requiring the services of a crew. The Hebrew word *tebah* used to describe this vessel occurs elsewhere in the Bible in this sense only in connection with the salvation of the baby Moses from the danger of drowning.[37] In both instances the building of an ark, rather than a ship, is intended to attribute the hero's deliverance solely to the will of God, and not to any human skill.[38]

The motivation for the Flood

Clear and unambiguous in the biblical account is the moral aspect of the events described.

> The Lord saw how great was man's wickedness on earth, and
> how every plan devised by his mind was nothing but evil all
> the time . . . The earth became corrupt before God, the earth
> was filled with injustice. When God saw how corrupt the
> earth was, for all flesh had corrupted its ways on earth, God
> said to Noah, "I have decided to put an end to all flesh, for
> the earth is filled with lawlessness because of them."
> (6 : 5, 11–13)

Far from unambiguous, however, is the motivation for the flood in the Mesopotamian versions. The Sumerian story is too fragmentary and no certain conclusion can be drawn from it about the reasons for the deluge.

The Gilgamesh narrative is completely silent on the matter, due either to the fact that the action of the gods was capricious, or to the irrelevancy of the motive in the context of the larger epic. Less easily understandable is the failure of Berossus to account for the disaster. Only in the Atrahasis epic do we get some glimmer of an explanation. Here the flood is part of a larger epic cycle dealing with various punishments visited upon mankind for its sins. In both the Old Babylonian and Assyrian fragments of the epic it is reported, though not explicitly in connection with the flood, that

> The land became wide, the people became numerous,
> The land bellowed like wild oxen
> The god was disturbed by their uproar
> Enlil heard their clamor
> And said to the gods:
> "Oppressive has become the clamor of mankind,
> By their uproar they prevent sleep . . ." [39]

The meaning of this passage is obscure. It may possibly indicate no more exalted motivation for the flood than that the sleep of the gods was disturbed. On the other hand, some scholars find an analogy in the description of the evil of Sodom and Gomorrah,

> The Lord said, "The cry of Sodom and Gomorrah is so great, and their sin so grave! I will go down to see whether they have acted altogether accordingly to the outcry that has come to Me."   (18 : 20–21)

And again,

> For we are about to destroy this place, because the outcry against them before the Lord has become so great that the Lord has sent us to destroy it."   (19 : 13)

If the "bellowing" and "uproar" of mankind that so disturbed the gods in the Atrahasis epic be indeed a metaphor for human wickedness, we would then have a moral motivation for the deluge punishment in a Mesopotamian version.[40] It should also be pointed out that after it was all over Ea asked Enlil how he could have brought on the flood so senselessly. "Lay upon the sinner his sin, lay upon the transgressor his transgression," he said to him, in the words of the Gilgamesh version.[41] This statement may well indicate nothing more than the capriciousness of Enlil's action. On the other hand, it may also imply a demand for some moral basis for divine behavior.

This uncertainty about the moral aspects of the deluge reflected in the myths is not accidental. Although the gods were often interested in encouraging human ethical behavior, this was not necessarily their exclusive or even primary interest. As we emphasized in the previous chapter, the inability to produce a divinely sanctioned, absolute, standard of right and wrong was among the inherent limitations of mythological polytheism.

The salvation of the hero

A similar situation exists regarding the salvation of the hero.

> Noah was a righteous man; he was blameless in his age; Noah walked with God . . . Then the Lord said to Noah, "Go into the ark, you and all your household, for you alone have I found righteous before me in this generation. (7 : 1)

The Bible leaves no doubt as to God's motivations. The choice of Noah is inspired solely by his righteousness; caprice or partiality play no role in the divine resolution.

In none of the Mesopotamian versions is any reason given for the divine favor to one individual. The Sumerian Ziusudra is the only hero who seems to have been thought of as pious and god-fearing.[42] Yet nowhere is it explicit or implied that his righteousness was the one and only cause of his favored treatment. On the contrary, one has constantly the impression that the moral reason played little part in the decision. Utnapishtim was saved only because Ea, by means of a ruse, managed to outwit Enlil.[43] The same technique of indirect communication is employed by the deity in informing Ziusudra.[44] It is quite clear that were it not for the deception of the particular god whose favorite the hero was, Enlil would have ignored any considerations of personal integrity.

The moral sin

The prominence of the moral dimension in the biblical narrative is in accord with the Israelite monotheistic conception of God as being primarily concerned with ethics and morality. The God of the Bible is not a remote deity, inactive and ineffective. Having created the world, He did not remove himself from humanity and leave man to his own devices. On the contrary, He is very much concerned with the world He created and is directly interested in human behavior.

The story of the Flood, like that of Sodom and Gomorrah, presupposes the existence of a universal moral law governing the world for the infraction of which God, the Supreme Judge, brings men to account. It asserts, through the medium of the narrative, that man cannot undermine the moral basis of society without endangering the very existence of civilization. In fact, society, by its own corruption, actually may be said to initiate a process of inevitable retribution.

This emphasis upon the themes of human evil and individual righteousness is an outstanding characteristic of all biblical literature. The fact that only Noah was saved because only he was righteous implies clearly that the rest of his generation was individually evil and that therefore, what appears to be collective retribution on the part of God is, in the final analysis, really individual. It is of no consequence whether the individual guilt of all but one member of any given generation is statistically probable. We are concerned here, not with the historicity of the narrative, but with the essential religious concepts which underlie it. The significance of the story lies not in the framework of the history of the ancient world, but in the sphere of religious thought and the spiritual development of mankind.

This consciousness of individual responsibility does not obscure the social orientation. The sins of the generation of the flood are subsumed under the term *ḥamas,* the definition of which is "injustice, lawlessness, social unrighteousness." [45] This is the same sin for which the heathen city of Nineveh was to be destroyed[46] and for which "sulphurous fire" rained down upon Sodom and Gomorrah. In the latter case, the prophet Ezekiel tells us explicitly that the cause of the destruction of Sodom was her callous disregard of the existence of poverty amidst an economy of plenty. In a daring comparison between that ancient symbol of evil and his contemporary Jerusalem, he says,

> See, this was the guilt of your sister Sodom: pride, surfeit of
> food and prosperous ease . . . she did not aid the poor and
> needy.   (E Z E K . 16 : 49)

The story of the Flood, therefore, as recounted in the Book of Genesis,
is of profound importance as a landmark in the history of religion. The
idea that human sinfulness finds its expression in the state of society,
and that God holds men and society accountable for their misdeeds, is
revolutionary in the ancient world. No less remarkable is the fact that
the Bible, dealing with non-Israelites, does not conceive of their sin in
what we should call today—in flagrant misuse of the word—"religious"
terms. That is to say, he does not accuse them of idolatrous or cultic
offenses. The culpability of the generation of the flood lies strictly in the
socio-moral sphere.

The mythological contrast

In our discussion of the Creation story, we had occasion to note the
inseparable link between mythology and polytheism. We contrasted the
highly imaginative language of the *Enuma Elish* with the simple majesty
of Genesis. Much the same situation exists in the present instance.

From a literary point of view, the biblical story is probably the poorer
for its monotheistic rendering. It records very simply,

> And on the seventh day, the waters of the Flood came upon
> the earth . . . All the fountains of the great deep burst apart
> and the flood-gates of the sky broke open. The rain fell upon
> the earth forty days and forty nights.   (7 : 10–12)

In the entire story the Bible has left no room for any force at work other
than the will of the one God.

In striking contrast, the flood episode in the *Epic of Gilgamesh* is satu-
rated with mythology. See how the onset of the deluge is there described.

> With the first glow of dawn,
> A black cloud rose up from the horizon.
> Inside it Adad thunders,
> While Shullat and Hanish go in front,

Moving as heralds over hill and plain.
Erragal tears out the posts,
Forth comes Ninurta and causes the dikes to follow
The Anunnaki lift up the torches,
Setting the land ablaze with their glare.
Consternation over Adad reaches to the heavens,
Who turned to blackness all that had been light.
(The wide) land was shattered like (a pot!)
for one day the south-storm (blew,)
Gathering speed as it blew, (submerging the mountains,)
Overtaking (the people) like a battle.
No one can see his fellow,
Nor can the people be recognized from heaven.[47]

Note the multiplicity of divine beings who share in the work. Adad is the god of storm and rain; Shullat and Hanish are his two heralds; Erragal who pulls out the dams of the subterranean waters is Nergal, god of the nether world; Ninurta who broke the dykes is the irrigation god, and the Annunaki are the divinities of the lower regions.

While considering the mythological contrasts, one may not ignore a close parallel found in a phrase that seems to be a direct verbal echo of the Babylonian tradition. In both versions the first human act performed after the disembarkation from the ark or boat was the bringing of a sacrifice. Just as "the Lord smelled the pleasing odor" of Noah's oblation, so "the gods smelled the sweet savor" of that of Utnapishtim.[48] Here the parallel ends, for in the biblical account there is nothing remotely resembling the repugnant sequel of the Gilgamesh version that "the gods crowded like flies" around the burnt offering. Clearly, this is meant to be taken literally, for the pagan gods, being subservient to matter, were thought to be in need of material sustenance. One of the universal beliefs of paganism was that the gods required food and drink to sustain their immortal and supramundane quality. Unlike Noah, Utnapishtim offered a libation as well as an animal sacrifice. The destruction of mankind by the flood had deprived the gods of food and drink for a prolonged period; hence, their immoderate, greedy, response.[49]

It cannot be determined with certainty what the Bible had in mind by describing God in such human terms as inhaling the pleasing odor of Noah's sacrifice. But we may note the delicate rephrasing of the incident and the deliberate sloughing off of the accompanying obnoxious details. Moreover, whereas in the Gilgamesh story the sacrifice is the prologue to quarrels and mutual recriminations among the gods, in the Bible it is introductory to the divine blessing of man and the covenant made with him. Finally, it is not without interest that the same Hebrew phrase employed in the Noah story is, in later ritual usage, a technical term divested of its literal meaning and signifying divine acceptance of man's attempt to find conciliation with his Maker.[50]

This use of mythological terminology as a vehicle for the expression of exalted ideas is already familiar to us from the Creation story. Here, too, the Hebrew writer has adopted language reminiscent of mythic connections. The very word *mabbul,* translated "Flood," is now recognized as having denoted originally the heavenly, or upper, part of the cosmic ocean.[51] "The fountains of the great deep" are none other than the primeval sea.

In other words, the Deluge is directly connected with Creation. It is, in fact, the exact reversal of it. The two halves of the primordial waters of chaos which God separated as a primary stage in the creative process, were in danger of reuniting. To the Bible, the Flood is a cosmic catastrophe. This explains why Genesis, unlike the Mesopotamian versions, is completely silent about the city in which the hero lived and why reference is repeatedly made to *"man's* wickedness on *earth"* (6:5), to the fact that *"the earth"* became corrupt, *the earth* was filled with injustice . . . , *all flesh* had corrupted its ways *on earth* (11f.), and God decided to put an end to *"all flesh,"* "to destroy them *with the earth"* (11:13), "to destroy *all flesh* under the sky" (11:17).

Now this kind of universalistic terminology, and this concept of the Flood as a returning to primeval chaos, has profound moral implications. For it means that in biblical theology human wickedness, the inhumanity of man to man, undermines the very foundations of society. The pillars, upon which rests the permanence of all earthly relationships, totter and collapse, bringing ruin and disaster to mankind.

This idea is one of the dominant themes of Scripture and runs like a thread of scarlet throughout its literature. The Psalmist, in excoriating the perversion of justice in the law courts, makes use of the same motif. He denounces the exploitation by the wicked of the poor and the fatherless, the afflicted and the destitute. Through such deeds, he says, "all the foundations of the earth are shaken."[52]

The new creation

The connection between Creation and the Flood is a very real one in biblical theology, especially in the biblical interpretation of human history. Reference has already been made to the fact that in both Mesopotamian and Hebrew traditions, the Flood episode constitutes an epochal juncture in the history of the world. But this is the only important similarity. Beyond this, the story of Noah is developed in the Bible to a degree and in a way that has no parallel in Mesopotamian sources.

In the Bible, Noah's birth is represented in the genealogical lists as the first after Adam's death. This reinforces the notion of Noah as the second father of mankind and emphasizes the idea of the immediate post-diluvial period as a new beginning to life on earth. The covenant between man and God symbolizes, furthermore, a new relationship between the Deity and His world. Noah's ark is thus the matrix of a new creation. That is why only his immediate family is taken aboard, and why there are no other human passengers, no other relatives, no friends, no ship-builders as in the Mesopotamian accounts.

Moreover, Noah received the same divine blessing as Adam, "be fertile and increase" (1:28; 9:1). Just as genealogical lists follow the Creation story,[53] so the "Table of Nations" [54] expressing fulfillment of the blessing, comes after the Flood story. The lineage of all nations is traced back to a common ancestor, Noah.

This schematization of human relationships, artificial though it be, is an unparalleled notion in the world picture of any people in ancient times. Its comprehensiveness and universality prefigure the idea of the brotherhood of man.

The blessing, the covenant, and the rainbow

The biblical preoccupation with human relationships, the peculiar social orientation of the religion of Israel, is powerfully brought out through another incident superficially common to the Mesopotamian and Hebrew versions. The two heroes, Noah and Utnapishtim, are both recipients of divine blessings after the disaster is all over.

In a moving passage in the Gilgamesh epic, we are told that after suppressing his anger at the discovery that some human had escaped the flood, the god Enlil took Utnapishtim and his wife by the hand, led them to the boat, and made them kneel down on either side of him. Then, touching their foreheads, he granted them the gift of immortality and removed them from human society. Such is the climax of the most celebrated Mesopotamian version of the flood story.[55]

This scene, it will be noticed, is thoroughly devoid of any universal significance, completely empty of any didactic values. It contains no message of comfort to mankind, no promise for the future, no offering of security. It is a reflection of the inherent limitations of the polytheistic system.

Far different is the treatment of the biblical writer. First of all, God reassures man that universal destruction will never again be visited upon the world. Then, He promises that the rhythm of life is to be restored and the orderly processes of nature, the beneficent gifts of God, will once more be resumed.

"Never again will I doom the world because of man . . . nor will I ever again destroy every living being as I have done. So long as the earth endures, seedtime and harvest, cold and heat, summer and winter, day and night, shall not cease."

(8 : 21f.)

This is followed by the divine blessing to Noah and his sons, not to withdraw from the world, but to be fertile and to increase, to replenish the earth and to utilize the resources of nature for the benefit of mankind.[56]

The divine promise and blessing are sealed for all eternity by a covenant.

"I now establish My covenant with you and your offspring to come . . . I will maintain My covenant with you: never again shall all flesh be cut off by waters of a flood, and never again shall there be a flood to destroy the earth."

(9 : 9–11)

This covenant is strictly an act of divine grace, for it involves no corresponding obligation or participation on the part of man. God binds Himself unconditionally to maintain His pledge to all humanity. Finally, God sets the rainbow in the sky as a symbolic guarantee of the covenant.

"This is the sign of the covenant that I set between Me and you, and every living creature with you, for all ages to come. I have set my bow in the clouds and it shall serve as a sign of the covenant between Me and the earth. When I bring clouds over the earth, and the bow appears in the clouds, I will remember My covenant between Me and you and every living creature among all flesh, so that the waters shall never again become a flood to destroy all flesh. When the bow is in the clouds, I will see it and remember the everlasting covenant between God and all living creatures, all flesh that is on earth. That . . . shall be the sign of the covenant that I have established between Me and all flesh that is on earth."

(9 : 12–17)

It is unclear whether the Hebrew writer is here explaining what he considers to be the true cause of the origin of the rainbow, or whether an existing celestial phenomenon is being endowed henceforth with new significance. Either way, this particular idea is most unusual in biblical literature. Parallels may indeed be cited for phenomena of nature, such as a cloud or fire, achieving special symbolic prominence.[57] But in such cases, the symbolism is individual, local and temporal, not universal and eternal as in the case of the rainbow.

The rainbow story contains yet another interesting feature. The motif of the bow is not uncommon in ancient Near Eastern mythology. In *Enuma Elish,* Marduk suspended in the sky his victorious bow with which he had defeated Tiamat and set it as a constellation.[58] Elsewhere in Babylonian astronomy we find that a number of stars grouped together in the shape of a bow were mythologically identified with the accoutrements of the war goddess. A magic bow is also a prominent feature of a Canaanite myth dealing with the relationship of the youth Aqhat to the bellicose goddess Anath. The Bible itself, in several poetic texts, makes mention of God's bow.[59] Always, the word *qeshet* designates a weapon of war. Only in the context of the divine covenant does this word acquire the meaning of "rainbow," [60] and here alone of all Near Eastern symbolism the divine bow does not have astral significance.

The rainbow episode was thus another Israelite break with contemporary notions. It is not impossible that the numerous biblical references to a divine bow and arrow are echoes of some ancient Hebrew epic. The Flood story, however, has identified the bow with the rainbow rather than a constellation, because the former is closely associated with rain and readily lends itself to a connection with the Deluge. More important is the fact that the symbol of divine bellicosity and hostility has been transformed into a token of eternal reconciliation between God and Man.

The rainbow motif is completely absent from the Mesopotamian versions for the obvious reason that they have no universalistic setting and that the notion of an unconditionally binding convenant between the gods and mankind would have been inconsistent with the inherently capricious nature of pagan gods.

Some would draw a parallel between the rainbow and the passage in the Gilgamesh epic which relates how, when the gods partook of Utnapishtim's sacrifice, Ishtar lifted up her jewelled necklace and swore that she would ever be mindful of the days of the flood and never forget them.[61] However, not only is this act not accompanied by any promise or assurance about mankind's future, but worse still, the oath came from the lips of just that member of the Mesopotamian pantheon most notorious for faithlessness. Elsewhere in the same epic it is related that Ishtar tried to seduce Gilgamesh, but the hero rejected her advances on the grounds that she had never before proved constant in love and that her perfidy was public knowledge.[62] Contrast this with the fact that the great prophet of the time of the Babylonian Exile could cite God's oath to Noah as a source of comfort and assurance to the unfortunate of his generation.[63]

The foregoing study of the biblical Deluge story leaves no room for doubting the direct connection between it and the Mesopotamian tradition. Yet a closer look at the two and a careful understanding of the purposes of the Bible leave us with quite a different impression. The Hebrew version is an expression of the biblical polemic against paganism. This assault is carried on, not on the level of dialectics, but indirectly and inferentially. Through an inspired process of selection, revision and addition, whether deliberate or intuitive, the original material has been so thoroughly reshaped as to become an entirely new and original creation purged of its polytheistic dross. What in the Mesopotamian tradition was apparently of local importance became in the Bible a major event of cosmic significance. What there is largely casual and contingent has become here causal and determinative. Like the Creation narrative, that of Noah and the Flood has been made into a vehicle for the expression of some of the most profound biblical teachings, an instrument for the communication of universal moral truths, the medium through which God makes known what He demands of man.

1. Frazer, *Folklore*, I, pp. 104-361.
2. That the Genesis flood story is derived from a northern Mesopotamian version is likely from the mention of Ararat; see Wright, *Bib. Ar.*, p. 119. For a possible Amorite origin of the name Noah, see J. Lewy in *Mélanges Syriens*, (Paris, 1939), I, p. 273ff. *SpG*, p. 42, suggests the possibility of a Hurrian medium of transmission.
3. For the different Mesopotamian versions, see A. Heidel, *The Gilgamesh Epic*; A. Parrot, *The Flood and Noah's Ark*, pp. 24-40. See, also, W. G. Lambert, *JSS*, V (1960), pp. 113-123.
4. See P. Schnabel, *Berossos*, esp. pp. 172-184.
5. For English translations, see R. Campbell Thompson, *The Epic of Gilgamesh*; Heidel, *op. cit.*; E. A. Speiser in *ANET*, pp. 72-99; N. K. Sandars, *The Epic of Gilgamesh*.
6. See S. N. Kramer, *JAOS*, LXIV (1944), pp. 7-23, 83; *idem* in Garelli, *GSL*, pp. 59-60.
7. On the representation of the Gilgamesh epic in art, see H. Frankfort, *Cylinder Seals*, pp. 62-67; cf., also, pp. 73, 90, 176; P. Amiet in Garelli, *GSL*, pp. 169-173; G. Offner, *ibid.*, pp. 175-181.

8. See A. Goetze and S. Levy, *Atiqot*, II (1957), pp. 108–115, (English ed. 1959, pp. 121–8).

9. For the archaeological documentation, see A. Parrot, *op. cit*, pp. 45–53; Wright, *Bib. Ar.*, p. 120.

1 0. For the interweaving of the J and P documents see, *SkG*, p. 147f.

1 1. EZEK. 14:14; ISA. 54:9. For the epic substratum, see Cassuto, *Noah*, pp. 16–22. On the Ezekiel references, see S. Spiegel in *LGJV*, I, pp. 305–355; M. Noth, *VT*, I (1951), pp. 251–60.

1 2. GEN. 5; 11:10–26.

1 3. *ANET*, p. 265; Th. Jacobsen, *The Sumerian King List*, p. 77.

1 4. Heidel, *op. cit.*, p. 227. A small Sumerian tablet, independent of the King List, also lists ten ante-diluvian kings; see W. G. Lambert, *JSS*, V (1960), p. 115.

1 5. Lambert, *ibid*, p. 116.

1 6. Gilgamesh, XI:14; *ANET*, p. 93.

1 7. *ANET*, p. 44.

1 8. *Ibid.*

1 9. Gilgamesh, XI:24; *ANET*, p. 93.

2 0. *ANET*, p. 105.

2 1. Heidel, *op. cit.*, p. 117.

2 2. Gilgamesh, XI:28ff., 57ff.; *ANET*, p. 93.

2 3. GEN. 16:14; cf. Gilgamesh, XI:65.

2 4. Gilgamesh, XI:27; *ANET*, p. 93.

2 5. *ANET*, p. 105.

2 6. Gilgamesh, XI:88; *ANET*, p. 94.

2 7. *ANET*, p. 105.

2 8. Gilgamesh, XI:133; *ANET*, p. 94.

2 9. Heidel, *op. cit.*, p. 118.

3 0. Gilgamesh, XI:140; *ANET*, p. 94.

3 1. Gilgamesh, XI:146–154; *ANET*, p. 94f.

3 2. Heidel, *op. cit.*, p. 117.

3 3. Gilgamesh, XI:155–161; *ANET*, p. 95.

3 4. Heidel, *op. cit.*, p. 117.

3 5. Gilgamesh, XI:189–95; *ANET*, p. 95.

3 6. Gilgamesh, XI:113–126; *ANET*, p. 94.

3 7. EXOD. 2:3–5.

3 8. See Cassuto, *Noah*, p. 40f.

3 9. *ANET*, p. 104; cf. p. 105f.

4 0. J. J. Finkelstein, *Commentary*, Nov. 1958, p. 436f. It is of interest to compare the complaint of the Hyksos ruler Apophis to the Theban king Sekenenre that the hippopotami in Thebes, 400 miles away, disturbed his sleep! See G. Steindorff and K. C. Seele, *When Egypt Ruled the East*, p. 28.

4 1. Gilgamesh, XI:179ff.; *ANET*, p. 95.

4 2. *ANET*, p. 44, cf., also, Schnabel, *op. cit.*, p. 181.

4 3. Gilgamesh, XI:20ff.; *ANET*, p. 93.

4 4. *ANET*, p. 44.

4 5. Cf. the contrast between *hamas* and "justice" in EZEK. 45:9; Job 19:7.

4 6. JONAH 3:8.

4 7. Gilgamesh, XI:96–112; *ANET*, p. 94.

4 8. Gilgamesh, XI:159ff.; *ANET*, p. 95.

4 9. See de Vaux, *AI*, p. 449f.

5 0. Cf. AMOS 5:21f.

5 1. See J. Begrich, *ZS*, VI (1928), pp. 135–153.

5 2. PS. 82:5.

5 3. GEN. 4:17f.; 5:1–32.

5 4. *Ibid.*, 10:1–32.

5 5. Gilgamesh, XI:189–196; *ANET*, p. 95.

5 6. GEN. 9:1–7.

5 7. EXOD. 13:21; 16:10; LEV. 16:2.

5 8. *Enuma Elish,* VI:84–92; *ANET*, p. 69. See *SkG*, p. 173.

5 9. HAB. 3:9ff.; PS. 7:13; LAM. 2:4.

6 0. *Qeshet* in this sense is elsewhere found only in EZEK. 1:28.

6 1. Gilgamesh, XI:162–165; *ANET*, p. 95.

6 2. Gilgamesh, VI:1–79; *ANET*, p. 83f.

6 3. ISA. 54:9.

CHAPTER III

The Tower of Babel

GENESIS 11:1-9

All the earth had the same language and the same words. And as men migrated from the east, they came upon a valley in the land of Shinar and settled there. They said to one another, "Come, let us make bricks and burn them hard." —Brick served them as stone, and bitumen served them as mortar. —And they said, "Come let us build a city, and a tower with its top in the sky, to make a name for ourselves;[1] else we shall be scattered all over the world." The Lord came down to look at the city and tower which man had built, and the Lord said, "If, as one people with one language for all, this is how they have begun to act, then nothing that they may propose to do will be out of their reach. Come, let us, then, go down and confound their speech there, so that they shall not understand one another's speech." Thus the Lord scattered them from there over the face of the whole earth; and they stopped building the city. That is why it was called Babel (Babylon), because there the Lord confounded the speech of the whole earth; and from there the Lord scattered them over the face of the earth.

(11:1-9)

Introduction

This story of the "Tower of Babel," as it is popularly called, is not likely to find its parallel or prototype in Babylonian literature.[2] For one thing, a native of Babylon would hardly look upon the building of his great city as displeasing to the deity. For another, there is the opprobrious interpretation of the name of the city, so that to this day "Babel" in English implies meaningless speech. At the same time, the surprise expressed at the use of brick and bitumen as building materials stamps the author as a foreigner not accustomed to conditions in lower Mesopotamia. Finally one cannot but sense that a general air of satirical hostility to pagan nations pervades the story.

On the other hand, the narrative reveals, as we shall see, an astonishingly intimate knowledge of Babylonian building techniques, displays some remarkable verbal correspondences with cuneiform literary sources, and features some typically Mesopotamian motifs.

Yet paradoxically enough, the story exhibits a complete lack of understanding of the true nature and purpose of the building project. In fact, it seems to assume that the city of Babylon was never completed.[3] No one would ever know from the nine-verse saga that the locale of the incident was to become the mighty cultural, religious and political center of a great empire. To add to the mystery, it might be mentioned that although quite early in biblical exegesis the "Tower of Babel" came to symbolize human vainglory and sinful rebellion against God, the narrative nowhere explicitly defines the sin of the sons of man, so that the cause of divine anger is difficult to understand. Moreover, it is exceedingly strange that so fruitful a source of later legendary embellishment as is this story is never again referred to in the Hebrew Bible.[4] The prophets frequently castigate Babylon as typifying pagan arrogance and insolent oppression,[5] but they never cite the "Tower of Babel," as they do Sodom and Gomorrah, to illustrate their discourse.

The ethnological framework

No solution to these problems is possible if the story be considered in isolation from its wider context. The ethnological setting in which it has been placed must be taken into account if we are to understand the writer's historiosophic purposes.[6]

It will be noted at once that the saga of the building enterprise follows immediately upon the "Table of Nations."[7] The various races of men are portrayed as all having sprung from a single stock. Mankind is differentiated into three branches of one family, each being traced back to one of the sons of Noah.

> The sons of Noah who came out of the ark were Shem, Ham and Japheth ... and from these the whole world branched out. (9 : 18f.)

The genealogical tables begin with a formula,

> These are the lives of Shem, Ham and Japheth, the sons of Noah: sons were born to them after the Flood. (10 : 1)

They conclude with another formula,

> These are the groupings of Noah's descendants according to their origins, by their nations, and from these the nations branched out on the earth after the Flood. (10 : 32)

This emphatic reiteration of the common ancestry of post-diluvial men, and the stress upon their national divisions, serves two immediate purposes. It points up the natural, non-magical approach of the Bible to the problem of the rapid increase of humanity after the Flood, and it expresses at the same time the notion that this natural proliferation is in accord with the divine will. For the repeopling of the earth is a matter of great concern to God. He blessed Noah and his sons with the words,

> Be fertile and increase, and fill the earth.
> (9 : 1)

By way of contrast, the Mesopotamian sources so far discovered are not clear on this point. There is some evidence from the Atrahasis Epic for a belief that the earth became repopulated by means of practical magic and the recitation of spells.[8]

A good example of such a mythological approach is the Greek legend of Deucalion and Pyrrha. These sole survivors of the flood pleaded with Zeus to renew mankind. In response, they were told to cast the bones of their mother behind them. This they properly understood to mean that they were to pick up stones from the earth and throw them over their shoulders. Those handled by Deucalion became male humans, while those thrown by Pyrrha became women.[9]

To get back to the narrative in Genesis, the fulfillment of the divine will is not merely to be seen in the natural human response to the divine command. The rise of ethnological divisions is equally part of God's scheme of history and the "Table of Nations" delineates these divisions and their interrelationships.

It is worthwhile paying attention to the formulaic summaries following each of the national groupings.

> (These are the sons of Japheth) by their lands—each with its language—their clans and their nations.   (10 : 5)

> These are the descendants of Ham, according to their clans and languages, by their lands and nations.   (10 : 20)

> These are the descendants of Shem, according to their clans and languages, by their lands, according to their nations.
>   (10 : 31)

In each case, mention is made of territorial, linguistic and national diversity. However, in the "Tower of Babel" story we observe that the text tells nothing of ethnological divisions. God's activities deal only with the confusion of speech and the world-wide distribution of the human race. We may conclude, therefore, that the biblical writer accepts ethnic diversity as a natural product of the multiplication of the human species in accordance with the divine blessing and will. But the rise of linguistic diversity and the dispersal of mankind over the face of the globe have to be separately accounted for. This, then, is one of the functions of the "Tower of Babel" narrative.

One language

The Bible is strangely silent on the phenomenon of language itself. It has no myths to explain its origins. It has no observations to make on the universality of human speech. It assumes, very simply, that mankind once possessed an original common language. The Hebrew author was attracted only by the incredible diversity of tongues that characterizes the human race.[10]

The belief that there was once a time when all peoples of the earth spoke one language may possibly have been current in ancient Mesopotamia. A Sumerian mythological tablet inscribed before 2000 B.C.E. tells of a golden age in dim antiquity when:

> The whole universe, the people in unison, to Enlil in one tongue gave praise.[11]

However, it is not at all necessary to assume that the Bible made use of the Sumerian myth. As we have seen, the basic unity of mankind is a cardinal theme in the Creation and Flood stories. If all men are envisaged as constituting ultimately one great family with a common ancestry, then inevitably there must have been a time when men also shared a common language.[12] So it becomes necessary to explain how a polyglot humanity came into being. The Babel narrative is thus in the first place etiological and complementary to the preceding chapter; it provides the necessary historical background.

The dispersal of mankind

It must not be thought, however, that the interests of the Bible were solely antiquarian. The confounding of human speech was not an end in itself. It was only the means by which God's true purpose could be accomplished, namely, that men should spread out over the whole earth.

Now the primary motive of the city-and-tower builders of the Babel story was precisely to guard against this eventuality. Man had fulfilled part of the divine blessing—"be fertile and increase"—but he had balked, apparently, at "filling the earth." The building project was thus a deliberate attempt to thwart the expressed will of God, something that would interfere with the unfolding of the divine scheme of history. It is in this light that the sin of the builders must be viewed and the vexation of God be regarded.[13]

The first eleven chapters of the Book of Genesis constitute a kind of

universal history of mankind. Thereafter, the interest of the Bible nar-
rows and focuses almost exclusively upon the fortunes and destinies of
Abraham and his clan. The narrative is moving toward the two control-
ling and paramount themes of all the Torah and prophetical literature—
the election of the people of Israel and the centrality of the Land of Israel
in that people's relationships with God. It will be readily understood,
therefore, why the rise of ethnological, linguistic and territorial divisions
among the sons of men is of such concern to the Bible, and why the
actual act of building the city and tower is of secondary importance. This
transition from the universal to the particular, this discrimination of the
Hebrew patriarchs from mankind at large, is furnished by the "Tower
of Babel" story.

Two singularities of the wider narrative, one contextual, the other
stylistic, serve to hint at the shifting center of attention. Preceding the
genealogies of Chapter 10 is a strange digression about the drunkenness
of Noah.[14] Whatever interpretation be put upon the story, one thing
above all is certain, and that is the emphasis upon the virtue and piety
of Shem, patriarch of the Semites, and his elevation to a position of divine
favor. Then, in the Table of Nations itself, the order of Noah's three sons
is deliberately reversed, so that the delineation of the descendants of
Shem, ancestor of Israel, has a climactic effect.

The rise of idolatry

The change of scene from the story of mankind in general to the story of
the people of Israel which is signified by the Tower of Babel narrative,
also marks another turning-point in biblical historiosophy. A careful
scrutiny of Scripture shows that it regards monotheism as the original
religion of mankind. According to this view, not a trace of paganism is
to be found in the world until the rise of ethnic divisions among the
children of men. That is to say, a universal monotheistic era in human
history is thought of as coming to an end with the generation of the dispersal of mankind.[15]

This idea is not explicitly stated in the sources. But it is tacitly assumed
to be the case that the appearance of idolatry is coeval with the rise of
nations. Henceforth, the knowledge of the true God is regarded as being
the exclusive possession of Abraham and his descendants. The other
peoples of the world, as distinct from individuals like Abimelech, for

example, are considered to have been polytheistic from the beginning. The stage is thus set for the launching of the people of Israel upon its historic course as a "light to the nations," [16] as the bearer of the message of monotheism to the world.

"Come let us build us a city"

The text clearly implies that the author conceived mankind after the Flood as being nomadic until, in the course of their wanderings, men chanced upon a valley in the land of Shinar.[17] Whatever the origin of this name, it is certain from several biblical passages that it here corresponds to the region known as Sumer and Akkad in the lower Tigris-Euphrates Valley.[18] Here men set about building Babylon, the first post-diluvial city.

Interestingly enough, a similar tradition was preserved by Berossus who, in concluding his own version of the flood story, tells us that after Xisuthros was transferred to the realm of the gods, the other survivors "went to Babylon, dug up the writings at Sippar, founded many cities, erected temples, and (so) rebuilt Babylon." [19] It is not unlikely that the biblical account and that of Berossus both stem from a common tradition. However, there is one significant difference between the two. Whereas Berossus assumes that Babylon existed before the flood and was simply restored afterwards, it is implicit in the biblical account that Babylon was not founded until after the Flood.

Berossus, of course, was familiar with Mesopotamian tradition, crystallized in the *Enuma Elish* epic ascribing the building of the terrestrial city of Babylon, together with its celestial counterpart, to the gods themselves at the creation of the world.[20] The Bible, by transferring the founding of the city to post-diluvial times, is in this way tacitly combating the polytheistic myth. Moreover, it extends this anti-pagan polemic still further, by presenting the founding of Babylon as a disastrous alienation from God and by indulging in deliberate word-play on the name of the city.

Babylon, Hebrew *Babel,* was pronounced *Babilim* by the Mesopotamians. The name is apparently non-Semitic in origin and may even be pre-Sumerian.[21] But the Semitic inhabitants, by popular etymology, explained it as two separate Akkadian words, *bab-ilim,* meaning "the gate of the god." This interpretation refers to the role of the city as the great religious center. It also has mystical overtones connected with the concept of "the navel of the earth," the point at which heaven and earth meet. The Hebrew author, by his uncomplimentary word-play substituting *balal* for *Babel* has replaced the "gate of the god" by "a confusion of speech," and satirized thereby the pagan religious beliefs.

". . . and a tower"

Sometime around the middle of the 5th century B.C.E., the famous Greek historian Herodotus paid a visit to Mesopotamia. Among his observations and impressions is a detailed report on the city of Babylon.[22] A few decades ago his account was being treated with considerable skepticism. However, with the progress of modern archaeology confirming much of his material this attitude has given way to a healthy respect for its general reliability.[23]

Among the numerous items of information that Herodotus records is the fact that still standing in his time was the sacred enclosure of Babylon and that in the center rose a solid multi-tiered tower. It is universally agreed by modern scholars that Herodotus and the Bible are both describing none other than the famous ziqqurat that was closely related to the Esagila, the complex of buildings comprising the temple of Marduk.

The word "ziqqurat" is derived from an Akkadian verb *zaqaru* meaning, "to rise up high." It was used specifically for the great towers constructed at the holy places. The ziqqurat was the most outstanding feature of a Mesopotamian city and dominated its entire area. Not every city had its temple tower, but most did, and some had more than one. So far, over thirty such have been unearthed in excavations carried out at more than twenty-five different sites, with the greatest concentration being found in lower Mesopotamia.[24]

The architecture of the ziqqurats was not uniform; some were rectangular, some square. But in general, they were massive, lofty structures, with the tower rising from its base in a succession of receding stages, each approached by an external ramp or stairway.

The ziqqurat at Babylon to which our biblical narrative refers, was one of the largest and most famous of all. Equipped with seven diminishing stories, it rose to a height of about 300 feet from a square base of the same dimensions. The whole vast structure was adorned with two sanctuaries, one at the summit, and one at the base.[25]

We shall deal later with the purpose and function of the ziqqurat. At the moment our attention is arrested by a curious notation of the Bible.

"Come let us make bricks and burn them hard."

The rise of monumental temple architecture, the construction of such spectacular edifices on so colossal a scale, was only made possible by the invention of the brick. Long before 3000 B.C.E. men had learned to fashion building material by molding mud or clay and drying it in the sun. Later on, the value of the invention was enhanced by the discovery of the technique of baking bricks in ovens. This was found to help bear the crushing weight of the high buildings.[26]

Now it is curious that Scripture has gone out of its way to remark upon the materials used in the construction of the Tower of Babel. Our curiosity turns to surprise when we learn that the core of the ziqqurat consisted of a solid mass of crude sun-dried bricks, encased in an outer coating of kiln-fired brick walls. Moreover, it is also a fact that in Mesopotamia oven-burnt bricks were generally reserved for use in the construction of palaces and temples, whereas the employment of sunburnt bricks exclusively was confined to common houses.

The important role of the brick in Mesopotamian architecture is reflected again and again in Akkadian texts. A bi-lingual version of the creation story speaks of a time when "no brick was laid, no brick-mold was formed," [27] a clear recognition of the great material revolution which the invention of the brick brought about. *Enuma Elish,* referring specifically to the founding of Babylon by the gods and their building of the temple and staged-tower in honor of Marduk, tells that, "for one whole year they molded bricks." [28] Akkadian building inscriptions which hail the achievements of the great kings repeatedly emphasize the making of the bricks. What is more, we now know that the molding of the first brick constituted an important rite in the construction or repair of a temple and that this act was accompanied by elaborate ceremonies.[29]

"Brick served them as stone and bitumen served them as mortar"

The wonderment of Scripture was aroused by two other distinguishing characteristics of the Tower building. Although the use of kiln-fired brick was practically unknown in Palestine in the pre-biblical periods, sun-dried clay bricks were widespread. But the hills of Palestine provided an abundant source of stone and that, in fact, was the most important building material in the country. In contrast, stone was exceedingly rare in southern Mesopotamia. The exclusive use of bricks was to the Bible a noteworthy peculiarity.

Even more unusual was the utilization of bitumen as mortar. In Egypt and Palestine the mortar was of the same material as the bricks.[30] But only in Mesopotamia was bitumen used extensively for building purposes. Due to the poor quality of the fuel it was not possible to obtain high temperatures for the kilns. As a result, the bricks were quite fragile and porous. To counteract this, a bituminous mastic was used to add to their compressive strength and impermeability.[31]

These peculiarities of Mesopotamian construction techniques find literary expression in numerous Babylonian building inscriptions where "with bitumen and burnt-brick" is a standard formula.[32] Herodotus, as well as the Bible, was struck by the same fact. In describing the construction of a moat, he records as follows:

> As fast as they dug the moat the soil which they got from the cutting was made into bricks, and when a sufficient number were completed they baked the bricks in kilns. Then they set to building . . . using throughout for their cement hot bitumen.[33]

In the light of all the foregoing we cannot but express astonishment at the remarkable familiarity of Scripture with Mesopotamian technology in the historical period. Furthermore, the conclusion is inescapable that our story is told from the standpoint of a non-Mesopotamian.

"With its top in the sky"

It has been customary to see in this passage the key to the meaning of the Tower of Babel story, and to interpret it as implying an attempt to storm heaven in insolent rebellion against God. We have already pointed out, however, that the sin of the generation lay in quite a different direction, and that it actually consisted of resistance to the divine will that the children of men be dispersed over the whole world. The soundness of this conclusion may be judged from several lines of evidence.

In the first place, there is no biblical analogy for the notion that it is possible for men physically to storm heaven. Further, from what we know of Mesopotamian religion the idea would have been thoroughly whimsical to the tower builders. Moreover, where the description is used elsewhere in the Bible it means nothing more than a great height. Thus the cities of Canaan are said to have walls "sky-high." [34] Finally, the expression is actually a stereotype in Mesopotamian inscriptions, used particularly with reference to the building or repair of ziqqurats. As early as the beginning of the second millennium B.C.E., Gudea, Sumerian ruler of Lagash, says of the temple of Eninnu that "it rose from earth to heaven." [35] A text from Nippur addresses a tower "whose peak reaches the sky." [36] Hammurabi (eighteenth century B.C.E.) gives himself the epithet, "raiser up of the top of Eanna" and it is related of him that "he built the temple tower . . . whose top is sky-high." [37] In the seventh century B.C.E., Esarhaddon informs posterity that he "raised to heaven the head" of the temple of Ashur, he "made high its top up to heaven." [38]

Most interestingly, it is just with respect to the temple of Marduk in Babylon that the phrase is persistently used. The temple itself was known as the "Esagila," which means, "the house of the lifting up of the head." A passage in the *Enuma Elish,* in a word-play on the name, says that the gods "raised high the head of Esagila." [39] Nabopolassar (626–605) and Nebuchadrezzar (605/4–562) both repaired this temple and both recorded the fact in numerous inscriptions which stress the "raising high of the head" of the tower "to rival the heavens." [40]

The biblical phraseology cannot be divorced from this literary tradition. In describing the desire of the builders to erect a tower "with its top in the sky," the writer once again displays his intimate knowledge, not only of the Babylonian scene, but also of the technical terminology of the building inscriptions.

"*To make a name for ourselves*"

The same conclusion must be reached in respect of still another detail of the story. The descendants of Noah wanted to "make a name" for themselves. At first glance this appears to have been part of the motivation of the builders. Yet a closer look reveals that the sentence is parenthetical. The desire for fame is perfectly human and not in itself reprehensible. Indeed, the granting thereof is part of the divine promise to Abraham. [41] In the light of the other parallels with Mesopotamian custom it is more than likely that here, too, the text cloaks a well-known Sumerian, Assyrian and Babylonian practice.

The names of most of the important kings were associated with building projects which were not only pleasing to the gods, but which also ensured the monarch's eternal posthumous fame. The name and titles of the builder were inscribed on bricks and cylinder seals and deposited in the foundations of the ziqqurats.[42]

Of Gudea of Lagash a temple inscription records that "on account of the great name which he made for himself he was received among the gods into their assembly."[43] Esarhaddon writes that "monuments, inscriptions with my name I made and within it I set."[44] Nebuchadrezzar, who restored the very ziqqurat of which the Bible speaks, records in a commemorative inscription, "the fortifications of Esagila and Babylon I strengthened, and made an everlasting name for my reign."[45]

The function of the ziqqurat

If we have repeatedly emphasized the surprising familiarity of the Hebrew writer with Babylonian conditions, it is not solely for the purpose of illuminating the biblical text, as important as that may be in itself. Rather it is because this very point serves to focus our attention upon a paradoxical situation. To put it simply, our story, which shows such familiarity with Babylonian conditions, exhibits no knowledge whatsoever of the true function of the tower or ziqqurat and the part it played in Mesopotamian religion.

The prime motivation of the builders is said to have been the consolidation of the group unity. This is undoubtedly valid to a limited extent. The very construction activity itself, carried out on a colossal scale and involving as it did large masses of people, implied a considerable concentration of authority and organization. The monumental edifice that resulted was a source of pride to every citizen, so that it served the entire community, politically, socially and religiously as an effective, cohesive force.[46] This feeling is well reflected in the building inscriptions. Nebuchadrezzar writes, "under its (Babylon's) everlasting shadow I gathered all men in peace."[47]

It is also not unlikely that Scripture envisaged a single center to house all the offspring of the sons of Noah, and that the ziqqurat, as the most familiar and outstanding feature of the landscape, would serve as a sort of landmark beckoning reassuringly to any who had lost his way.[48] Yet, the fact remains that our narrative is conspicuously and strangely silent about the real role of the ziqqurat as we now know it to have been. This ignorance cannot be overlooked. It is in such sharp contrast to the situation in other respects that it cries out for explanation.

If we speak, however, of the "true function" of the ziqqurat, it is not to imply that there are no major problems in connection with it still awaiting solution.[49] Nevertheless, we are entitled to draw upon the considerable body of important information that archaeology and the study of comparative religion have placed at our disposal.

Modern scholars are well-nigh unanimous that the ziqqurat symbolized a mountain. To understand what this means it has to be realized that the holy mountain played an important role in most religions in ancient times. Rooted in the earth with its head lost in the clouds, it was the meeting point of heaven and earth. As such, it became the natural arena of divine activity. Here on its heights the gods had their abode, here they gathered in fateful assembly, and here they revealed themselves to man. Being the obvious channel of communication between heaven and earth, the holy mount was looked upon as the center of the universe, the "navel of the earth," the very *axis mundi*.[50]

The association of the ziqqurats with the mountain motif is revealed by the names so many of them bore.[51] That of Nippur was called, "the house of the mountain." At Ashur there was "the house of the mountain of the universe." "The house of the link between heaven and earth" was situated at Larsa. The most famous ziqqurat of all, the subject of our biblical story, was that of Babylon, known as the *E-temen-an-ki*, "the house of the foundation of heaven and earth."

In the flat alluvial plain of Mesopotamia, the ziqqurat constituted a man-made holy mountain in miniature. By way of the stairs or ramp connecting each stage with the other, the god was believed to descend from his ethereal abode to make his presence manifest below. The ziqqurat was thus a means by which man and god might establish direct contact with each other, and the construction of it would be an expression of the human desire to draw closer to the deity, an act of deep piety and religious fervor on the part of man.[52]

The anti-pagan polemic

Now it seems hardly conceivable that the biblical writer, who otherwise knew the Babylonian setting in such intimate detail, should really have been ignorant of the religious function of the tower. If, then, he is quite silent on this subject and portrays the story of its building as an act of arrogant defiance of the will of God, it can only have been intentional. We have to conclude, and there is much evidence in support, that the Tower of Babel saga is a continuation of the anti-pagan polemic of the preceding Creation and Flood stories. The Bible has deliberately selected the mighty city of Babylon with its famed temple of Marduk as the scene for a satire on paganism, its notions, mythology and religious forms. This theme has already been touched upon above in connection with the departure from the tradition of Berossus and the word-play on the name "Babylon."

Let us now examine the anti-pagan polemic in greater detail. We first note the attitude of contempt for that which was the focus for Babylonian national pride, in the reference to the clay bricks and bitumen. Emphasis upon the utilization of so perishable a substance as brick in place of stone underscores the impermanent nature of the edifice.[53] In fact, since we are told that "they stopped building" as a result of God's intervention, the writer must have believed that the city remained unfinished. It is quite probable, therefore, that the saga was inspired by the spectacle of Babylon and its ziqqurat lying in ruins. Such was the case, for instance, after the Hittite raid on the city about 1600 B.C.E.[54]

No less emphatic, if more subtly expressed, is the opposition to a typical Mesopotamian notion about temple building. "The Lord came down to look at the city and tower which *man* had built." The Hebrew term employed here for "man"—*bnei ha'Adam*—is one that is heavily charged with temporal significance. It is man, the earthling, puny and mortal, in contradistinction to the Deity.[55] *Enuma Elish,* the great creation myth of Babylon, describes how the gods erected the Esagila in that city to the greater glory of Marduk.[56] According to Mesopotamian religious psychology the gods were intimately associated with all phases of temple construction. Through their revelation the project was usually initiated, and priests would consult the omens to determine the gods' will at every stage of the operations. Akkadian cylinder seals pictorially represent the gods participating in all the manifold chores which the building of a great edifice entailed.[57] The biblical stress on the strictly human nature of the enterprise breathes a different spirit, one of opposition and protest against this polytheistic concept.

The same may be said of another peculiarity of the narrative. Twice God "came down," once to survey the human scene, and then again to confound men's speech. The identical expression is used of God's intervention at Sodom and Gomorrah.[58] There is no doubt that the phrase smacks of anthropomorphism. Yet the writer could not have intended a literal meaning restrictive of God's omniscience, for the decision to "go down" already implies prior knowledge of affairs from on high. Moreover, as we shall see, God's unlimited power is one of the leading themes of the story. Rather, the writer is demonstrating the ultimate inadequacy of even the most grandiose of human endeavors. Men wished to build a tower with its top in the sky. According to all accepted notions, this ziqqurat was to be a physical link between the divine and human realms. The Bible, by stressing that God "came down," sweeps away such a fancy. Before God's infinite superiority, elevation is meaningless and even the sky-capped tower becomes a puny creation. God's transcendence is absolute and His independence of materiality complete. Not the monumental achievements of human ingenuity, but only the human heart can forge a link with God.

In similar vein, the absolute supremacy of the divine will is demonstrated by the repetition of certain phrases. Men built a tower lest they be "scattered." Twice, the text records that the Lord "scattered" them. Men initiated their rebellious labors with the reiterated summons, "come let us . . ." God expresses his superior determination to thwart man's efforts by the same phrase. The clash of human and divine wills is thus disposed of.

Finally, the writer has used the Tower of Babel story to give voice to a major theme in biblical teaching. The emergence of idolatry is, as we have seen, made coeval with the generation of the city-and-tower builders. The urbanization of society, the growth of material civilization and the rise of monumental architecture may all, from the Bible's point of view, involve a retrograde step in man's spiritual progress.[59] This is a theme that receives its fullest treatment in the prophetic activity of a much later age. But it is highly significant that it appears for the first time at the very inception of Israel's history.

NOTES TO CHAPTER III

1. See further p. 73f. for a somewhat different understanding of the syntax.
2. E. A. Speiser, *Orientalia*, XXV (1956), pp. 317–323 (cf. *SpG*, p. 75f.), regards the account in *Enuma Elish*, VI:60–62 (*ANET*, p. 69), as the ultimate inspiration for our story.
3. All critics assign the Babel narrative to J. While it is certain that this narrative must once have been part of a more extensive tale (cf. G E N . 11:6) connected, perhaps, to G E N . 3:22ff., there is no need to divide it into two separate recensions, as does *GuG*, pp. 92–97. See H. Gressman, *The Tower of Babel*, p. 2; J. Pedersen, *Israel*, I–II, p. 248f.; 520 n.; O. E. Ravn, *ZDMG*, XCI (N. f. 16), (1937), p. 361; Cassuto, *Noah*, pp. 160ff.; Speiser, *Orientalia, loc. cit.*, p. 322.
4. See, however, the Greek to I S A . 10:9.
5. I S A . 13:19; 14:4ff.; 47:7; J E R . 51:53.
6. See Cassuto, *Noah*, p. 96f.
7. G E N . 10.
8. *ANET*, p. 100. See E. Kraeling, *JAOS*, LXVII (1947), p. 183; A. Heidel, *The Gilgamesh Epic*, p. 259f.
9. See Kraeling, *op. cit.*, p. 182; R. Graves, *The Greek Myths*, I, pp. 13ff.; 140, n. 4.
1 0. Cf. E. Ullendorff, *BJRL*, XLIV (1961–62), p. 455f.

1 1. See E. Kraeling. *JBL*, LXVI (1947), p. 284; S. N. Kramer, *JAOS*, LXIII (1943), pp. 191–194; *idem*, *SM*, p. 107, *idem*, *SBO*, III (1959), p. 193.

1 2. That this was Hebrew was, of course, taken for granted and frequently stressed in medieval sources. See Ginzberg, *Legends*, V, p. 205f.; Baron, *SRH*, VII, pp. 14f., 27, 241, n. 64; N. Allony, *OYS*, V (1962), p. 22, n. 6; A. S. Halkin, in *BOS*, p. 241 & n. 37. For the corresponding Greek ideas on the subject of the diversity of languages, see J. Guttmann, *OLD*, pp. 585–594.

1 3. For this interpretation, see Josephus, *Antiquities*, I:IV:1, on which see Ginzberg, *Legends*, V, p. 204, n. 90; the commentaries of RashBam and Ibn Ezra *ad loc.*; Cassuto, *Noah*, p. 154. This would explain why the prophets did not use the story to illustrate the arrogance of Babylon.

1 4. GEN. 9:20–26.

1 5. See Kaufmann, *Toldot*, II, p. 412f.; and in *Molad*, XVII (1959), pp. 336ff.

1 6. ISA. 42:6; 49:6.

1 7. GEN. 11:2.

1 8. Cf. *ibid.* 10:10. See E. Kraeling, *JBL*, LXVI (1947), p. 280, esp. n. 6.

1 9. See Kraeling, *ibid.*, p. 281; *JAOS*, LXVII (1947), p. 179f.

2 0. *Enuma Elish*, VI:56–64; 114f.

2 1. See *GuG*, p. 95; I. Gelb, *JIAS*, I (1955), pp. 1–4.

2 2. Histories, I, §§ 179–183.

2 3. O. E. Ravn, *Herodotus' Description of Babylon*.

2 4. See M. A. Beek, *Atlas of Mesopotamia*, 142ff.

2 5. For a detailed description, see L. H. Vincent, *RB*, LIII (1946), pp. 403–440. See, also, A. Leo Oppenheim, *BA*, VII (1944), pp. 54–63.

2 6. See Oppenheim, *ibid.*, p. 54; G. Childe, *Man Makes Himself*, p. 91; C. Singer, *et al.*, *A History of Technology*, I, p. 467f.

2 7. See Heidel, *BG*, p. 62, l. 3; cf. p. 63, l. 36; p. 65, ll. 27, 72; Kramer, *SM*, p. 61.

2 8. *Enuma Elish*, VI:60; *ANET*, p. 68; Heidel, *BG*, p. 48.

2 9. See Frankfort, *Kingship*, pp. 271–74.

3 0. Franken, *Primer*, p. 131, points out that bricks of Iron Age Palestine, especially in the Jordan Valley area, were laid without any kind of mortar between them.

3 1. See Forbes, *SAT*, II, pp. 67–74. Note his observation, p. 73, that bituminous mortar did not come to be used in the city of Babylon until the time of Hammurabi.

3 2. See S. Langdon, *Building Inscriptions*, where the phrase *ina kupri u agurri* ("with bitumen and burned brick") occurs scores of times. Cf. the proverbs cited in *ANET*, p. 425 and Lambert, *BWL*, p. 249.

3 3. Histories, I, § 179.

3 4. DEUT. 1:28; 9:1.

3 5. Barton, *RISA*, p. 213, A:IX:11; p. 225, A:XX:9; p. 227, A:XXI:23; p. 237, B:I:1; p. 255, B:XXIV:9.

3 6. See Beek, *op. cit.*, p. 142f.

3 7. *ANET*, p. 270, § 36; Driver and Miles, II, pp. 9, 122.

3 8. F. R. Steele, *JAOS*, LXXI (1957), p. 6.

3 9. *Enuma Elish*, VI:62.

4 0. Langdon, *op. cit.*, pp. 48f., 6off.

4 1. GEN. 12:2.

4 2. An echo of this practice is to be found in the midrashic interpretation of Gen. 11:4, on which see Ginzberg, *Legends,* V, p. 203, n. 88.

4 3. Barton, *op. cit.,* p. 231, ll. 20f.

4 4. See n. 38.

4 5. Langdon, *op. cit.,* p. 75.

4 6. *Before Philosophy,* p. 141.

4 7. Langdon, *op. cit.,* pp. 89, 171.

4 8. Frazer, *Folklore,* I, p. 362.

4 9. See A. Parrot, *The Tower of Babel,* pp. 59ff.; Moscati, *FAO,* p. 52.

5 0. On this subject see A. J. Wensinck, *The Ideas of Western Semites;* W. H. Roscher, *Der Omphalosgedanke;* H. Frankfort, *The Birth of Civilization,* pp. 56, 59; M. Eliade, *Cosmos and History,* pp. 12ff. de Vaux, *AI,* pp. 279ff.

5 1. See Beek, *op. cit.,* pp. 142ff.

5 2. See E. A. Speiser, *IEJ,* VII (1957), pp. 203, 206; Hooke, *BAR,* p. 42.

5 3. See Cassuto, *Noah,* p. 157.

5 4. See Wright, *Bib. Ar.,* p. 45.

5 5. For the use of *adam* in contrast to God, cf. N U M . 23:19; D E U T . 4:28, 32; I S A M . 15:29; I I S A M . 7:14; 24:14; I I K I N G S 19:18; I S A . 31:3; 38:11; P S . 11:4; 14:2; 82:6f.; 115:16.

5 6. *Enuma Elish,* VI:49–51.

5 7. See H. Frankfort, *Cylinder Seals,* p. 76; *idem, Kingship,* p. 274; A. S. Kapelrud, *Orientalia,* XXXII (1963), p. 56f. In connection with the last-mentioned article, it should be noted that in the case of the Jerusalem temple, the initiative is ascribed to David, and the project actually received divine discouragement (I I S A M . 7:2ff.).

5 8. G E N . 18:21.

5 9. See Wellhausen, *Prolegomena,* p.302f. Cf. Wright, *OTAE,* p. 53. It is probably not coincidental that the Bible makes Cain, a murderer, the first city-builder (G E N . 4:17).

CHAPTER IV

The Patriarchal Period

GENESIS 12-50

With the genealogies following the Tower of Babel narrative, the first section of biblical literature draws to a close. The universal history of mankind contained in Genesis 1-11 gives way to a narrowing of focus. Henceforth, the interest of Scripture centers primarily upon the people of Israel. The rest of the Book of Genesis concerns itself with the formative, or patriarchal, period. The wanderings and fortunes of Abraham, Isaac and Jacob and the divine promises to them, the emergence of the tribes and their descent to Egypt—all are described in more or less detail.

The problems of chronology

When did all this take place? It is one thing to speak of the patriarchal age, quite another to determine the exact period in history into which it fits. No external sources have, as yet, been uncovered that refer by name to any of the patriarchs or to any of the personages associated with them. Without such synchronistic controls we have solely the biblical data to fall back on, and here, unfortunately, the problems are thoroughly complex.[1]

The length of time covered by the patriarchal period can actually be very simply calculated. Abraham set out from Haran for Canaan in the seventy-fifth year of his life.[2] Twenty-five years later, his son Isaac was born.[3] Jacob came into this world when his father Isaac was sixty years old[4] and was himself one-hundred and thirty when he migrated with his family to Egypt.[5] There thus elapsed a total of two hundred and ninety years from the birth of Abraham to the end of the period, or two hundred and fifteen years from the exodus from Haran to the descent to Egypt.

The complications arise when we attempt to fit this period into the framework of history. Israel's sojourn in Egypt lasted, according to one report, four hundred and thirty years.[6] Solomon built his temple four hundred and eighty years after the Exodus,[7] which would make a total of exactly twelve hundred years after the birth of Abraham (290 + 430 + 480). Since the temple building is synchronized with the fourth year of Solomon's reign,[8] i.e. ca. 958 B.C.E., it should be possible to fix the birth of the patriarch at ca. 2158 B.C.E. and the migration from Haran at ca. 2083 B.C.E.

This calculation, however, is beset with numerous difficulties. The four hundred and thirty years for the duration of the Egyptian episode indeed accord well with the divine declaration to Abraham that his descendants would be strangers in another land for four hundred years.[9] But they conflict with another prediction that the period of national homelessness would last four generations,[10] a time-span well established in the later genealogical tables. Levi, born to Jacob in Mesopotamia, was the father of Kohath, grandfather of Moses.[11] This would make the four hundred and thirty year duration of the Egyptian sojourn indefensible.[12] Interestingly, the Samaritan and Greek versions of the Pentateuch imply two hundred and fifteen years,[13] but even this figure would not be easy to reconcile with just four generations from Levi to Moses.[14]

Another difficulty lies in the four hundred and eighty years said to have elapsed between the Exodus and the temple building.[15] This would place the Exodus at ca. 1440 B.C.E., a date quite unacceptable in the light of several converging lines of evidence which place the great event at least one hundred and sixty years later.

The conflict in the sources between the calculation according to years and that according to generations cannot be satisfactorily resolved. Impressive arguments have been mustered by scholars to place the Abrahamic period either at the beginning or about the middle of the second millennium B.C.E.[16] We shall have to await further evidence for a more definite solution to the problem. However, it is well worth turning our attention to a closer examination of the biblical chronology for this period.

Number harmony

PERSONALITY	EVENT	AGE IN YEARS	SOURCE
Abraham	Migrated from Haran	75	GEN. 12:4
	Married Hagar	85	16:3
	When Isaac was born	100	21:5
	Died	175	25:7
Sarah	When Isaac was born	90	17:17
	Died	$127 = 2 \times 60 + 7$	23:1
Isaac	Married Rebekah	40	25:20
	When Jacob and Esau were born	60	25:26
	When Esau married	100	26:34
	Died	$180 = 3 \times 60$	35:28
Jacob	Descended to Egypt	130	47:9
	Died	$147 = 2 \times 70 + 7$	47:28
Joseph	When sold to Egypt	$17 = 10 + 7$	37:2
	When rose to power	30	41:46
	Died	110	50:26

It will surely have been noted that the four hundred and eighty figure mentioned above is the product of 12×40. Both of these factors have symbolic or sacred significance in the Bible and the ancient Near East. The number forty, especially, designates a fairly long period of time in terms of human experience.[17] This immediately raises the question whether the biblical numbers relevant to the patriarchal period are not meant to be schematized and rhetorical, rather than literal. A close study of the year numbers reveals a combination of the sexagesimal, or six-based, system that prevailed in Mesopotamia with the decimal system in use in Egypt, with the occasional addition of the sacred number seven.[18] The years for significant events are expressed in exact multiples of five, or in multiples of five, plus seven. The accompanying chart illustrates the point.

To the evidence of this chart should be added one or two other significant numbers. Abraham lived seventy-five years in the home of his father and seventy-five years in the lifetime of his son. He was one hundred years of age at the birth of Isaac and he lived one hundred years in Canaan. Jacob lived seventeen years with Joseph in Canaan and a like number with him in Egypt. Joseph's one hundred and ten years happen to coincide with the Egyptian ideal life span,[19] while the one hundred and twenty years of Moses correspond to the maximum term of life imposed on the human race.[20] Finally, the life spans of the three patriarchs constitute a number series when factored; the coefficients decrease by two, while the squared numbers increase by one:[21]

	LIFE SPAN		FACTORS
Abraham	175 years	=	7×5^2
Isaac	180 years	=	5×6^2
Jacob	147 years	=	3×7^2

It is clear that the biblical chronologies of the patriarchal age are not intended to be accurate historical records in our sense of the term. They fall within the scope of historiosophy, or philosophy of history, rather than historiography. We are not dealing with simple annals or chronicles. The numbers used are an expression of the biblical interpretation of history as the unfolding of the divine plan on the human scene. Schematized chronology, the featuring of neatly balanced periods of time, thus constitutes the poetic superstructure, the rhetorical framework for the biblical exposition of certain profound ideas about human events and their inner, deeper, meaning. The patriarchal year numbers inform us, not about the precise passage of time, which is of relatively minor importance, but about the ideas that animate the biblical narrative. If the text has Sarah bearing a child at the age of ninety[22] when she was, as is explicitly stated, beyond the child-bearing stage,[23] it is but a poetic way of describing the emergence of the people of Israel as an extraordinary event. The use of numerical symmetry is Scripture's way of conveying the conviction that the formative age in Israel's history was not a series of haphazard incidents, but the beginning of the fulfillment of God's grand design. Not blind chance, but the hand of God is at work preparing the way for the emergence of the people of Israel. In other words, the patriarchal chronologies constitute paradigmatic, rather than pragmatic history.

The source material

Does this then mean that the patriarchal narratives are merely symbolic and not to be regarded as factual? Are they in the same categories as the stories related in the first eleven chapters of Genesis?

Not so long ago it was accepted as one of the finalities of scholarship that the documents that make up the Book of Genesis, chapters 12–50, were thoroughly untrustworthy for any attempted reconstruction of the times about which they purport to relate. The events described were regarded as a late collection of folkloristic tales originating on the soil of Canaan and it was thought to be naive in the extreme to expect them to yield any reliable information about the beginnings of the history of Israel.

"We attain to no historical knowledge of the patriarchs," wrote the chief proponent of this school of thought, "but only of the time when the stories about them arose in the Israelite people; this later age is here unconsciously projected, in its inner and its outward features, into hoar antiquity, and is reflected there like a glorified mirage."[24]

This judgment was inadequate, even in the light of nineteenth-century critical methods. It overlooked the remarkable fact that the origins of Israel as related in the Bible are not hidden in the mists of mythology. The Hebrew patriarchs are not mythological figures, not gods or semi-gods, but intensely human beings who appeared fairly late on the scene of history and whose biographies are well rooted in a cultural, social, religious and legal background that ought to be verifiable. It is not to be wondered at that in recent years a thorough-going revolution has taken place in the scholarly attitude to the patriarchal narratives; in fact, no period in biblical history has been so radically affected. Irrespective of the dating applied to the Pentateuchal documents, one thing has emerged crystal clear. The traditions of the Book of Genesis are now acknowledged to be an authentic reflection of the age with which they claim to deal. Those narratives have come to be accepted as the starting point for the reconstruction of the patriarchal period, in its general outlines, and for the history of the religion of Israel.

This dramatic change in scholarly attitudes has resulted from two independent developments in biblical and Near Eastern studies. The first involves a re-evaluation of the internal biblical evidence;[25] the second results from some spectacular archaeological discoveries in the lands of the ancient world.

The Mesopotamian background—its inconvenience

The close connections between the literature of the first eleven chapters of the Bible and that of Mesopotamia have been fully examined in the preceding pages of this book. That it was the land between the two rivers in the east, rather than Canaan or Egypt, that left the greatest imprint upon Israel's early traditions should not be at all surprising. The biblical sources are emphatic and consistent about the Mesopotamian origins of the patriarchs, and the narratives describe the continued contacts with the native land even after the migration to Canaan. It was to his kinsmen in the Haran area that Abraham sent to find a wife for his son Isaac.[26] It was to this same place that Jacob repaired when he fled from the wrath of Esau.[27] Here he spent a good part of his adult life and here, too, found his wives and begat, with one exception, all his sons, the fathers of the future tribes.

However, this intimate association with Mesopotamia ceases with Jacob's return to Canaan, and is not again encountered in the Bible. There could not be any conceivable reason either for inventing these traditions or for abruptly discontinuing them at the end of the patriarchal period. They must, therefore, represent an authentic historical situation.

This argument may be strengthened by yet another peculiarity of the narratives. Their foreign origin and associations make Abraham, Isaac and Jacob always strangers and aliens in Canaan. They are wanderers and tent-dwellers ever on the move, with no roots in the soil and much dependent upon the goodwill of the inhabitants. It must be admitted that this is a very unusual and inconvenient tradition for a people that laid eternal claim to the land of Canaan as a national home. It is, in fact, highly significant that Israel never made conquest or settlement the basis of its rights to its national territory. Its title to the land derived solely from the everlasting validity of the divine promise to the patriarchs. It is this very inexpediency that authenticates the traditions of the Book of Genesis relative to the Mesopotamian origins of Israel.

The religious contrasts

Much the same conclusion as to the antiquity of the patriarchal narratives may be derived from the simple fact that they have preserved materials offensive to the later religious consciousness of Israel.

Abraham is said to have married his paternal half-sister,[28] although such a union is prohibited by later Torah legislation.[29] Jacob was married simultaneously to two sisters, a situation repugnant to the morality of another age.[30] The stories of Judah's relationship with his daughter-in-law Tamar,[31] and Reuben's affair with his father's concubine and the mother of his half-brothers,[32] are recorded despite their objectionable character. All these events can hardly be retrojections of later "ideals."

Abraham is reported as planting a sacred tree where he invoked the name of the Lord,[33] although such a practice was obnoxious in later times.[34] We are further told that Jacob set up sacred pillars (*maṣṣebot*) at Bethel[35] and Gilead,[36] although such cultic objects were later regarded as Canaanite abominations to be destroyed,[37] and not to be imitated even in the worship of the true God.[38] The patriarchs built altars and offered animal sacrifices, but no mention is made of temples or priests in this connection.[39] This, too, is in direct variance to the religious ideas and cultic forms of a later age.

The contrasts in inter-tribal relationships

Pursuing the same line of enquiry with regard to the picture of tribal relationships as presented in the Book of Genesis, a similar conclusion emerges. The contrasting historical situation, as compared with later times, is striking.

If Reuben is represented as Jacob's first-born son, it must reflect a time when the tribe bearing that name was the most powerful. Reuben always has pride of place in the lists of Jacob's offspring.[40] Yet the biblical sources show clearly that the tribe of Reuben enjoyed no such

Genealogical Table of the Patriarchs

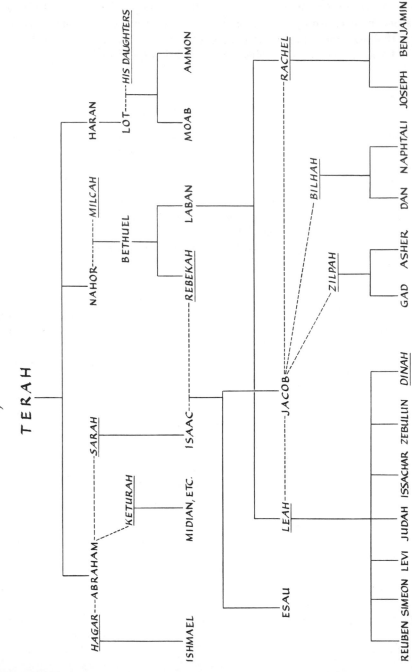

supremacy in the post-patriarchal history of Israel.[41] The identical situation applies to the fortunes of the tribe of Manasseh. Since it was very early eclipsed by Ephraim,[42] there is absolutely no reason why Manasseh should have been depicted as the first-born of Joseph unless the story represents an authentic tradition about the one-time supremacy of that tribe. In the patriarchal narratives Levi displays none of the priestly interests which later characterized the tribe. He is depicted as a warlike and ruthless adversary who collaborates with Simeon in predatory expeditions.[43] But Levi took no part in the wars of conquest in which Simeon was the partner of Judah who subsequently absorbed that tribe.[44] Here, again, the information of the Book of Genesis must reflect the true situation in pre-conquest times.

The inter-ethnic contrasts

In the period of the conquest of Joshua, and for a long time after, relationships with the inhabitants and neighbors of Canaan were generally marked by outright hostility. This contrasts very strongly with the atmosphere of peaceful and harmonious contacts that characterize the patriarchal period. Abraham, Isaac and Jacob wander freely through the country, make pacts with the local peoples,[45] and purchase land from them.[46] Melchizedek blesses Abraham who thereupon gives him a tithe.[47] There is no tension recorded between the religion of the patriarchs and that of their neighbors. Neither Ishmael nor Esau is portrayed as an idolater.

The attitude to the Arameans is particularly illuminating. From the time of David, and through most of the period of the monarchy, Aram was the warring rival of Israel.[48] But the Book of Genesis does not hesitate to make Nahor, brother of Abraham, the grandfather of Aram,[49] to identify the house of "Laban the Aramean" with Abraham[50] and to assign to Isaac and Jacob Aramean wives.

Israel waged a war of extermination against the Canaanites, yet Judah lived peacefully among them and intermarried with them.[51] Simeon, too, took himself a Canaanite wife.[52] In biblical literature, Edom is the implacable enemy of Judah. But Edom[53] is the brother of Jacob.

Still more striking is the role of Egypt in the lives of the patriarchs as contrasted with later history. Abraham descends to Egypt;[54] Isaac would do so if not forbidden by God;[55] Joseph spends all his adult life there and marries the daughter of an Egyptian priest;[56] Jacob and his entire family settle there and are very well received by the Egyptians.[57] Yet in all the stories of the conquest of Canaan, and until the time of Solomon, Egypt is neither a political nor military factor and of all the external cultural and religious influences upon biblical Israel, that of Egypt was the least.

Finally, the picture of the Philistines in the patriarchal age differs radically from that of the later historical books.[58] They are not organized in five coastal city-states led by *Seranim*,[59] but dwell in the vicinity of Beer-sheba and are ruled by the "King of Gerar."[60] They are far from being the principal enemy of Israel, as they were from the days of the Judges until their subjection by David.

All this shows that the patriarchal traditions about the mixed ethnic origins of Israel and the associations with the local inhabitants and neighbors of Canaan, are not retrojections of later history, but authentic reflexes of a true historic situation. The biblical material was not reworked in the spirit of later ideas, experiences and legislation.

The extra-biblical sources

The most startling confirmation of the conclusion about the archaic nature of the patriarchal materials results from archaeological excavation of a few sites in Mesopotamia and elsewhere. The material, largely epigraphic, has completely revolutionized our understanding of the formative period in Israel's history and has illuminated in a most unexpected manner, many a biblical text.

The outstanding site from the point of view of the sheer wealth of relevant materials is the town of Nuzi, twelve miles or so southwest of the modern Kirkuk in northeast Iraq. Excavated between 1925 and 1931, it yielded many thousands of clay tablets comprising mainly public and private archives. The legal, social and business activities of the leading citizens of the town over a few generations are meticulously recorded in these documents which date from the fifteenth and fourteenth centuries B.C.E. when the population was overwhelmingly Hurrian.

This people, we now know, infiltrated middle Mesopotamia about the beginning of the 3rd millennium B.C.E. By the middle of the second millennium, or just about the time of these records from Nuzi, the Hurrians were at the height of their power and constituted the dominant

ethnic element in the kingdom known as Mitanni in northern Mesopotamia. They had also spread out widely over Syria and Palestine.[61]

What makes the archives of Nuzi so significant for the study of the
patriarchal period of the Bible is the fact that one of the most important
political and religious centers of the Hurrians was the town of Haran in
northwest Mesopotamia. Nuzi and Haran were both part of an integrated
ethnic and cultural area, so that the picture of life and custom as it
emerges from the Nuzi texts would apply equally to Haran.[62]

Now Haran is the most prominent place-name connected with the
origins of the patriarchs. Here Terah lived with his family and from here
Abraham set out for the promised land.[63] His kinsmen stayed on in
Haran for generations and it was, as has already been mentioned, to this
same area that Abraham sent for a wife for Isaac.[64] It was in the Haran
area, too, that Jacob spent so many years of his life, married and raised
his family.[65] The reconstruction of life in this place was bound to
illuminate the patriarchal narrative, and this it has indeed done to an extent that is remarkable and to a degree of detail that is truly astonishing.[66]

If we travel westward from Nuzi to the modern Tell Hariri on the
right bank of the middle Euphrates, we come to the site of the ancient
town of Mari, about seven miles northeast of Abou Kemal near the
Iraqi-Syrian border. Excavations at Mari were begun by French archaeol-
ogists in 1933 and continued for several years, in the course of which
it became apparent that here once stood the capital of a highly important
state. Situated strategically on the highway from southern Mesopotamia
to Syria and Palestine, Mari was under the control of western Semites.
It was one of the largest and richest commercial and political centers
in Mesopotamia in the third millennium and in the first centuries of the
second millennium B.C.E. The great palace of the king was one of the
show places of the ancient world. It covered no less than seven acres and
contained about three hundred rooms, halls and courts. This magnifi-
cent edifice was found in a fine state of preservation and the royal archives
of the eighteenth century King Zimri-Lim have yielded approximately
twenty thousand clay tablets. About one quarter of these comprise the
royal diplomatic correspondence from many kingdoms of western Asia.
The rest are economic and administrative records.[67]

These documents constitute a rich source of material for Mesopotamian history; they also are of the greatest importance for understanding
the early history of Israel. Most of the persons mentioned are, like the
patriarchs, western Semites, and the close ties that existed between Mari

and the Haran area naturally arouse the interest of the student of the Bible. The dominant ethnic group at Mari was the Amorites, the people most frequently mentioned in Scripture, with the exception of the Canaanites. In the second millennium, Amorite tribes had spread out over Palestine, Syria and northern Mesopotamia. How numerous they were in Canaan in the time of Abraham may be seen from the fact that the chief reason against the immediate fulfillment of God's promise of the conquest of the country was that "the sin of the Amorite was not yet complete" (15:16). Abraham was linked to the Amorites in an alliance of mutual assistance,[68] and we know that the language of this people was very closely linked to that of the Canaanites and the patriarchs. The excavations at Mari, like those at Nuzi, have thus provided fruitful source materials for biblical studies.

The family of Shem

Between the Tower of Babel episode and the life of Abraham is interposed a long genealogical chain delineating the descendants of Shem, son of Noah.[69] The purpose is clearly to provide the bridge between two epoch-making events in history as seen from the biblical perspective. These lists, however, are of special interest to the historian for several reasons. Of thirty-eight names connected with the patriarchal family, no less than twenty-seven are never found again in the Bible.[70] This fact, alone, makes it highly unlikely that the narratives are products of later inventiveness, and increases the probability that they reflect historic traditions actually derived from patriarchal times. Furthermore, quite an appreciable proportion of these names conforms to the onomastic, or name giving, patterns common to the Western Semites during the first part of the second millennium B.C.E. But most important of all is a surprising discovery involving these personal and place-names.

We have already referred to the city of Haran from which Abraham migrated to Canaan. This place, together with its neighbor Nahor[71] is very frequently mentioned in the Mari texts. Interestingly, the name Nahor was borne also by Abraham's grandfather[72] and brother.[73] This identity of place and personal names is not uncommon in ancient Near Eastern literature and occurs, too, with other members of Abraham's family. Terah designates a town near Haran, and the same is true of the names Serug, Terah's grandfather,[74] and Peleg, grandfather of Serug.[75]

Every one of these names is peculiar in the Bible to the ancestors of the patriarch, and at the same time each denotes a place-name in the area in which the family resided. This fact, brought to light by the Mari texts, constitutes striking additional or independent confirmation of the authenticity of the Genesis traditions about the associations of the patriarchs with northern Mesopotamia.[76]

The name Abram, or Abraham, has not so far turned up in precisely the Hebrew form, but a closely-connected name occurs in Akkadian texts.[77] In sixteenth century Babylonian texts, Laban, the name of Jacob's uncle, was an epithet of the moon-god, the chief deity of Haran. The noun is found as a component of several old Assyrian and Amorite personal names.[78] Jacob itself occurs numerous times as the basic element of Semitic personal and place-names throughout the Fertile Crescent in the first half of the second millennium B.C.E.[79]

Among the most intriguing of all the names in the Mari texts is that of the Semitic tribe repeatedly cited as the Bini-Yamina. The epithet means, "sons of the right-hand," i.e. southerners. The tribe had pasture lands south of Haran, and its rebellious and predatory nature was a constant source of worry and trouble to the kings of Mari in the eighteenth century.[80] The history of this tribe as it emerges from these texts readily calls to mind the description of the tribe of Benjamin in Jacob's last blessing.

> "Benjamin is a ravenous wolf; In the morning he consumes
> the foe, and in the evening, he divides the spoil."
>
> (49 : 27)[81]

1. For the chronological problems, see R. de Vaux, *RB*, LIII (1946), pp. 328–36; H. H. Rowley, *From Joseph to Joshua*, pp. 57–108.
2. GEN. 12:4.
3. *Ibid.*, 21:5.
4. *Ibid.*, 25:26.
5. *Ibid.*, 47:9.
6. EXOD. 12:40.
7. I KINGS 6:1.
8. *Ibid.*
9. GEN. 15:13.
1 0. *Ibid.*, v. 16.
1 1. EXOD. 6:16–20; NUM. 3:17–19; 26:58–59; I CHRON. 6:1–3.
1 2. W. F. Albright, *BASOR*, 58 (1935), p. 16; *FSAC*, p. 242f., takes the 430 years as from the Era of Tanis, i.e., from the Hyksos foundation of that city ca. 1720.
1 3. See SAM., LXX to EXOD. 12:40.
1 4. The four generation tradition is consistent, too, for the offspring of Joseph (GEN. 50:23; NUM. 32:39f.). Kaufmann, *Toldot,* II, p. 1, n. 1, and C. H. Gordon, *The Ancient Near East*, p. 113f., prefer the generation tradition as the more reliable.

See, however, Wright, *Bib. Ar.*, p. 50, n. 5, and W. F. Albright, *BASOR*, 163 (1961), p. 50f., and n. 70.

1 5. I KINGS 6:1.

1 6. See J. Bright, *A History of Israel*, pp. 74ff. D. N. Freedman in *BANE*, pp. 204ff.

1 7. Cf. NUM. 14:34; JUD. 3:11; 5:35; 8:28. On this number, see W. H. Roscher, *Die Zahl 40*.

1 8. On this and the following chart, see U. Cassuto in *LGJV* (Hebrew), pp. 381–390; *EBH*, IV, col. 247–49.

1 9. See below p. 226.

2 0. GEN. 6:3.

2 1. Cited by J. Meysing, in the name of Schildenberger, in *CNI*, XIV (1963), p. 26.

2 2. GEN. 17:17.

2 3. *Ibid.*, 18:11.

2 4. J. Wellhausen, *Prolegomena*, p. 318f.

2 5. For the following examination of the internal biblical evidence, see Kaufmann, *Toldot*, I. pp. 187–211; II, pp. 1–32.

2 6. GEN. 24:4ff.

2 7. *Ibid.*, 28:2, 10.

2 8. *Ibid.*, 20:12.

2 9. LEV. 18:9, 11; 20:17; DEUT. 27:22; cf. II SAM. 13:13; EZEK. 22:11.

3 0. LEV. 18:18.

3 1. GEN. 38:16.

3 2. *Ibid.*, 35:22; I Chron. 5:1; cf. GEN. 49:4.

3 3. *Ibid.*, 21:33.

3 4. DEUT. 16:21; cf, EXOD. 34:13; DEUT. 12:3.

3 5. GEN. 28:18, 22; 31:13; 35:14.

3 6. *Ibid.*, 31:44–52.

3 7. EXOD. 23:24; 34:13; DEUT. 7:5; 12:3.

3 8. LEV. 26:1; DEUT. 16:22.

3 9. GEN. 12:7f.; 13:4, 18; 22:9; 26:25; 31:54; 33:20; 35:1, 3, 7; 46:1.

4 0. *Ibid.*, 35:23; 46:8f.; EXOD. 1:2; II CHRON. 2:1.

4 1. Cf. GEN. 49:3; DEUT. 33:6; JUD. 5:15ff.

4 2. GEN. 48:1–20.

4 3. *Ibid.*, 34; 49:5f.

4 4. JOSH. 19:9; JUD. 1:3.

4 5. GEN. 14:13; 21:22–32; 26:28–31.

4 6. *Ibid.*, 23:2–20; 33:19.

4 7. *Ibid.*, 14:20.

4 8. For the history of Aramean-Israelite relationships, see B. Mazar, *BA*, XXV (1962), pp. 98–120.

4 9. GEN. 22:21.

5 0. *Ibid.*, 24:38.

5 1. *Ibid.*, 38:2.

5 2. *Ibid.*, 46:10; EXOD. 6:15.

5 3. Edom is Esau, GEN. 36:1.

5 4. *Ibid.*, 12:10–20.

5 5. *Ibid.*, 26:2.

5 6. *Ibid.*, 41:50–52.

5 7. *Ibid.*, 47:7–10.

5 8. On the problem of Philistines in Canaan in the patriarchal period, see Kaufmann, *Toldot*, II, pp. 304ff.; J. M. Grintz in *Schorr Festschrift*, pp. 96–112; *Tarbiz*, XVII(1945/6), pp. 32ff; XIX(1947/8), p. 64; S. Abramsky, *Beth Mikra*, XIV(1962), p. 102f.; Gordon, *op. cit.*, p. 121f. On the Philistines in general, see J. C. Greenfield in *IDB*, III, col. 791–95.

5 9. I SAM. 5:8.

6 0. GEN. 20:2; 21:31–34; 26:1, 8, 14, 33. On the identification of Gerar, see Y. Aharoni, *IEJ*, VI(1956), pp. 26–32; M. Naor in *Sefer Biram*, pp. 74–81.

6 1. On the Hurrians, see E. A. Speiser, *JWH*, I(1953), pp. 311–327; *EBH*, III, col. 58–62; *WHJP*, I, pp. 153–6; 158–61; H. G. Guterbock, *JWH*, II(1955), pp. 383ff.

6 2. On Haran, see A. Parrot, *Abraham et son Temps*, pp. 36ff.

6 3. GEN. 11:31–12:4.

6 4. *Ibid.*, 24:2, 10.

6 5. *Ibid.*, 27:43; 28:10; 29:4.

6 6. For an extensive bibliography on this subject see R. J. Tournay in *DBS*, vi, col. 671–74. For a useful and cautious summary of the patriarchal period in the light of modern scholarship, see J. M. Holt, *The Patriarchs of Israel*.

6 7. See G. E. Mendelhall, *BA*, XI(1948), pp. 1–19; Ch-F. Jean, *DBS*, V, col. 883–905; A. Malamat, *EBH*, IV, col. 559–79; J. C. L. Gibson, *JSS*, VII(1962), pp. 44–62.

6 8. GEN. 14:13.

6 9. *Ibid.*, 11:10–32.

7 0. A complete list, together with the statistics, is to be found in S. Yeivin, *Beth Mikra*, XVI(1963), p. 15f. reprinted in his *MTYA*, p. 48f.

7 1. GEN. 24:10.

7 2. *Ibid.*, 11:22ff.

7 3. *Ibid.*, v. 26.

7 4. *Ibid.*, 10:25; 11:20–23.

7 5. *Ibid.*, 10:25; 11:16–19.

7 6. On these names, see R. de Vaux, *RB*, LV(1948), p. 324; Albright, *FSCA*, pp. 236ff.; *BASOR*, 163 (1961), p. 46.

7 7. See R. de Vaux, *RB*, LIII(1946), p. 323.

7 8. See J. Lewy, *HUCA*, XVIII(1943–44), pp. 434, n. 39, 455ff.

7 9. See D. N. Freedman, *IEJ*, 13 (1963), pp. 125–126 and the sources cited there in n. 1.

8 0. On the Benjamin question, see H. Tadmor, *JNES*, XVII(1958), pp. 129ff.; A. Parrot, *op. cit.*, pp. 42–48; A. Malamat in *EBH*, IV, col. 572: K. D. Schunck, *Benjamin*.

8 1. Cf. JUD. 20:16; I CHRON. 12:2.

CHAPTER V

From Mesopotamia to Canaan

GENESIS 12

Terah took his son Abram, his grandson Lot the son of Haran, and his daughter-in-law Sarai, the wife of his son Abram, and they set out together from Ur of the Chaldeans for the land of Canaan; but when they had come as far as Haran, they settled there. (11 : 31)

The genealogical lists close with information about the family of Abraham. The passage here cited plainly establishes the fact that it came to Haran from some other place, and that the original intention was to migrate to the land of Canaan. We are given no reasons for Terah's exodus from Ur, nor any motivation for wanting to go to Canaan. Whatever the cause, it was apparently independent of any divine call. It was only after the family had interrupted the journey at Haran that the word of the Lord came to Abraham saying:

"Go forth from your native land and from your father's
house to the land that I will show you."   (12 : 1)

The problem of Ur

Four times biblical sources mention Ur as the original point of departure. We are told that Haran, Abraham's brother, died while the family
still lived in the city.[1] After the patriarch had arrived in Canaan, God
appeared to him as the One "who brought you out from Ur of the
Chaldeans" (15:8). Many centuries later, the small community of Jews
who had returned from the Babylonian exile recalled the fact that God
had chosen Abraham and had brought him forth from "Ur of the
Chaldeans."[2]

Despite the general silence of Scripture on the family fortunes at Ur,[3]
and notwithstanding the centrality of the city of Haran and its environs
in the patriarchal stories,[4] the association with Ur must reflect an authentic tradition since it is difficult to find a reason for its invention.

The difficulty, however, lies with the designation "Ur of the Chaldeans." The name "Chaldeans" as applied to lower Mesopotamia does
not appear before the eleventh century B.C.E., many hundreds of years
after the patriarchs. The city Ur itself could not have been called "of
the Chaldeans" before the foundation of the Neo-Babylonian empire
in the seventh century B.C.E. The characterization therefore, as distinct
from the tradition, would seem to be anachronistic.[5]

If the biblical Ur be indeed the ancient city of that name situated
on the Euphrates in lower Mesopotamia, then we know that the child-
hood of Abraham was spent in one of the foremost centers of culture in
the world of his day. Excavations of the site have shown that Ur reached
the peak of its prosperity between the twenty-first and twentieth centuries B.C.E. About 1950 B.C.E. it was destroyed by the Elamites, never
again to resume its former position.[6] The decline of the city would
perhaps have been an important factor in the migration of Terah.[7]

It is of particular interest that the family went from Ur to Haran, for
both cities were important centers of the worship of the moon-god Sin.
In fact, the Abrahamic family names Terah, Sarah, Milcah and Laban,
all reflect traces of a connection with moon worship.[8] The pagan antecedents of Abraham, well remembered in biblical times, may indeed
refer to the official moon cult at Ur and Haran:

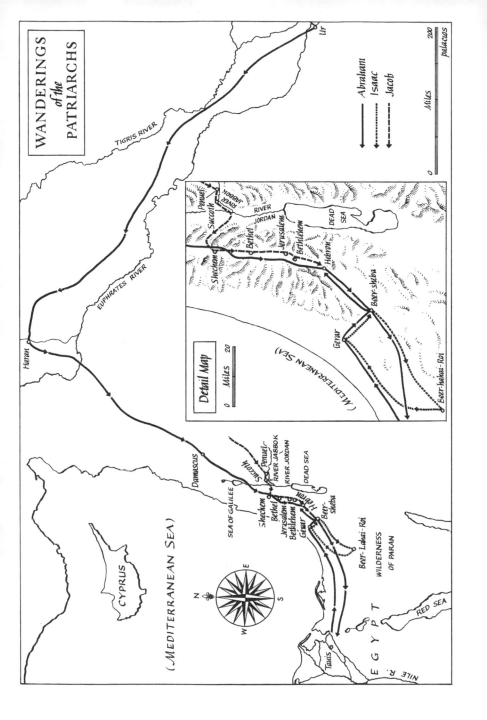

WANDERINGS of the PATRIARCHS

TIGRIS RIVER

EUPHRATES RIVER

Ur

Haran

Abraham
Isaac
Jacob

Miles
0   200
palacuos

Detail Map

Miles
0   20

Shechem
Penuel
Succoth
RIVER JABBOK
RIVER JORDAN
Bethel
Jerusalem
Bethlehem
DEAD SEA
Hebron
Beer-sheba
Gerar
Beer-lahai-Roi

(MEDITERRANEAN SEA)

Damascus

SEA OF GALILEE

Shechem
Bethel
Penuel
Succoth
RIVER JABBOK
RIVER JORDAN
Jerusalem
Bethlehem
Hebron
DEAD SEA
Gerar
Beer-sheba
Beer-Lahai-Roi

WILDERNESS OF PARAN

CYPRUS

(MEDITERRANEAN SEA)

N
E
S
W

E G Y P T

Tanis

NILE R.

RED SEA

"Your fathers lived of old beyond the Euphrates, Terah the
father of Abraham and of Nahor; and they served other gods."

(JOSH. 24 : 2)

As has been noted, the original intention of Terah was to make his way
to Canaan. From what we now know of the history of the second millennium B.C.E. it would be difficult to separate this migration from the extensive movements of peoples which were going on in the Near East. All
over the ancient world masses were on the march, radically altering ethnic
and political patterns.[9] Viewed against this broader background, the
attachment of Terah and his family to the migratory stream of Semites
wending their way from East to West was hardly more than a trivial incident. Yet to biblical historiosophy it became a stirring event of universal
significance, productive of far-reaching consequences for mankind as a
whole, and constituting a major turning point in human history.

The Bible expresses these ideas in its own idiom and through its own
literary medium. We have already seen how it used the device of schematized chronology as the rhetorical framework for historiosophy. It is no
accident that exactly ten generations separate Noah from Adam and that
exactly ten more bring us to the birth of Abraham, another epochal
juncture in history from the Bible's viewpoint. Just as a divine communication to Noah transforms a natural phenomenon into a purposeful event,
so God's command to Abraham, "Go forth!" converts a routine migration
into a fateful movement, inaugurating the birth of a new nation whose
history and destiny are to acquire unique purpose. Once this consciousness of meaning was reached, it was not difficult to reinterpret, in
retrospect, the original exodus from Ur as also belonging to the divine
plan. Hence, God can later be described as addressing Himself to Abraham as the One who brought him out of Ur.[10]

The divine promise

The order to Abraham to go forth from his father's house was accompanied by an assurance that the patriarch was to become the progenitor of a
"great nation" (12:2). Since this was not the kind of promise that could
possibly be fulfilled in the lifetime of the recipient, it was something that
had to be accepted on faith. Certain it is that Scripture intended to emphasize just this aspect of Abraham's personality and the magnitude of
his act of faith.

We had previously been told that Sarah was barren,[11] so that God's pledge of nationhood taxed the patriarch's credulity to the full. Nor was the vagueness of the ultimate destination—"the land that I will show you" (12:1)—calculated to arouse an enthusiastic response; while the migration from Haran involved for Abraham the agonizing decision to wrench himself away from his family in the sure knowledge that he was not likely ever again to see his father. In point of fact, Terah lived in Haran for another sixty years after he bade farewell to his son.[12]

It might appear somewhat strange that the divine promise of nationhood should have necessitated a sacrifice of this nature. Could not the ancestral soil of Mesopotamia have witnessed the birth of Israel? The answer to this question may perhaps be sought in the very nature of Mesopotamian civilization as contrasted with the destiny of the nation yet to emerge.

The land between the Tigris and Euphrates rivers was already heir to a tradition of hoary antiquity by the time the first of the patriarchs arrived on the scene. It could justifiably boast of monumental achievements and rightly take pride in the success of its administrative accomplishments. Intensive agriculture and extensive foreign trade sustained a stratified society controlled through a highly centralized royal authority with its professional bureaucracy and an elaborately organized temple government. But it was not a situation that would be likely to encourage a challenge to its basic conservatism. The burden of tradition lay very heavily upon the ancient Near East, above all in the sphere of religion. The overcrowded, changeable pantheon resting upon a mountain of complex mythological symbolism, served to accentuate the inherent deficiencies of paganism in providing satisfactory answers to the problems of existence. The ever-present pall of anxiety that hung over Mesopotamian life is the measure of the failure of its civilization, religiously speaking. Consequently, it is not to be wondered at that the fulfillment of God's purposes in history through the mediation of a new people required a radical break with the past and the finding of a new and more fruitful soil.[13]

It should be noted that the divine blessing, bestowed while Abraham was still in Haran, made no mention of the gift of land. This would have detracted from the act of faith involved in heeding the simple command, "Go forth!" It would also have been a meaningless promise, being contingent upon the patriarch's obedient response to the divine call. No sooner, however, had the destination been reached than the divine word came once again to declare that that very land through which Abraham journeyed would become the possession of his offspring.[14] The promise of nationhood was supplemented by the grant of national territory, two themes that henceforth dominate biblical history and theology.

The pivotal nature of the divine promise may be gauged from the numerous times it is repeated to the patriarchs and cited in later literature, usually in times of crises. No sooner had Abraham received the picture of a glorious future than the contrasting reality of the present asserted itself. There was famine in the land, and the patriarch was forced to depart for Egypt.[15] No sooner had he arrived than he found himself confronted with personal danger of a different kind.[16] These two incidents are of special interest to the historian. Their incorporation into the patriarchal narratives has a significance of its own in the understanding of the historiosophical purposes of Scripture.

The descent to Egypt

That Abraham should have left Canaan for Egypt in time of famine accords well with what we know of conditions in the second millennium B.C.E.[17] An excellent illustration is the report of an Egyptian frontier official sent to his superior, the "Scribe of the Treasury," concerning Edomite shepherds to whom permission was given to cross into Egypt for seasonal pasturing of their flocks in the Delta. He writes:

> We have finished letting the Bedouin tribes of Edom pass the fortress, to keep them alive and to keep their cattle alive.[18]

Isaac, too, it will be remembered, had intended to descend to Egypt in time of famine in Canaan,[19] and the ultimate migration of the tribes of Israel was the result of the same cause.[20] Egypt, of course, unlike Canaan, was not dependent upon seasonal rainfall. Its fertility derived from the less capricious rise and fall of the life-giving Nile.

The wife-sister motif

One of the strangest of the patriarchal narratives is that recording the attempt by Abraham to ward off personal danger by passing off his wife as his sister.[21] This wife-sister motif occurs only in the Book of Genesis where it is repeated no less than three times. Abraham is again forced to resort to the device in his dealing with Abimelech, King of Gerar.[22] The explanation that Sarah was indeed Abraham's half-sister[23] is not adequate to explain Isaac's experience.[24]

Recent research in the Nuzi archives sheds totally new light on this problem.[25] There was an institution, peculiar it would seem to Hurrian society, which may be described as "wife-sistership." "Sistership" in Nuzi did not necessarily have anything to do with blood ties, for it could indicate a purely legal status. One document reads as follows:

> Tablet of sistership of Akkulenni son of Akiya, whereby he sold his sister Beltakkadummi as sister to Hurazzi son of Ennaya.[26]

Interestingly enough, another document records that the same gentleman sold the same lady as a wife to the same Hurazzi.

> Tablet of marriage-contract of Akkulenni son of Akiya, contracted with Hurazzi son of Ennaya . . . Akkulenni shall give his sister Beltakkadummi as wife to Hurazzi.[27]

In other words, Beltakkadummi enjoyed the dual status of wife-sistership which endowed her with superior privileges and protection, over and above those of an ordinary wife.

In the light of this situation, it must be assumed that Sarah and Rebekah were both holders of this wife-sister privilege, peculiar to the society from which they came and in which the legal aspects of their marriage were negotiated. The patriarchal narratives have faithfully recorded the unique institution of wife-sistership. However, in the course of transmission, until finally incorporated into the scriptural story, the very uniqueness of the socio-legal institution of wife-sisterhood was bound to be misunderstood in the context of an entirely different civilization, and the patriarchal events connected with it were completely reinterpreted and reused for a different purpose. They have been worked into a narrative that gives a critical judgment on Canaanite moral standards.

Affirmation of the promise

The famine in the land of promise and the physical danger that
threatened to engulf Abraham and Sarah exemplify one of the characteristic features of the patriarchal stories. The hopes generated by the divine
assurance of nationhood and national territory seem to be in perpetual
danger of miscarrying. Reality always falls short of the promise. Yet
the purposes of God cannot be frustrated, and the hand of Providence
is ever present, delivering the chosen ones. Hence the recurring theme
of peril and reaffirmation of the promises throughout the Book of
Genesis.

No sooner was Abraham back once more on the soil of Canaan, than
fresh trouble developed over rival claims to the limited pastureland
available.[28] The quarrel with Lot was amicably settled and at once
evoked God's renewed and strengthened reassurance.

> "Raise your eyes and look out from where you are, to the
> north and south, to the east and west, for I give all the land
> that you see to you and your offspring forever. I will make
> your offspring as the dust of the earth, so that if one can count
> the dust of the earth, then your offspring too can be counted.
> Up, walk about the land, through its length and its breadth,
> for I give it to you."   (13 : 14–17)

The entire land is now actually given to Abraham himself, as well as
to his offspring, for all eternity, and the promise of nationhood is made
more explicit through the use of picturesque language. It is quite
probable that God's order to "walk about the land" etc. (v. 17), preserves some ancient contract formula describing the performance of a
symbolic physical act that legally validated title to land received by
gift.[29]

The patriarchal wanderings

The divine promises were not intended to bring quiet and repose to their
recipients. The possession of the land was, after all, not the same thing
as ownership. The latter had been endowed and was irrevocable. But
possession was still far beyond the horizon. The nation did not yet exist.

The patriarchs are for this reason wanderers, constantly on the move.

It must not be thought, however, that the fathers of the people of Israel were desert nomads. This was once a widely held view that has been completely overthrown. In the first place, even had the desert nomad represented an undesirable image, it is hard to see why the Bible should have suppressed the fact since it preserved such other inconvenient traditions as the mixed ethnic origins of Israel and the lack of Canaanite roots, not to mention the glaring contradictions between patriarchal customs and the Torah legislation.

Secondly, the fathers were essentially ass nomads, not camel nomads. The true nomadic Bedouins are men of the desert, since the camel allows them to roam freely over vast distances.[30] The use of the ass allows no such freedom, and the ass was the regular beast of burden of the patriarchs according to the scriptural accounts. Abraham set out for Mount Moriah on an ass;[31] Simeon and Levi found asses but no camels, among the loot of Shechem;[32] Joseph's brothers mounted asses to go down to Egypt to buy food;[33] it was not camels that Joseph sent to transport his father from Canaan,[34] and there is no reference to camels among the animals that the hard pressed Egyptians sold to Joseph in return for food.[35] It is true that the camel is mentioned in connection with Abraham,[36] Jacob[37] and Joseph.[38] It is also true that camel bones have been found in the ruins of a house at Mari which dates from about 2400 B.C.E.,[39] and that an eighteenth-century tablet from the city of Alalakh includes the camel among a list of domesticated animals.[40] Yet the beast does not figure in Egyptian texts and art from the times of the Pharaohs and is, significantly, not to be found in the Mari archives which are replete with information about nomadic tribes.[41] The effective domestication of the camel as a widely used beast of burden does not appear to have taken place before the twelfth century B.C.E.[42] It is totally misleading, therefore, to draw upon the bedouin mode of life to illustrate that of the patriarchs who were primarily sheep and cattle raisers and, as such, restricted in the scope of their wanderings.

Abraham, Isaac and Jacob were tent-dwellers, not city-builders. But their travels took place between the great urban centers. They had dealings with kings,[43] possessed slaves,[44] retainers,[45] silver and gold,[46] and might possibly have participated in the international caravan trade. They seem to have been in the first stages of settling down and of urbanization. Lot, the shepherd, landing up as a resident of Sodom may well be symptomatic of a more general movement on the part of recently migrated tribes. Isaac sowed the land successfully,[48] while Joseph, who tended the sheep, dreamed of sheaves of corn in a field,[49] indicating the association of sheep-rearing with soil cultivation at that time. In other words, the patriarchs were semi-nomads who moved in the vicinity of urban or semi-urban areas.[50]

There was nothing haphazard, however, about these peregrinations.[51] Were we to trace them on a map we should soon notice that the patriarchs avoided the northern part of Canaan, shunned the coastal plain and kept away from the plain of Esdraelon and the Jordan Valley. On the other hand, they continually wandered between sites in the central mountain range and the Negeb. This means that they avoided the well-inhabited areas and stuck to the sparsely populated hill country, and it fits in with the fact that Dothan, Shechem, Bethel and Gerar are all known to have existed by the year 2000 B.C.E. As far as the Negeb is concerned, surveys of the area have uncovered over half a dozen important Middle Bronze I sites, proving that even fairly large numbers of sheep, cattle and human beings could readily have found food and water in their journey to and from Egypt.[52]

1. GEN. 11:28.
2. NEH. 9:7.
3. JOSH. 24:2f. speaks only of "beyond the River," omitting both Ur and Haran. Surprisingly, Ur is not mentioned among the Mesopotamian cities in GEN. 10:9–12.
4. GEN. 12:1 "native land and father's home" refers to Haran, not Ur. The same phrase in 24:4f. also undoubtedly refers to the Haran area.
5. For a thorough review of the Ur problem see A. Parrot, *Abraham et son Temps*, pp. 14–18. For ancient traditions placing Ur in the north, see I. Ben-Shem in *OLD*, pp. 86ff. In recent years, Lods, *Israel*, p. 187, suggested a northern location as a solution to the problem. On the basis of cuneiform documents from Ugarit and Alalakh, C. H. Gordon, *JNES*, XVII (1958), pp. 28–31 (cf. his *Before the Bible*, pp. 287ff.; *Ancient Near East*, p. 132f.), also argues strongly for a northern Ur. On this see H. W. F. Saggs, *Iraq*, XXII (1960), pp. 200–209; W. F. Albright, *BASOR*, 163 (1961), p. 44; A. F. Rainey, *IEJ*, XIII (1963), p. 319. For a divergent point of view on "Chaldean," see P. Artzi in *OLD*, pp. 71–85. On the LXX to GEN. 11:31, see W. F. Albright, *BASOR*, 140 (1955), p. 31f.
6. For the history of the city, see L. Woolley, *Ur of the Chaldees*; A. Parrot, *op. cit.*,

pp. 19–52. Cf., also, Albright, *FSAC*, p. 236, and his description of Ur in *BASOR*, 163 (1961), p. 44 as "the greatest commercial capital that the world had yet seen."

7. This, of course, is based on an assumption of an early dating for Abraham.
8. See J. C. L. Gibson, *JSS*, VII (1962), p. 54.
9. See de Vaux, *RB*, LV (1948), pp. 321ff. and the citations in Parrot, *op.cit.*, p. 40, n.1.
1 0. GEN. 15:8.
1 1. *Ibid.*, 11:30.
1 2. This can be determined by the following data: Terah was 70 when Abraham was born (GEN. 11:26), and the latter was 75 when he left Haran (*ibid.* 12:4). Terah would have then been 145. He died aged 205 (*ibid.* 11:32). It should be noted that according to the Samaritan version Terah was 145 at his death. This would then have coincided with the year of Abraham's departure from Haran. This tradition has been preserved in Acts 7:4.
1 3. See E. A. Speiser, *IEJ*, VII (1957), p. 210f.
1 4. GEN. 12:7.
1 5. *Ibid.* v. 10.
1 6. *Ibid.* vv. 11–20.
1 7. See Wilson, *CAE*, p. 258; Montet, pp. 11–14.
1 8. *ANET*, p. 259.
1 9. GEN. 26:1–2.
2 0. *Ibid.* chaps. 42–46.
2 1. *Ibid.* 12:11–20.
2 2. *Ibid.* 20:1–18.
2 3. *Ibid.* 20:12.
2 4. *Ibid.* 26:6–11.
2 5. See E. A. Speiser, *IEJ*, VII (1957), p. 212f.; and esp. in *BOS*, pp. 15–28.
2 6. *AASOR*, X (1930), p. 60.
2 7. *Ibid.* p. 59.
2 8. GEN. 13:5–12.
2 9. This is the view of R. Eliezer in B. Bathra 100[a]. Cf. JOSH. 18:4; 24:3; EZEK. 33:24.
3 0. See de Vaux, *AI*, p. 3f.
3 1. GEN. 22:3, 5.
3 2. *Ibid.* 34:28
3 3. *Ibid.* 42:26f.; 43:18; 44:3, 13.
3 4. *Ibid.* 45:23.
3 5. *Ibid.* 47:17.
3 6. *Ibid.* 12:16; chap. 24 passim.
3 7. *Ibid.* 30:43; 31:17, 34; 32:8, 16.
3 8. *Ibid.* 37:25.
3 9. See Parrot, *op. cit.*, p. 89.
4 0. See A. Goetze, *JCS*, XIII (1959), p. 37; but see W. G. Lambert, *BASOR*, 160 (1960), p. 42f.
4 1. See Albright, *FSAC*, p. 165; S. Moscati, *The Semites in Ancient History*, p. 59.
4 2. This problem has generated a literature of considerable dimensions. See Albright,

FSAC, p. 164f.; *ARI*, pp. 90f., 227; *JBL*, LXIV (1945), p. 287f.; *JNES*, V (1946), p. 25, n. 14; *BASOR*, 163 (1961), p. 38, n. 9; J. P. Free, *JNES*, III (1944), pp. 187–193; B. S. J. Isserlin, *PEQ* LXXXII (1950), pp. 50–53; R. Walz, *ZDMG*, CI (1951), pp. 29–51; CIV (1954), pp. 45–87; *Actes du IVᵉ Congres International des sciences anthropologiques et ethnologiques*, III (1956), pp. 190–204; M. W. Mikesell, *SJA*, II (1955), pp. 236ff.; Forbes, *SAT*, II, pp. 187–204; Bodenheimer, *AMBL*, pp. 4, 7, 12, 37, 160, 173ff., 178; C. H. Gordon, *The Ancient Near East*, pp. 84, 124.

4 3. GEN. 12:15ff.; 14:20; 21:22; 26:9ff.

4 4. *Ibid.* 12:16, *et al.*

4 5. *Ibid.* 14:14.

4 6. *Ibid.* 13:2, *et al.*

4 7. See C. H. Gordon, *JNES*, XVII (1958), pp. 28–31; W. F. Albright, *BASOR*, 163 (1961), pp. 36–54. See also, S. Yeivin, *Beth Mikra*, XVI (1963), pp. 14, 28f. For a discussion of the meaning of the root *shr* in GEN. 34:10, 21, see E. A. Speiser, *BASOR*, 164 (1961), pp. 23–28 and Albright's note, *ibid.*, p. 28.

4 8. GEN. 26:12.

4 9. *Ibid.* 34:7.

5 0. Cf. Wellhausen, *Prolegomena*, p. 31, n. 1; M. Haran in *OLD*, p. 50, who point out that the patriarchs generally stuck to the periphery of Canaanite towns, rarely actually entering them.

5 1. See R. de Vaux, *RB*, LVI (1949), pp. 15f.

5 2. See N. Glueck, *BA*, XVIII (1955), pp. 2–9; *Rivers in the Desert*, p. 60.

CHAPTER VI

The Battle of the Kings

GENESIS 14

One of the most unusual of the patriarchal stories, and at the same time one of the most perplexing, is that relating the "battle of the kings."

Five Canaanite kings had been paying allegiance for twelve years to Chedorlaomer, ruler of Elam. When they finally decided to assert their independence, a coalition of four eastern monarchs organized a punitive expedition against them. Carried out on a grand scale, the invasion succeeded in routing the rebels. Among the casualties of the city of Sodom was Lot, Abraham's nephew, who was taken prisoner together with his family and possessions. As soon as Abraham received the news he mustered his three hundred and eighteen retainers and set off in hot pursuit of the invaders. In a night encounter Abraham defeated them north of Damascus, rescued the captives and retrieved the loot.

On his victorious return home, the patriarch received the blessing of Melchizedek, King of Salem, to whom he paid tithes. He also turned down an offer to share personally in the spoils of war.

This narrative does not, at first glance, seem to be organically related to either the preceding or subsequent events in the life of Abraham. It has a literary, annalistic style all its own. It is replete with detailed information of a geographic and ethnic nature. It is the only chapter in the Book of Genesis that connects a patriarch with great historic events that bring him out onto the international stage. The nature of the subjection of Canaanite kings to a distant monarch and the exact form which their rebellion took is not stated. Equally uncertain is whether the suppression of the revolt was the sole objective of the eastern coalition or whether it was part of a larger enterprise. The tone of the story is more secular than religious, the latter note appearing only toward the end. The *dramatis personae* are not otherwise attested, and some of the place-names are unknown. The account has no parallel in Near Eastern records and cannot therefore be easily fitted into the framework of history. Finally, the image of Abraham as a military chief and hero is remarkable and unique.

Its antiquity

It is now recognized that this entire account is based upon a document of great antiquity.[1] The prose style has preserved indications of an archaic substratum in verse form. For instance, the names of the Canaanite Kings are arranged in two alliterative pairs, Bera-Birsha and Shinab-Shemeber.[2] The language contains some unique or very rare words and phrases. One such, *hanikh* (v. 14), meaning "an armed-retainer," appears but this once in the Bible, but is found in the Egyptian execration texts of the nineteenth-eighteenth centuries B.C.E. and in a fifteenth-century B.C.E. cuneiform inscription from Taanach, Israel.[3]

It will be noticed that only four of the local monarchs are mentioned by name, the fifth being called simply, "the king of Bela" (v. 2). Had the whole episode no historical foundation, the writer would surely not have been at a loss for a name. The ancient source behind the biblical account must no longer have preserved the information and Scripture adhered faithfully to it.

The names of the Eastern kings likewise have about them an air of verisimilitude. While they cannot be connected with any known historic personages, three of the four can certainly be associated with the early Near Eastern onomasticon. Arioch now has its counterpart in the name

Arriwuk, also found in the Nuzi documents as Ar-ri-uk-ki. Chedorlaomer contains two elements, each of which is known separately from Elamite sources. The first means "servant" and the second is the name of a deity. Tidal is a northwest Semitic transcription of the Hittite royal name Tudhalias.[4]

The wealth of geographical detail is particularly illuminating. The scene of the decisive military invasion is described as "the Valley of Siddim, now the Dead Sea." In other words, we are told that the valley no longer existed at that time when the story achieved its final literary form, for the waters of the Dead Sea had by then encroached upon the once flourishing area;[5] but the original name was carefully reproduced. This tendency to preserve the ancient toponyms, while at the same time supplementing them with the place-names used in later times, is meticulously applied throughout.[6] Sometimes the additional name served to identify the location for the Israelite reader no longer familiar with the site. Typical in this respect are the notations, "El-paran which is by the wilderness" (v. 6), "En-mishpat which is Kadesh"[7] (v. 7), "the Valley of Shaveh which is the Valley of the King" (v. 17). In addition, there are three sets of double place-names, Ashteroth-Karnaim, Shaveh-Kiriathaim and Hazazon-Tamar.[8] In each case, the second name is known to us from Israelite times. In the case of Ashteroth-Karnaim, they were separate, but closely neighboring cities, the second flourishing after the decline of the first.[9] We may assume also that in each of the other pairs, the first name represents the archaic pre-Israelite designation strange to later generations. In the case of Dan (v. 14), a town representing the northern extremity of the Land of Israel, only the later, Israelite, name is anachronistically given, the earlier Laish having, for some reason, been here omitted.[10]

The list of defeated peoples, like the inventory of cities, bears all the hallmarks of having been based on a chronicle of great antiquity. Rephaim is an ethnic term generally designating the very early pre-Israelite inhabitants of the land. By the time of Moses they had all but disappeared and had been endowed in the popular imagination with the attributes of aboriginal giants.[11] The Emim were the earliest settlers in the land of Moab[12] and the Horites of Mt. Seir were dispossessed by the Edomites in the thirteenth century B.C.E.[13]; yet the text does not anachronistically refer to either Moab or Edom. The Zuzim are otherwise unknown, but may be identical with the Zamzumim.[14] Only the Amalekites and Amorites were still extant at the time of the Israelite occupation.

The invasion route

The invasion route followed by the eastern kings is of considerable interest.[15] Its topographic soundness has been effectively demonstrated in the light of extensive archaeological surveys undertaken in recent years. We do not know the identity of the places of origin of the invaders except for Elam, the territory lying north of the Persian Gulf, west of the Tigris river in modern Iran. Shinar is here undoubtedly Babylonia, the area containing ancient Sumer and Akkad.[16] Ellasar may possibly be the royal city of Ila(n)zura, situated East of the Euphrates between Charchemish and Haran, mentioned in the Mari texts.[17] Goiim is totally unknown and may perhaps be simply the usual Hebrew word for "nations," indicating that the name of the home-town of King Tidal was lost. However, once the coalition of kings reached the west we can trace fairly accurately their destructive path, even though a precise identification of some of the place-names is not yet possible.

The invaders traversed the entire length of the country east of the Jordan from north to south. From Karnaim in Bashan they passed on to Ham in north Gilead down through the Plains of Moab and continued across the hill-country of Edom as far as Elath on the Gulf of Akaba. They then turned northwest crossing the Negeb to Kadesh-Barnea.[18] From here they made another abrupt turn, this time to the northeast towards the Valley of Siddim in the area now a lagoon south of the Lisan of the Dead Sea. In this Valley they fought a decisive battle routing the five kings of the cities of the Plain.

It so happens that this route coincides with the King's Highway,[19] the international road running in practically a continuous straight line from north to south in Transjordan, which served as the ancient caravan route bearing the products of the south Arabian lands to the Red Sea. If our story of the invasion be factual, it would mean that several highly developed areas of permanent sedentary occupation must have existed in early times along the route followed. Extensive archaeological surveys of Transjordan and the Negeb have indeed shown this to have been the case during what is known as the Middle Bronze I period, i.e. between the twenty-first and nineteenth centuries B.C.E. A civilization of a high order of achievement flourished throughout this period, and a truly amazing number of settlements has been discovered. Strangely enough, there occurs a complete and sudden interruption in settled life in Transjordan and the Negeb just at the end of the period, apparently as a result of some historic catastrophic invasion that systematically wiped out everything

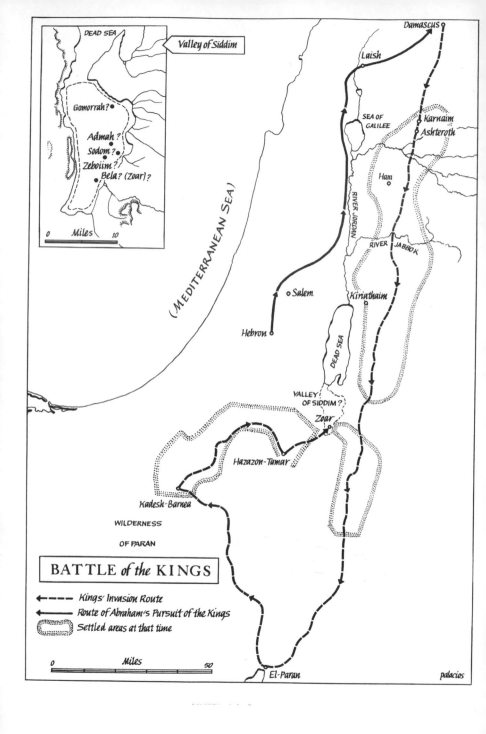

DEAD SEA

Valley of Siddim

Gomorrah?●

Admah ?●
Sodom ?●
Zeboiim ?●
● Bela? (Zoar)?

0   Miles   10

Damascus ○

Laish

SEA OF
GALILEE

Karnaim ●
Ashteroth ○

Ham ○

RIVER JORDAN

RIVER JABBOK

(MEDITERRANEAN SEA)

○ Salem

Kiriathaim ○

Hebron ○

DEAD SEA

VALLEY
OF SIDDIM ?

Zoar

Hazazon-Tamar

Kadesh-Barnea

WILDERNESS

OF PARAN

BATTLE of the KINGS

╌╌╌◀ Kings' Invasion Route
───◀ Route of Abraham's Pursuit of the Kings
⬭ Settled areas at that time

0   Miles   50

El-Paran

palacios

in its path. For the next six hundred years, Transjordan remained desolate until the founding of the Kingdoms of Edom and Moab in the thirteenth century B.C.E. In the Negeb, the break in civilization lasted nearly a thousand years.[20]

In the light of all this, it is not unreasonable to assume that the story of the battle of the Kings in the Book of Genesis preserves an authentic echo of a great military expedition which put an end to the Middle Bronze I settlements. The annals recording the catastrophic events may well have furnished the basis for the biblical account.

Abram the Hebrew[21]

The attentive reader will have observed that up to this point Abraham remains wholly detached from the course of events. In fact, the twenty-four-verse chapter is almost exactly divided between the account of the invasion and the story of Abraham's intervention. The isolation of the patriarch fits in with the picture of the fathers as strangers and wanderers in the land. So long as Abraham was outside the path of hostilities he was not likely to become involved. The capture of Lot, however, altered the complexion of the entire episode as far as he was concerned, and it is this development that rescued the account of the invasion from oblivion. Our narrative provides a perfect example of biblical historiosophy. The aim is not the simple narrative of historic events but their use for the illumination and illustration of the biblical understanding and interpretation of the historical process. With the intervention of Abraham, the secular annalistic nature of the account changes abruptly and the intertwining of the events of the ancient military chronicle with the life of the patriarch transforms the secular record into a religious document.

Abraham assumes a central role in the second part of the story. He and his mere three hundred and eighteen retainers[22] put to flight the victorious armies of the four powerful kings. True, he has two Amorite allies, Eshkol and Aner, as well as Mamre, but so thoroughly obscured is their part in the drama that the only other mention of them, and that somewhat offhand, is in connection with the distribution of the loot.[23] It is Abraham who occupies the center of the stage. Yet the terseness of the account of this campaign, in contrast with the unusually great detail of the preceeding one, is very striking. There is no suggestion here of Abraham's great military prowess, and never again is this aspect of his personality and career so much as alluded to. Melchizedek, who came to greet him on his return ascribes the victory entirely to God, and Abraham tacitly assents. How insecure the patriarch really was may be seen from the next chapter in which God has to reassure him of His protection.

"Fear not Abram, I am a shield to you."

(15 : 1)

This delicate shift in the tenor of the narrative from a secular annal to a religious document, is further extended in the dealings with the King of Sodom. In response to a generous offer to hand over the entire spoils of war, Abraham indignantly, disdainfully and almost insultingly swears before the Lord that he would not take so much as a thread or sandal strap or anything belonging to the King, lest the monarch be able to claim that he made Abraham rich.[24] This attitude is easily understandable in the light of the remark in the preceding chapter that the inhabitants of Sodom "were very wicked sinners against the Lord" (12:13). Doubtless, the mention of Lot and the Sodomites in chapter thirteen was decisive in fixing the juxtaposition with this story in which the King of Sodom appears so prominently. And Abraham's treatment of the King must have been conditioned by Sodom's evil reputation.

Abraham's rejection of any profit from his campaign points up at the same time the completely disinterested nature of his intervention which had as its only motive the rescue of his kinsman. Although Lot had quarreled with his uncle and had chosen to live among the Sodomites of his own free will, yet he was still a member of the family and clan and the ties of blood imposed a sense of solidarity and responsibility upon the patriarch so that he could not stand by indifferent to Lot's fate.

The incident with Melchizedek, King of Salem and priest of "God Most High," is most puzzling. It interrupts the continuity of the narrative.[25] If Salem be identical with Jerusalem, as is suggested by its use elsewhere in parallel with Zion,[26] then we are dealing with a Canaanite king. Yet he blesses Abraham in the name of God using the very epithets that the patriarch himself employs in his dialogue with the King of Sodom. Moreover, Abraham acknowledges Melchizedek's blessing by paying him a tithe.

There is some evidence to suggest that the incident here recorded was once part of a fuller tradition about Melchizedek. This shadowy figure appears once again in biblical literature referring to a king of Israel as being divinely endowed with sacral attributes, "after the order of

Melchizedek."²⁷ This would make sense only if the symbolism were easily understood. It may be assumed, therefore, that a story about this Canaanite priest-king of Jerusalem was well known in Israel.²⁸

As to the divine epithets used in the narrative, it is interesting to note that they are all paralleled in Canaanite religious texts.²⁹ In view of this, Abraham's oath to the King of Sodom³⁰ is particularly important. Unlike the case of Melchizedek, the text has here prefixed the tetragrammaton, YHWH, as though to leave no doubt as to the correct reference. We have here one more example of Israelite appropriation of ancient Near Eastern material, which is then transformed in terms of Israel's religious concepts. But this is not the whole of the story, for by giving a tithe to the priest, Abraham actually acknowledges that the deity of Melchizedek is indeed his own. The insertion of YHWH, therefore, can only be meant to emphasize the identity, not the difference, between the God of Melchizedek and the God of Abraham, known to the people of Israel as YHWH. This accords with the biblical idea of individual non-Hebrews who acknowledge the one God. Such a one was Jethro; another, Balaam; a third, Job. Melchizedek thus belongs to this category.³¹

Why did the narrative introduce the Melchizedek incident here at all? This question cannot be answered with any degree of certainty, though some plausible suggestions may be put forward.³² No other patriarchal story is connected with the city of Jerusalem. The fathers built altars at different places, but there is no association with the one place that was later to monopolize the Judean cult. Our story would thus fill in a lacuna. It places the antiquity of Jerusalem's sanctity back into the patriarchal age and makes it a center of pure divine worship acceptable to the religious consciousness of Israel. It also has Melchizedek, the priest-king of Jerusalem, taking the initiative in paying respect to Abraham, an act symbolic perhaps of the future submission of the city to the people of Israel. Lastly, the incident is the first example of the fulfillment of God's initial promise back in Haran that Abraham's name would become great and be invoked in blessings.³³

1. See W. F. Albright, *BASOR*, 163 (1961), p. 49; *SpG*, p. 106, goes so far as to date the narrative to "scarcely later" than the middle of the second millennium, and even raises the possibility (p. 101) that our Hebrew text may actually be a translation from an Akkadian original.
2. See Albright, *op. cit.*, p. 51f.
3. See *ANET*, p. 328f.; W. F. Albright, *JBL*, LVIII (1939), p. 96; *BASOR*, 94 (1944), p. 24; T. O. Lambdin, *JAOS*, LXXIII (1953), p. 150.
4. On these names, See W. F. Albright, *BASOR*, 163 (1961), pp. 49ff.
5. See Chapter VIII.
6. See Y. Aharoni, *IEJ*, XIII (1963), p. 32. For the Israelite change of ancient place-names, cf. N U M . 32:38, 41f.
7. See the discussion on this place by H. Bar-Deroma, *PEQ*, XCVI (1964), pp. 101–134, esp. pp. 111ff., 118f.
8. On this place, see Y. Aharoni, *op. cit.*, pp. 30–39 (=*Eretz-Israel*, V (1958), pp. 129–134, in Hebrew).
9. On these places and their identity, see W. F. Albright, *BASOR*, 19 (1925), pp. 14–16; 35 (1929), p. 10. For a similar combination of two independent place-names, cf. Kadesh-Barnea, on which see W. F. Albright, *BASOR*, 163 (1961), p. 37, n. 4.

1 0. Cf. J U D . 18:7, 27ff. With the anachronism here, cf. D E U T . 34:1.

1 1. D E U T . 2:11, 20; 3:11.

1 2. *Ibid,* 2:10.

1 3. Cf. G E N . 38:20f.; D E U T . 2:12.

1 4. Deut. 2:20; so identified in the *Genesis Apocryphon,* col. xxi, l. 29.

1 5. On this, see Aharoni, *EYBH,* pp. 32f., 43, 61f., 123f.

1 6. Cf. G E N . 10:10.

1 7. See G. Dossin, *Syria,* XX (1939), p. 109.

1 8. On these names, see above n. 9.

1 9. Cf. N U M . 20:17; 21:22.

2 0. See N. Glueck, *BA,* XXII (1959), pp. 82–97; *Rivers in the Desert,* pp. xi, 11, 68f., 72–77, 105ff.; W. F. Albright, *BASOR,* 163 (1961), pp. 36–40.

2 1. The relationship of the biblical "Hebrew" to the Near Eastern Ḥabiru is still a moot point. These latter appear all over the Fertile Crescent in documents covering a time-span of nearly 1000 years. While the Ḥabiru may originally have derived from a common racial stock, the term in the written sources is clearly an appellative designating a distinct social group, either slave or military, characterized by perpetual rootlessness, wide geographic dispersion and ethnic diversity. Interestingly, all uses of "Hebrew" in Genesis occur in connection with non-Israelites; thus: 14:13; 39:14, 17; 40:15; 41:12; 43:32. On this subject see T. J. Meek, *Hebrew Origins,* pp. 7–14; J. Bottéro, *Le problème des Ḥabiru;* M. Greenberg, *The Hab/piru;* Kaufmann, *Toldot,* I, p. 739f. II, pp. 7–11, 328–334; M. P. Gray, *HUCA,* XXIX (1958), pp. 135–202.

2 2. On this number, see C. H. Gordon, *JNES,* XIII (1954), p. 57.

2 3. G E N . 14:13, 24.

2 4. *Ibid.* v. 23.

2 5. *Ibid.* v. 21 would seem naturally to follow v. 17; see below n. 28.

2 6. P S . 76:3. On Albright's suggestion in *BASOR,* 163 (1961), p. 52, to emend *Shalem,* to *shelomoh,* see S. Abramsky, *Beth Mikra,* XIII (1962), pp. 105–109; *OLD,* pp. 144ff.; S. Yeivin, *Beth Mikra,* XVI (1963), p. 38, n. 235; M. Haran, *OLD,* p. 49, n. 20. For the post-biblical tradition identifying Salem with Jerusalem, see Josephus, *Antiquities,* 1:10:2; the Targum *ad loc.; Genesis Apocryphon,* col. XXII, l. 13.

2 7. P S . 110:4.

2 8. On Melchizedek, see J. Liver, *EBH,* IV, col. 1154–57. The insertion of the Melchizedek incident between G E N . 14:17 and 21 must have been conditioned by the identity of the divine epithets used by the priest-king and Abraham; cf. vv. 18, 19, 20 with v. 22.

2 9. See H. G. May, *JBL,* LX (1941), pp. 115–118; G. Levi Della Vida, *JBL,* LXIII (1944), pp. 1–9; Albright, *FSAC,* p. 247f.; B. W. Anderson in *IDB,* II, p. 412.

3 0. G E N . 14:22.

3 1. See Kaufmann, *Toldot,* I, pp. 224, n. 4; 736, n. 28; *RI,* pp. 221, 224, 294.

3 2. See U. Cassuto, *Eretz-Israel,* III (1954), p. 17f.

3 3. G E N . 12:2f.

CHAPTER VII

The Covenant

GENESIS 15-17

The structure of chapter 15

It has frequently been noted that chapter 15 is a composition of originally heterogeneous elements.[1] In its present form, however, it is a harmoniously structured narrative divided into two dialogues and concluded with a summary.

The bipartite blessing of great posterity and of possession of the land is, as in chapter 12, separated into its individual components,[2] save that the promise of national territory presupposes the existence of a people and therefore incorporates also the blessing of offspring. In each section, God's pronouncement is followed by Abraham's expression of his misgivings. This, in turn, is succeeded by a divine reassurance, supported by the performance of some symbolic action. Each time God allays the doubts of the patriarch He employs and emphasizes a key word of the original question. Abraham complained,

"One of my household will be my heir"

(v. 3),

and God answered,

> "That one shall not be your heir; none but your very own
> issue shall be your heir"   (v. 4).

Abraham queried,

> "How shall I know?"
> (v. 8),

God replied,

> "Know well . . ."
> (v. 13).

The sequence of thought

There is no way of determining whether or not the great vision actually occurred immediately after the "battle of the kings," described in the previous chapter. It is of interest that neither the age of the patriarch, nor the locale of the event is recorded, contrary to the usual practice. These omissions are most likely deliberate and meant to stress that the divine promises, sealed by a covenant ceremonial, are eternally valid and free of all dependence on time and place.

On the other hand, through the literary form in which the narrative has been transmitted to us, the impression is conveyed that the vision was occasioned by the great peril in which Abraham had just found himself and which threatened to nullify all hope of posterity. From God's opening words,

> "Fear not, Abram, I am a shield to you; your reward shall
> be very great"   (v. 1).

it is obvious that Scripture is pursuing its pattern of reaffirming the promises following moments of trial and danger.

The Hebrew word for "shield" (*magen* v. 1) is connected with Melchizedek's invocation of God who "delivered" (*miggen* 14:20) the patriarch's enemies into his hands. The assurance of "great reward" is clearly to be associated with Abraham's refusal to have any part of the spoils of war.[3] The material reward so disdainfully spurned is to be vastly exceeded by a recompense of a different kind, even though the prospects were, as yet, only on the distant horizon. The very word designating the rejected possessions (*rekhush,* 14:21) is employed by God to describe the "great wealth" that Abraham's descendants would ultimately have (15:14).

The mention of Damascus is another point of contact between the two narratives,[4] as is also the word *berit.* Previously, reference was made to Abraham's allies, called in the Hebrew *ba'alei berit* (14:13); now God Himself becomes an ally of the patriarch by making a covenant (*berit,* 15:18) with him. Twice the Amorites are mentioned in the story of the "battle of the kings," and twice they appear in our chapter (vv. 16, 21).

Finally, there is every likelihood that Abraham's campaign in which a small group prevailed against powerful military opponents, is to be understood as signaling the fortunes of the patriarch's descendants against the formidable array of enemies listed in the last three verses of the chapter.

Abraham's heir

In the first dialogue with God, Abraham complained that material reward would be of little use to him since, having no offspring, his servant was to be his heir.[5] To this God replied with an emphatic promise of a natural born heir.[6] This cryptic conversation has taken on new meaning in recent years in the light of the Nuzi archives. It is now widely accepted that behind the biblical narrative lies the institution of adoption, widely recognized in ancient Near Eastern legislation and legal contracts, and commonly practised in the world of the patriarchs.[7]

Numerous documents from Nuzi show that it was a well-established custom for childless persons to adopt a stranger, even a slave, as a son. He owed his adoptive parents filial respect, maintained the estate, took care of their physical needs, and performed the funerary rites at their death. In return, the adopted son became the heir to the property. Sometimes, complications might arise were a natural son to be born after the adoption. The contracts, therefore, carefully set out the rights and obligations of both parties and often specifically provided for such eventualities. One such, dealing with a certain Shennima who was adopted by Shuriha-ilu, reads as follows:

> Shuriha-ilu, with reference to Shennima, (from) all the lands
> . . . (and) his earnings of every sort gave Shennima one
> (portion) of his property. If Shuriha-ilu should have a son
> of his own, as the principal (son) he shall take a double
> share; Shennima shall then be next in order (and) take his
> proper share. As long as Shuriha-ilu is alive Shennima shall
> revere him. When Shuriha-ilu [dies] Shennima shall become
> the heir.[8]

Another such arrangement is recorded as follows:

> The tablet of adoption belonging to Ehelteshup son of
> Puhiya; he adopted Zigi son of Akuya. "Accordingly, all my
> lands, my buildings, my earnings, my domestics, one (part) of
> all my property, I have given to Zigi." In case Ehelteshup has
> sons (of his own), they shall receive a double portion and Zigi
> shall be second. If Ehelteshup has no sons, then Zigi shall be
> the (principal) heir. . . . As long as Ehelteshup is alive, Zigi
> shall serve him; he shall provide him with garments.[9]

From Abraham's colloquy with God, we may reconstruct a situation in which the old couple, having despaired of begetting children, had adopted a servant after the manner of the times.[10] God's reassurance at this point becomes all the more meaningful.

Scripture records that Abraham "put his trust in the Lord and that God reckoned it to his credit" (v. 6). The patriarch was now firmly convinced that he would live to see the fulfillment of the promise of offspring. But what of the gift of the land?

The moral rationalization

Three stages are discernible in the unfolding of the divine promise of national territory to Abraham. Soon after the arrival in Canaan from Haran, he was told, "I will give this land to your offspring" (12:7). After the separation of Lot came the word, "I will give all the land that you see to you and your offspring forever" (13:15). Here Abraham is included among the beneficiaries, the gift is made irrevocable, and is protected by what is most likely a legal formality performed by the recipient.[11] With the vision in chapter 15, a new stage has arrived. Ownership of the land by Abraham is sealed by a covenant ritual in which God, Himself, plays the dominant role.

The subtle changes in the tense forms of the verb used each time are illuminating. "I will give" became "I give" and then "I hereby give" (15:18). The covenant actually marked the transference of real ownership. The future conquest under Joshua, in the biblical view, was but the conversion of ownership into possession.

We have earlier referred to the remarkable and unparalleled fact that Israel never made conquest or settlement the basis of its rights to its national homeland, but that it always regarded its sole title-deed to be the eternally valid divine promises. Even more striking is the moral rationalization of God's actions.

It is perfectly obvious that the biblical genealogical conception of the origins and growth of the people of Israel left no room for immediate occupation of the land. The idea of nationhood through a process of natural proliferation, rather than through the amalgamation or confederacy of existing tribes, meant that Scripture had no option but to envisage the realization of the divine promises only after the passage of many years.[12] But this "natural" explanation is not the one given here in the text. Instead, we are told that the delay was because "the iniquity of the Amorites will not be fulfilled until then" (v. 16).

This amazing explanation means that the displacement of the native population of Canaan by Israel was not to be accounted for on grounds of divine favoritism or superior military prowess on the part of the invading Israelites. The local peoples, here generically called "Amorites," had violated God's charge. The universally binding moral law had been flouted, just as in the days of Noah, and with the same inevitable consequences. The pre-Israelite inhabitants of Canaan had been doomed by their own corruption. Yet God's justice is absolute. In the days of the patriarchs the measure of the pagan sin was not yet complete and Israel would have to wait—and suffer—until God's time was ripe. Divine justice was not to be strained even for the elect of God, and even though its application related to the pagans.

This moral judgment of the Canaanites is reflected in several of the patriarchal stories and is reiterated many times in the Pentateuch. The sinfulness of the Sodomites[13] is, of course, the most prominent example;

another is the report of Abraham's visit to Gerar where he fears the consequences to his person of the local moral laxity, attributed to the absence of the fear of God.[14] The same idea doubtless accounts for the repetition of the incident in Isaac's day.[15]

The Priestly Code, seeking to purify and sanctify sexuality, outlaws certain patterns of behavior as being obnoxious to God. The passage concludes with the admonition:

> Do not defile yourselves in any of those ways, for it is by such that the nations which I am casting out before you defiled themselves. Thus the land became defiled; and I called it to account for its iniquity, and the land spewed out its inhabitants . . .   (LEV. 18 : 24f.)

This theme is repeated again and again.[16] It should be noted, too, that God judges Israel by the same strict moral standards.

> So let not the land spew you out for defiling it, as it spewed out the nation that came before it.   (LEV. 18 : 28)

Furthermore, there is no suggestion that Israel's right to the land results from any inherent superiority. On the contrary, the Book of Deuteronomy expressly warns against such a conceit.

> Say not to yourselves, "the Lord has enabled me to occupy this land because of my virtues. . . ." It is not because of your virtues and your rectitude that you will be able to occupy their country, but because of the wickedness of those nations the Lord your God is dispossessing them before you, and in order to fulfill the oath that the Lord made to your fathers, Abraham, Isaac, and Jacob. Know, then, that it is not for any virtue of yours that the Lord your God is giving you this good land to occupy; for you are a stiffnecked people."
>
> (DEUT. 9 : 4-6)

The form of the covenant

The elaborate ceremonial of the covenant between God and Abraham cannot fail to arouse curiosity. Unfortunately, the precise meaning of the various elements defies us, for the only other biblical parallel[17] is likewise without explanation, and there is plenty of evidence to show that Scripture has here utilized the outward forms of an ancient ritual in a disintegrated state.[18]

The peculiar Hebrew phrase "to cut a covenant" is derived from the practice of severing animals as the seal of a treaty. This custom is widely attested in ancient times and exists among primitive peoples to this day; particularly interesting are Hittite and Greek parallels.[19] It is generally believed that when the contracting parties passed between the severed pieces they thereby accepted the covenant obligations and invoked upon themselves the fate of the animals if the terms of the pact were violated.[20] But how could this latter apply to God? The smoke and the flame[21] are frequent symbols of the divine presence in biblical theophanies[22] (accounts of God's self-manifestation), and it is only these that "passed between the pieces." Abraham did not participate. Only God bound Himself to a solemn obligation, the patriarch having been the passive beneficiary.

What was the function of the particular animals chosen? Certainly, it was not sacrificial, as one might have expected, since there is no altar, no mention of blood, no suggestion of consumption by the heavenly fire or by Abraham. Nor is there any indication of the role of the birds. Are they a relic of some technique of obtaining oracles?[23] Or since the promise of posterity plays so prominent a part, are they perhaps fertility symbols, familiar to us from Akkadian, Canaanite and Greek mythological texts?[24]

Whatever the origins, the entire ceremony has undergone a radical transformation. The symbolism attached to the individual items was most likely forgotten already by the time the tradition was reduced to writing. The occult aspect, if ever there was one, has given way to a didactic purpose, namely, to provide the patriarch with an answer to his question,

"How shall I know that I am to possess it?"

(15 : 8)

The awesome spectacle that generated the "deep dark dread"[25] (v. 12) had as its sole purpose the strengthening of faith in God.

Turning from the ritualistic to the literary-juristic features of the covenant, an interesting comparative study is now possible.[26] From the Hittite empire records of treaties have survived which regulated relationships between the great kings and their inferior vassals. The documents usually contain a preamble identifying the author of the pact, after which follows a historical prologue describing the past relationships between the contracting parties. Then come the treaty stipulations, the obligations which the superior imposes upon the inferior. A close analysis of God's covenant with Abraham reveals that Scripture has here followed a similar legal pattern.

> "I am the Lord who brought you out from Ur of the Chaldeans," (v. 7)

constitutes the identification and historical introduction, while the subsequent speech of God defines the future relationships.[27] Incidentally, this same pattern is followed in the Decalogue.[28] Here again, Scripture made use of existing Near Eastern convention which it adopted for its own purposes. To what extent this is so may be gauged from the astonishing fact that the covenant completely lacks, as we have pointed out, mutuality. It is a unilateral obligation assumed by God without any reciprocal responsibilities being imposed upon Abraham. The use of established legal forms of treaty-making to express such a situation is a dramatic way of conveying the immutable nature of the divine promise. In a society in which the capriciousness of the gods was taken for granted, the "covenant between the pieces," like the covenant with Noah, set religion on a bold, new, independent course.

Hagar the concubine

The experience of the covenant ritual evoked no vocal response from Abraham. This silence must be interpreted as complete confidence in the fulfillment of the divine promise. It was ten years since the patriarch had parted from his father to set out for a new land and a new career.[29] Even before the initial migration to Haran, Scripture had carefully noted that "Sarai was barren, she had no child" (11:30). Now, after a decade of frustrated hopes, we are told once again that "Sarai, Abram's wife, had borne him no children" (16:1). The impatience of the matriarch had reached a critical point. In her desperation she resorted to a device that was to be imitated in similar circumstances by Rachel, but which is not to be found again anywhere else in the Bible.

Sarah brought her Egyptian maidservant, Hagar, to her husband saying,

"See, the Lord has kept me from bearing. Consort with my
maid; perhaps I shall have a son through her."   (16 : 2)

Rachel, having been denied the fruit of the womb, confronted Jacob
with a like situation declaring,

"Here is my maid Bilhah. Consort with her, that she may
bear on my knees and that through her I too may have
children."   (30 : 3)

Concubinage as a social institution has long been known to have existed
in ancient Babylon. The laws of Hammurabi mention it, but apparently
restrict its application to the case where the wife was a priestess.[30] Of
far more immediate interest are Nuzi contracts that actually stipulate that
should the wife prove to be childless she must provide her husband with
a slave-woman. One such document reads as follows:

(Miss) Kelim-ninu has been given in marriage to (Mr.)
Shennima. . . . If Kelim-ninu does not bear, Kelim-ninu shall
acquire a woman of the land of Lulu (i.e. a slave-girl) as wife
for Shennima.[31]

In these Nuzi documents it is clear that it is the husband who inserts
the stipulation in the marriage contract in order to guard against the
possibility of being left without an heir. In the biblical accounts it is
the wives who, out of despair, take the initiative. Their action may well
have been motivated by a popular belief that the adoption of the children
of the maidservant would prove to be a remedy for infertility.[32] The
immediate effect of Sarah's action, however, was to disturb domestic
harmony.

Sarah's experience with Hagar could not have been an uncommon side
effect of unions arranged in such circumstances. In a society which
regarded female sterility as a disgrace it is not to be wondered at that
Sarah "was lowered in the esteem" of her maidservant (16:4–5). Hammurabi's laws[33] provided for just such a development where, "because
she bore children, the female slave claimed equality with her mistress."
The law provided that although the mistress was not allowed to sell
her, the concubine was to be punished by having to resume her former
slave status. The Nuzi document previously cited, mentions that Miss

Kelim-ninu received a hand-maid as a marriage gift and specifies that the maid is to revere the mistress as long as she lives. These parallels with the biblical narrative indicate once again the dependence of the latter on an authentic, living tradition derived from the patriarchal period.

Peculiarly biblical is the account of the sequence of events. It is stated quite openly that Sarah treated Hagar harshly,[34] and as if to leave no doubt as to where the sympathies of Scripture lie, God, as the guardian of the weak and the suffering, reveals Himself to the lowly maidservant bringing her a message of comfort and hope. The God of Abraham is also the God of the Egyptian Hagar and He shows His concern for Ishmael, as yet unborn and not destined to belong to the people of Israel.

The change of name

Two dozen years had elapsed since that fateful day when Abraham had first set forth from Haran, and thirteen years had gone by since the birth of Ishmael. Sarah's pathetic experiment had failed. Once again, a divine reaffirmation of the promises of posterity and land was vouchsafed the patriarch, an occasion that marked another critical station in his spiritual odyssey.

> "And you shall no longer be called Abram, but your name shall be Abraham, for I make you the father of a multitude of nations." (GEN. 17 : 5)

The matriarch, too, was henceforth to be known by a new name, Sarah in place of Sarai.[35]

A true understanding of the meaning and significance of this event will not be possible without an appreciation of the function and importance of the name in the psychology of the ancient Near Eastern world.[36] To begin with, it must be observed that a name was not merely a convenient means of identification. The name of a man was intimately involved in the very essence of his being and inextricably intertwined with his personality. Hence, giving a name is connected with creativity. An Egyptian theogonic myth tells how the first god Atum brought other gods into being by naming the parts of his body.[37] In the Genesis cosmogony, God carefully gives a name to the first things He created, except that in the scriptural demythologizing process the order has become reversed. The designations no longer initiate creation, but complete it.[38]

Conversely, anonymity is equivalent to non-being. Thus, to "cut off the name" means to end existence, to annihilate,[39] and in Egypt, with its death-centered religion, the way to bring an end to the continued existence of a deceased person in the afterlife was by effacing his name from his tomb.[40] Alternatively, posterity may be expressed in terms of the name. The Torah legislates that when a man dies without issue his brother must take the widow as his wife and,

> The first son that she bears shall be accounted to the dead brother, that his name may not be blotted out in Israel.
>
> (DEUT. 25 : 6)

From all this it will be readily understood why the Bible invests name-giving with such great importance and why a change of name is an event of major significance. Throughout the Near East the inauguration of a new era or a new state policy would frequently be marked by the assumption of a new name expressive of the change on the part of the King. Amen-Hotep IV of Egypt, whose name meant "(The god) Amon-is-satisfied," signified the revolutionary new theology which he imposed on his people by altering his name to Akh-en-Aton ("He-who-is-serviceable-to-the-Aton," or "It-goes-well-with-the-Aton").[41] In the Bible, apart from Abram and Sarai, Jacob,[42] Joseph,[43] Hoshea (Joshua),[44] the Judean Kings Eliakim (Jehoiakim)[45] and Mattaniah (Zedekiah),[46] and Daniel and his friends[47] all experienced changes of name, symbolizing the transmutation of character and destiny. To be sure, the new appellation may be, as in the case of Abram-Abraham and Sarai-Sarah, nothing but a dialectic variant of the old, and scientific etymology cannot possibly explain Abraham as meaning "father of a multitude" (17:5). But this is of no importance, theologically speaking. The very fact of a new name distinguishes and even effectuates, to an extent, the transformation of destiny. The association with which the new name is charged is all that matters. The interpretation given to "Abraham" is clearly a piece of exegesis based on the original divine blessing.

> "I will make of you a great nation, and I will bless you;
> I will make your name great."   (12 : 2)

Now the patriarch is told that he will not only have an heir and be the progenitor of a nation but that he will even become the "father of a multitude of nations." This is how a "great name" is to be understood.

It will doubtless be noted that each of the patriarchs received his name of destiny from God Himself. If Isaac, alone, undergoes no change of name, it is only because his was divinely ordained even before birth.[48] In this way Scripture is expressing once again the idea of the God-given destiny of the patriarchs and the notion that the origins and fate of the people of Israel are central to the divine plan of history. It is probably this that accounts for the curious fact that the patriarchal names, as well as the names of great biblical heroes like Moses, Aaron, David and Solomon, are unique to their bearers, never being attached to any other personage in all of scriptural literature.

Circumcision

The turning-point in the life of Abraham is marked by a further affirmation of the divine covenant.[49] This time, however, the patriarch is no longer to be a passive onlooker, but is ordered to play an active role. The spiritual progression indicated by the change of name is to be supplemented by a physical alteration, a painful, self-inflicted act carried out in submission to the divine command.

The practice of circumcision is widely attested in the ancient world[50] and its origin in Israel is ascribed to the founding father of the nation. It is of historic interest that it is in Canaan, rather than Mesopotamia, that Israel is introduced to the institution, since it was not known in ancient Babylon and Assyria. On the other hand, Egyptians and other peoples practised it widely. A stela inscription of a man who describes himself as "a commoner of repute," possibly stemming from as early as the twenty-third century B.C.E., describes a mass circumcision ceremony in Egypt carried out on one hundred and twenty men.[51] A celebrated Sakkarah tomb painting from the Sixth Dynasty (2300–2000) actually depicts the rite performed by "mortuary priests" on boys.[52] Herodotus reported that the Egyptians practised circumcision "for the sake of cleanliness, considering it better to be clean than comely." He believed that other peoples borrowed the custom from them.[53] From the Book of Joshua it is clear that the Egyptians regarded lack of circumcision as a "reproach."[54] From the fact that of all the peoples with whom Israel came into close contact only the Philistines are derisively called "the uncircumcised,"[55] it may be inferred that this people was unique in that respect. This conclusion is confirmed by Jeremiah who mentions that, along with Judah, Egypt, Edom, Amon, and Moab also practised circumcision of the flesh.[56]

The story of Dinah and the Shechemites[57] and of Zipporah at the night encampment in the wilderness of Midian,[58] as well as the laws of the Passover,[59] show the consistency of the tradition ascribing the practice in Israel to pre-Sinaitic times. Our text relating God's command to Abraham assumes an understanding of the procedure to be followed even though no instructions are forthcoming. That is, God is not instituting a totally new and unknown rite, but is adapting and transforming an existing custom. That flint knives were used both by Zipporah[60] and Joshua,[61] although Canaan was then in the Bronze Age, is as much a testimony to the great antiquity of the practice of circumcision in Israel as a witness to religious conservatism.

The origin and meaning of a custom so old and so widely diffused cannot fail to be of absorbing interest to the anthropologist. Yet his conclusions will be of little relevance to the biblical scholar, except in so far as they help to point up the remarkable transformation of the rite in Israel. In the first place, circumcision is no longer a matter of social mores or the perpetuation of tribal tradition. It is now conceived of as being divinely ordained and as deriving its sanction solely from that fact. It has been transferred from the area of formality to the realm of law. Secondly, it cannot be abrogated. It must be kept, precisely because it is regarded as a divinely ordained institution, "throughout the ages" (17:9, 12), as "an everlasting pact" (17:14). Thirdly, the Bible shifted its performance from puberty to the eighth day of birth, a radical departure from well-nigh universal practice which not only marks the distinction in spiritual destiny between Isaac[62] and Ishmael, but even more importantly establishes another essential differentiation of the biblical institution of circumcision from its contemporary pagan counterpart. Finally, the rite has been invested with entirely new and original meaning. It is described both as a "sign of the covenant" and as a covenant itself.[63] It is an ineradicable token of the immutability of God's unilateral promises to Israel, and at the same time its operation constitutes a positive act of identification and dedication as a member of the covenanted community.[64] It thus became an indispensable part of the covenant concept, so that failure to perform the sacramental rite constitutes a breach of the covenant on the part of the Israelite. "Such a person shall be cut off from his kin" (*ibid.*). Having excluded himself from the religious community by deliberate choice, he cannot hope to be a beneficiary of the blessings of the covenant.

The new Abraham

With the alteration of his name and the performance of circumcision, the transformation of the patriarch is all but complete. Three times he had spoken with God and on each occasion his personal weal and woe had been the sole substance of his discourse.[65] Now, however, a revolutionary change is about to take place. The very next dialogue with God involves a concern for the welfare of others, a plea for the lives of the men of Sodom and Gomorrah.

1. For a summary of the widely divergent critical analyses, see A. Cazelles, *RB*, LXIX (1962), p. 321f.
2. G E N . 15:1ff., 7ff.
3. G E N . 14:22ff. It is quite likely that we are dealing in G E N . 15:1 with a play on words, for *mgn* in P R O V . 4:9 means, "to give a gift;" cf. C. H. Gordon, *Ugaritic Manual*, 3:1061.
4. G E N . 14:15; 15:2.
5. For a summary of exegesis on G E N . 15:2 *Dammeseq Eliezer*, see Cassuto in *EBH*, II, col. 675f. See, also, O. Eissfeldt, *JSS*, V (1960), p. 48f.; W. F. Albright, *BASOR*, 163 (1961), p. 47, and n. 54; *SpG*, p. 111f.
6. G E N . 15:3f.
7. See C. H. Gordon, *BA*, III (1940), p. 2f.; R. de Vaux, *RB*, LVI (1949), p. 25f.; I. Mendelsohn, *IEJ*, 9 (1959), pp. 180–183.
8. *ANET*, p. 105; cf. E. A. Speiser, *AASOR*, X (1930), pp. 31ff.
9. *Ibid.*, p. 30.
1 0. See W. F. Albright, *BASOR*, 163 (1961), p. 47 and n. 56.
1 1. G E N . 13:17.
1 2. Cf. G E N . 15:13, 16. On the problems involved in these passages, see chap. IV, n. 14.

1 3. Cf. G E N . 13:13; chaps. 18–19.

1 4. *Ibid.* 20:11.

1 5. *Ibid.* 26:6ff.

1 6. Cf. L E V . 20:23f.; I Kings 14:24.

1 7. J E R . 34:18ff.

1 8. See *SpG,* Notes to 15:9, 17.

1 9. For the Mari parallels, see Albright, *ARI,* p. 113; R. de Vaux, *RB,* LVI (1949), p. 24; G. E. Mendenhall, *BA,* XI (1948), p. 18; *BASOR,* 133 (1954), pp. 26ff.; M. Noth, *Gesammelte Schriften,* pp. 142ff. For the Qatna practice, see W. F. Albright, *BASOR,* 121 (1951), p. 21f.; *ibid.* 163 (1961), p. 46, n. 51. On Hittite and Greek parallels, see J. F. Priest, *JNES,* XXIII (1964), pp. 48–56.

2 0. Cf. the soldier's oath in *ANET,* p. 353f. On this interpretation, see Frazer, *Folklore,* I, pp. 399–428; G. Wallis, *ZAW,* LXIV (1952), pp. 57–61, who compares Jud. 19:29; I Sam. 11:7; J. Henninger, *Biblica,* XXXIV (1953), pp. 344–53.

2 1. G E N . 15:17.

2 2. E X O D . 3:2; 13:21; 14:24; 19:18; 24:16f.; 40:33, 38; N U M . 10:34; 14:14.

2 3. See A. Bentzen, *Introduction to the O. T.,* I, p. 185.

2 4. See C. H. Gordon, *Ugaritic Literature,* p. 58; M. Pope, *EL in the Ugaritic Texts,* p. 40; G. R. Driver, *Canaanite Myths and Legends,* p. 123.

2 5. See J. Lindblom, *HUCA,* XXXII (1961), p. 94f. Note, however, with Kaufmann, *Toldot,* I, p. 529, that the "deep sleep" and "deep dark dread" here followed the theophany, and cannot thus be included in the usual category of incubation.

2 6. See G. E. Mendelhall, *BA,* XVII (1953), pp. 50–76.

2 7. G E N . 15:13–16.

2 8. E X O D . 20:1–17; D E U T . 5:6–18.

2 9. G E N . 16:3.

3 0. See *ANET,* p. 172, §§ 144–147; R. de Vaux, *RB,* LVI (1949), p. 20f.; Driver and Miles, I, pp. 304–6.

3 1. *ANET,* p. 220; E. A. Speiser, *AASOR,* X (1930), p. 31f.

3 2. S. Kardimon, *JSS,* III (1958), pp. 123–26. G E N . 30:17f. would tend to substantiate this interpretation.

3 3. *ANET,* p. 172, § 146.

3 4. G E N . 16:6.

3 5. *Ibid.* 17:15.

3 6. See J. Pedersen, *Israel,* I–II, pp. 245–59; M. Noth, *Die Israelitischen Personennamen;* de Vaux, *AI,* pp. 43–46; cf. Albright, *FSAC,* p. 253, n. 76.

3 7. See Wilson, *CAE,* p. 59; *ANET,* p. 4.

3 8. Cf. G E N . 1:5, 8, 10; 2:19f., 23.

3 9. Cf. D E U T . 7:24; 9:14; 12:3.

4 0. See Wilson, *CAE,* p. 225.

4 1. *Ibid.,* pp. 215, 222; cf. 133.

4 2. G E N . 32:29; 35:10.

4 3. *Ibid.* 41:45.

4 4. N U M . 13:16.

4 5. I I K I N G S 23:24.

4 6. *Ibid.,* 24:7.

4 7. D A N . 1:7.

4 8. GEN. 17:19.

4 9. *Ibid.,* 17:6–8.

5 0. De Vaux, *AI,* 46ff.; cf. M. H. Segal, *JQR,* LII (1961), pp. 51–54; M. Haran, *OLD,* p. 62f.

5 1. *ANET,* p. 326.

5 2. *ANEP,* p. 629.

5 3. Herodotus, *Histories,* II: §§ 36f., 104; cf. Josephus, *Contra Apion,* II:13.

5 4. JOSH. 5:9.

5 5. JUD. 14:3; 15:18, etc.

5 6. JER. 9:24; cf. EZEK. 32:21ff.

5 7. GEN. 34:14ff. This passage would indicate that the inhabitants of Shechem were exceptional among the peoples of Canaan. A Hurrian origin, as suggested by *SpG,* p. 267, would readily account for the fact. See, however, GEN. 48:22.

5 8. EXOD. 4:24ff.

5 9. *Ibid.,* 12:43–48.

6 0. *Ibid.,* 4:25.

6 1. JOSH. 5:2–9.

6 2. GEN. 21:4.

6 3. *Ibid.,* 17:9f., 11, 14.

6 4. Cf. N. Eichrodt, *Theology of the O.T.,* p. 138.

6 5. GEN. 15:2, 8; 17:17.

CHAPTER VIII

Sodom and Gomorrah

GENESIS 18, 19

The story that converted the names of these two cities into an imperishable metaphor of human wickedness and divine retribution is well enough known. God's decision to destroy sinful Sodom and Gomorrah stirred Abraham to ask the immortal question, "Shall not the judge of all the earth deal justly?" (18:25). The patriarch pleaded for the revocation of the sentence for the sake of an innocent nucleus that might exist in the city. But, when even ten guiltless men were not to be found, God proceeded to execute His judgment. First, however, He sent two messengers to rescue Lot, Abraham's nephew, and his family. The Sodomites resented Lot's hospitality to the strangers and menacingly surrounded his home. Lot felt obligated to protect his guests even to the extent of offering his daughters in exchange. Only the quick action of the guests saved Lot and his family.

The narrative then continues with a description of the annihilation of the civilization of the area and the escape of Lot and his daughters.

The historical background

The frequent mention of this catastrophe in biblical literature shows that the event left an indelible impression upon the popular mind.[1] Even Greek and Latin historians like Strabo and Tacitus recorded it; though we cannot be entirely certain that they did not receive their information from Jewish sources.[2] However, whether or not the biblical narrative is based on a historical fact, the purposes of Scripture become abundantly clear if we consider that of the forty-seven verses devoted to the entire episode,[3] the description of the actual disaster occupies but six[4] and is terse almost to the point of obscurity. Obviously, the question of historical detail is of far less importance than the treatment of the theme. Nevertheless, since we are dealing with an event that is centered in the patriarchal age, we should be deficient in our understanding of the Bible if we neglected the historical aspect and failed to make full use of the materials that modern scholarship has placed at our disposal.

The first problem is a geographical one. If Sodom and Gomorrah are ever to yield their secrets to the spade of the excavator they have to be pinpointed on the map. But, despite the unenviable notoriety achieved by the "cities of the Plain," their exact location has never been discovered. They seem to have vanished irretrievably without leaving behind so much as a rubbish heap to tease the eager archaeologist. The most that we can hope for is to put together the scattered bits of data available so that we may be able to declare, with some degree of assurance, that Sodom and Gomorrah lay in this or that general direction. This exercise is not simply academic for, as we shall see, it brings the biblical text into sharper focus and puts the narrative and sequence of events in bolder relief.

Considering the biblical use of Sodom as a symbol of desolation and aridity, it comes as a great surprise to read a report about the cities in the story of Lot separating from his uncle, Abraham. In choosing Sodom as his domicile he was influenced, we are told, by the luscious fertility of the Jordan valley.

> Lot looked about him and saw how well watered was the whole plain of the Jordan, all of it—this was before the Lord had destroyed Sodom and Gomorrah—all the way to Zoar, like the garden of the Lord, like the land of Egypt.
>
> (13 : 10)

Explorations in recent years have shown that this description was indeed accurate, and applied particularly to the region south of the Lisan, that tongue-shaped peninsula that juts into the middle of the Dead Sea.[5] Several streams water the area around the eastern shore of this sea. Since the availability of an adequate water supply is a prerequisite for all urban settlement, there is a very good case for placing the lost cities to the south of the Lisan. This claim is strengthened by another piece of intelligence gleaned from the "Table of Nations" in the Book of Genesis. Sodom and Gomorrah constituted the southern extremity of the area of Canaanite occupation.[6] The significant omission of the great cities of Hebron and Jerusalem favors a southern situation for the "cities of the Plain."[7] Topographically, such a location would fit in very well with Genesis 19:28:

> And, looking down toward Sodom and Gomorrah and all the land of the Plain, he saw the smoke of the land rising like the smoke of a kiln.

The smoke of the ruined cities would be much more easily visible from Hebron in a southerly, rather than northerly, direction.

Another story about Abraham records a battle that took place in the Valley of Siddim, in the Dead Sea area, in which the kings of Sodom and Gomorrah participated. We are told that this Valley was "dotted with bitumen pits" (14:10). Now the presence of bitumen in considerable quantities is well known in the southern Dead Sea region. To this day, chunks of the material may be seen from time to time rising to the surface of the lake.[8]

To the mention of bitumen must be added that of salt.[9] Lot's wife is said to have turned into a "pillar of salt" (19:26), suggesting some grotesque salt-rock formation in the region.[10] Salt is also mentioned in connection with Sodom and Gomorrah in another context. In Moses' farewell speech he warns that a breach of the Covenant with God would bring ruin to the land, and he describes the state of affairs that would arise as follows:

> All its soil devastated by sulphur and salt, beyond sowing and producing, no grass growing in it, just like the upheaval of Sodom and Gomorrah. . . .   (D E U T . 29:22)

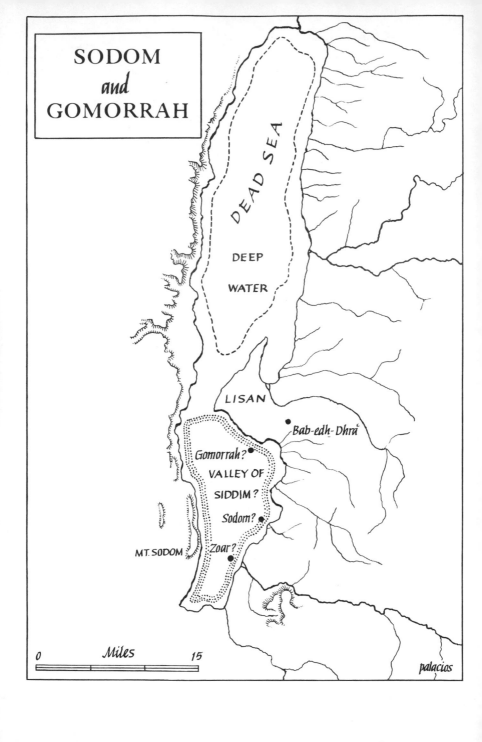

SODOM
and
GOMORRAH

DEAD SEA

DEEP

WATER

LISAN

Bab-edh-Dhra'

Gomorrah?

VALLEY OF

SIDDIM?

Sodom?

MT. SODOM

Zoar?

0   *Miles*   15

palacios

The prophet Zephaniah who prophesied concerning the lands of Moab and Ammon, says they will be like Sodom and Gomorrah, "a land possessed by nettles and salt pits and a waste forever" (Zeph. 2:9). In the entire Jordan-Dead Sea valley area there is only one region to which the mention of salt would be appropriate, and that is a salt mountain known to this day as "Mount Sodom," nearly six miles long and about six hundred and fifty feet in height, lying on the southwest shore of the Dead Sea.[11] Here, again, the data confirms a location for the lost cities in the area of the southern embayment of the Dead Sea.

Of all the scraps of evidence that have had to be fitted togther in jigsaw fashion, perhaps the most exciting come from a site called Bab-edh-Dhraʿ, standing in an empty plain about five hundred feet above the eastern Dead Sea shore.[12] Here were found remnants of a large fortified open-air enclosure. Over a fairly wide area of virgin soil were strewn an abundance of flint implements and pottery datable to the end of the third millennium B.C.E., and here and there were a number of primitive hearths. Not far off from the enclosure was a cemetery and some distance from it a group of fallen menhirs, or stone pillars. The relics showed clearly that the site had been used, though not continuously, for hundreds of years until the twenty-first century B.C.E.[13] Strangely enough, there is no sign of any permanent settlement in the entire region. Moreover, we know from archaeological surveys that in the period to which Bab-edh-Dhraʿ belonged, this part of East Jordan was populated largely by wandering Bedouins who certainly were incapable of constructing buildings like the fortified stronghold. Who, then, put up this structure and used this site, and for what purpose?

The stone pillars, the open-air hearths, and the implements and pottery all point to one conclusion. The place must have been a great open air sanctuary, a place of pilgrimage for people who lived in the valley down below. It was they who built the fortified enclosure to preserve both their holy place and the pilgrims from the ravages of the Bedouins during the periodic festivals. In other words, the material relics all presuppose the existence of a local civilization of which not a trace has remained. Bab-edh-Dhraʿ must have been sustained by the populace of cities which once were situated in what is now the southern embayment of the Dead Sea.

As a matter of fact, the great disproportion between the thirteen-hundred-foot water depth in the north end and the mere eight to fourteen feet in the extreme south, proves that the latter is of a far younger formation than the former. Indeed, there is plenty of evidence to show that the water level of the Dead Sea has been steadily rising for centuries as well as spreading southward.[14] In short, the area south of what is now known as the Lisan was once a plain in which stood Sodom and Gomorrah. This is what Scripture must have meant by its incidental remark that "the valley of Siddim is now the Dead Sea" (14:3). At some time or other occurred a great disaster that caused the waters of the Dead Sea to extend southward, completely submerging the entire inhabited area.

The nature of the catastrophe[15]

Can we now describe more closely the event that is behind the biblical description of the catastrophe?

> As the sun rose upon the earth . . . the Lord rained upon Sodom and Gomorrah sulphurous fire from the Lord out of heaven. He annihilated those cities and the entire plain and all the inhabitants of the cities and the vegetation of the ground.   (19 : 23–25)

Geologists have completely ruled out the possibility of a volcanic eruption in this part of the world. On the other hand, the Hebrew word translated here "annihilated" suggests the effects of an earthquake.[16] It is well known that the entire Jordan Valley is part of an immense system of rift valleys stretching from Syria in the north, down the Arabah to the Gulf of Akaba, and extending through the Red Sea to the Upper Nile Valley and on to Lake Nyasa in East Africa. This great fracture in the earth's crust was, of course, brought about by geological spasms.[17] Now, the whole tenor of the Sodom story suggests some unnatural and extraordinary happening, swift and sudden in its visitation. We are most likely, then, dealing with a description of one of the last earthquakes that shaped the lower Jordan Valley area. As is frequently the case, the earthquake was accompanied by lightning which ignited the natural gases and seepages of bitumen or asphalt and probably also petroleum, causing a terrible conflagration. This would also explain why, when Abraham looked down over the area, he saw "the smoke of the land rising like the smoke of a kiln" (19:28).

Abraham and the Sodom story

Unfortunately, no parallels to our story from extra-biblical Palestinian sources have yet turned up. It is unthinkable, however, that a devastating calamity such as overtook "the cities of the Plain" did not leave its impress upon the local Canaanite traditions. In fact, the existence of a more extensive popular version or, perhaps, several versions, of the saga in ancient times may be deduced from the scattered and fragmentary biblical citations which differ in some respects from the Genesis recension in the names of the cities involved and in the details of the description of the disaster. Our story concentrates mainly on Sodom; others speak of Sodom and Gomorrah; still others refer to Admah and Zeboiim as well,[18] while one source[19] restricts itself solely to these latter two. Again, our story makes no mention of salt as being part of the visitation, only of sulphurous fire descending from heaven. Deuteronomy 29:22 speaks of the soil being devastated by sulphur and salt.

We may assume, then, that in its original form, the Sodom and Gomorrah story was an independent narrative, unconnected with Abraham and his family.[20] The Bible has once again adopted the nucleus of a popular saga to rework it in accordance with its own ethico-religious purposes. This would explain the almost exclusive concentration on Sodom and the very brief description of the catastrophe.

The value of this kind of critical analysis does not lie in the disentanglement of the literary strands. That, of itself, would be of little interest to the non-specialist. Rather, it is the significance of the interweaving on the part of Scripture that arrests our attention, for the association of Abraham with the story becomes all the more remarkable.

Consider this. Abraham, the elect of God, the founder of the people of Israel and proponent of a faith which turned its back upon contemporary religious notions, and to which the conduct of the inhabitants of Sodom was utterly abhorrent, stands before God to plead for the lives of pagans of another race; pagans, what is more, who were to become the eternal symbol of human depravity. He neither rejoices at the downfall of evil, nor adopts an attitude of indifference. He feels a sense of kinship with those human beings of Sodom and a sense of involvement in their fate. In this way, the scriptural narrative has cast the father of the Jewish people in a representative role that foreshadows the later prophetic conviction of the destiny of Israel among the nations. The grafting of the personality of the patriarch onto an originally independent narrative is an astonishing and triumphant spiritual and moral achievement. Before its grandeur and everlasting relevance the question of historicity and source division pales into insignificance.

The sin of Sodom

Turning now from Abraham's involvement with Sodom to the nature of its sins, we may continue our investigation of the ideas that animated the story.

The first intimation of the moral standing of the inhabitants of Sodom is rather vague, being confined to the simple observation that they "were very wicked sinners against the Lord" (13:13). What it means, in the biblical concept, to "sin against the Lord" is soon vividly illustrated by the conduct of the Sodomites upon the arrival of the two messengers at Lot's home. Here we find them violently demonstrating their hostility to the strangers and lusting to indulge in unnatural vice.[21] But the most sweeping condemnation of the Sodomites is contained in the following passage:

> Then the Lord said, "The outrage of Sodom and Gomorrah is so great, and their sins so grave! I will go down to see whether they have acted altogther according to the outcry that has come to Me . . ."   (18 : 20–21)

The Hebrew words translated here "outrage" and "outcry" are really one and the same *(ṣeʿaqah-zeʿaqah)*. The identical description is repeated as the disaster approaches.

> For we are about to destroy this place; because the outcry against them before the Lord has become so great that the Lord has sent us to destroy it.   (19 : 13)

This thrice-repeated, generalized, designation of the Sodomite sin as an "outcry" appears to the English reader to be rather a mild appellation, hardly commensurate with the enormity of punishment. But this is one of those instances in which a Hebrew word cannot be adequately translated into another language. In the course of its linguistic metamorphosis the force of the original has become vitiated. The Hebrew root *ṣaʿaq/ zaʿaq* indicates the anguished cry of the oppressed, the agonized plea of the victim for help in some great injustice. A few examples of the Hebrew usage will suffice to illustrate the degree of poignancy and pathos, of moral outrage and soul-stirring passion that pervades the Hebrew word.

God heeded the "outcry" of Israel in Egypt against their taskmasters.[22] If any mistreat a widow or orphan God will heed the "outcry as soon as they cry out" and His "anger shall blaze forth" (Exod. 22:21–23). To Isaiah, an "outcry" is the very negation of justice and righteousness.

> And he looked for justice,
> but behold, bloodshed;
> for righteousness,
> but behold, an outcry.   (ISA. 5 : 7)

The Book of Job castigates the wicked who cause the "outcry" of the poor and afflicted to come before God.[23]

The "outcry" of Sodom, then, implies, above all, heinous moral and social corruption, an arrogant disregard of elementary human rights, a cynical insensitivity to the sufferings of others.[24] The prophet Ezekiel, speaking in the name of God, powerfully sums up the iniquity of Sodom and Gomorrah as follows:

> Behold, this was the guilt of your sister Sodom. She and her
> daughters had pride, surfeit of food, and prosperous ease,[25]
> but did not aid the poor and the needy. They were haughty,
> and did abominable things before me; therefore I removed
> them, when I saw it.   (EZEK. 16 : 49–50)

The indictment of Sodom, it will be remembered, is highly reminiscent of the Flood account. Indeed, the "violence" spoken of there is, in content, identical with the "outcry" here. In both cases, the evils on which the Bible dwells are not those of dishonoring, or offending God, in the pagan meaning of the terms.[26] It is not the neglect of sacrificial gifts, the disregard of an oracular utterance, or the making of a false oath that arouses the ire of the Deity. The sins are entirely on the moral plane, and of idolatry there is not so much as a whisper. As with the Flood, the Sodom and Gomorrah narrative is predicated upon the existence of a moral law of universal application for the infraction of which God holds all men answerable. *The idea that there is an intimate, in fact, inextricable, connection between the socio-moral condition of a people and its ultimate fate is one of the main pillars upon which stands the entire biblical interpretation of history.*[27] The theme is central to the Flood story, basic to the Sodom and Gomorrah narrative and fundamental to the understanding of the Book of Jonah. It constitutes the Torah's vindication of God's action in destroying the inhabitants of Canaan before the invading Israelites.

> Do not defile yourselves in any of those ways, for it is by such that the nations which I am casting out before you defiled themselves. Thus the land became defiled; and I called it to account for its iniquity, and the land spewed out its inhabitants.   (L E V. 18 : 24–25)[28]

The theme receives full expression in the oracles of Amos[29] and thereafter dominates the prophetic consciousness.

The doctrine of the absolute supremacy of the moral law can have at times dangerous consequences. It is clear from our story that Lot, in offering hospitality to the strangers, had violated the norms of the society in which he lived, and the angry citizens soon came to give vent to their sense of outrage. We have here what must be the first example in the literature of the world of the problem of the moral conscience of the individual in opposition to the collective concept of the group. The Bible declares tacitly, but unequivocally, through the medium of our narrative, that all socially approved actions and all societal patterns must take second place to the higher obligations which the moral order of the universe imposes upon men.

The concept of God

In some of the previous chapters we have had the opportunity of gaining insight into the concept of God as portrayed in the early Pentateuchal narratives. We stressed there Israel's revolutionary notion of God, universal, independent of nature, and completely lacking in capriciousness—all this in contrast to the pagan notions. The story of Sodom and Gomorrah emphasizes two of these attributes.

The universality of God is presumed throughout the story. He rules the pagans, judges their deeds, decides their fate and executes His decisions. He is "the Judge of all the earth" (18:25). His universality finds its expression, above all, in that He punishes the pagans solely for moral corruption. That is to say, God is assumed to be the architect of a societal pattern which is universal in scope. Not only may the non-believer fully share in it, but he is, in fact, fully responsible for its maintenance.

Above all, the Bible is concerned with the problem of divine justice. Just because God is universal and omnipotent mankind needs assurance that His mighty power is not indiscriminately employed and that His ways are not capricious. God must act according to a principle that man can try to understand, and that principle is the passion for righteousness.

Thus, when Abraham asks the questions, "Will you sweep away the innocent along with the guilty? Shall not the Judge of all the earth deal justly?" (18:23-25), it is taken for granted that the respective answers cannot possibly be other than a resounding, "Of course not!" "Indubitably!"

This unshakeable faith in divine right inevitably engenders human expostulation with God. Significantly enough, the argument is heard at two critical junctures in Israel's history. In the style of Abraham, founding father of the nation, the prophet Jeremiah who witnessed the destruction of the kingdom of Judea, exclaims,

> Righteous art thou, O Lord . . . yet, I would plead my case before you. Why does the way of the wicked prosper? Why do all who are treacherous thrive? (JER. 12 : 1)

This kind of relationship between man and God would, of course, not have been possible in the contemporary pagan world, for, as we have frequently pointed out, the gods could give men no assurance that their actions were dictated by anything other than mere whim. An illuminating example from Babylonian wisdom literature is the "Poem of the Righteous Sufferer," about a pious man whose world crashed about him despite his punctilious attention to the cultic demands of his gods. He complains that in the pantheon there is a complete transvaluation of values. The gods do not operate according to any intelligible norms.

> What is good in one's sight is evil for a god.
> What is bad in one's own mind is good for a god.
> Who can understand the counsel of the gods in the midst of heaven?

> The plan of a god is deep waters, who can comprehend it?
> Where has befuddled mankind ever learned what a god's
>   conduct is?[30]

By way of sharp contrast, our Sodom and Gomorrah story is at great
pains to demonstrate that God's actions are strictly just. In the first
place, God accepts Abraham's basic arguments.[31] Then, long before
the narrative unfolds, the very first time the Bible mentions the inhabitants of Sodom, we are informed that they "were very wicked sinners
against the Lord" (13:13). When the wickedness of the city reaches
intolerable proportions, God makes a personal investigation of the facts.

> I will go down to see whether they have acted altogether
> according to the outcry that has come to Me.   (18 : 21)

The facts in this case are all too obviously verified and at the moment
of punishment the messengers tell Lot,

> We are about to destroy this place; because the outcry against
> them before the Lord has become so great that the Lord has
> sent us to destroy it.   (19 : 13)

To show that not a single innocent Sodomite could be found, contrary to Abraham's expectations, the Bible is very deliberate in its choice
of words in depicting the angry scene outside Lot's home.

> . . . The townspeople, the men of Sodom, young and old—all
> the people to the last man[32]—surrounded the house.
>   (19 : 4)

All this detail is but another way of emphasing the righteousness of God's
judgment and of justifying His actions, something that is of vital importance to Abraham, for he has been singled out to

> instruct his children and his posterity to keep the way of the
> Lord by doing what is just and right.   (18 : 19)

A conviction of God's absolute justice and right is indispensable to
the fulfillment of the mission imposed upon him. Of course, the problem
of the contradiction between this conviction and the apparent realities

of life is an inevitable development of this conception of God. But it belongs to a later stage of biblical literature, finding its supreme expression in the Book of Job.

The absence of repentance

One of the notable deficiencies of the Sodom and Gomorrah saga, as indeed of the Flood narrative, is the complete absence of the theme of repentance. Noah did not call upon his contemporaries to repair their ways, and neither Abraham nor the messengers warned the Sodomites of the impending disaster in the hope of arousing them to atonement.

What a contrast with the story of Jonah! There, the reluctant prophet gives the sinful city of Nineveh forty days' notice of the punishment about to descend upon it. Sure enough, the penitent response of the contrite citizens succeeds in averting the evil decree.

This theme of repentance plays a major and indispensable role in the theological outlook and religious teachings of the great literary prophets. They pound away at it incessantly. They deeply lament the inability of the people to understand it and accept it. It becomes part of the great prophetic vision about "the end of days." But it is not to be found in the Noah and Sodom narratives. It can only be that these belong to the earliest traditions of Israel and were formulated at a time when the doctrine of repentance had not yet been developed. Nevertheless, the announcement of the forthcoming events to Abraham, giving him the opportunity to plead for the Sodomites, is the first stage on the road towards it.

The doctrine of merit

The character of Lot and his role in the story are both somewhat hazy and contradictory. On the one hand, a seemingly incidental observation contains an implied aspersion on his sense of values.

> Lot looked about him and saw how well watered was the whole plain of the Jordan . . . like the garden of the Lord. . . .
> Lot settled in the cities of the Plain, pitching his tents near Sodom. Now the inhabitants of Sodom were very wicked sinners against the Lord. (13 : 10, 12–13)

The Bible seems to suggest that economic advantage was more important to Lot than the moral compromises in which he was bound to
become involved through unavoidable association with the depraved
Sodomites.

On the other hand, the narrator surely desires to stress, with approval,
Lot's warm hospitality to the strangers in striking contrast to the behavior of his neighbors. Hospitality, it should be noted, was a sacred
duty in the Near East and bestowed upon the guest the right of asylum.
It was the responsibility of the host to protect his guests even at the risk
of exposing himself to danger, and Lot fulfilled that obligation to the
letter.[33]

Yet the worthiness of Lot's actions is certainly impaired by the way
he handled the predicament in which he found himself. To the modern
reader his willingness[34] to allow his daughters to be violated is utterly
incomprehensible, even if allowance be made for the fact that the story
reflects an age and a society in which daughters were the property of
their fathers. At any rate, it is to be noted that the salvation of Lot, unlike
that of Noah, is not attributed to his righteousness. The Bible underlines
this fact by reporting that it was due to "the Lord's mercy on him"
(19:16), and that "when God destroyed the cities of the Plain . . . God
was mindful of Abraham and removed Lot from the midst of the up-
heaval" (19:29). That is to say, not because of his intrinsic merit was
Lot saved, although he was certainly superior to his neighbors, but
through the merit of Abraham. It is a curious fact that in this situation
we actually have a fulfillment in another form of the purport of Abraham's dialogue with God. The patriarch had established the principle
that the wrathful judgment of God could be averted through the merit
of an innocent nucleus; so God delivered Lot from the catastrophe
through the merit of Abraham. This "doctrine of merit" is a not infrequent theme in the Bible and constitutes the first of many such incidents in which the righteousness of chosen individuals may sustain
other individuals or even an entire group through its protective power.[35]

Thus, the king of Gerar is informed by God in a dream that Abraham
would effectively intercede for him to save his life.[36] When Israel was
in danger of annihilation after worshipping the golden calf, the interces-
sion of Moses achieved a renunciation of the punishment.[37] A similar
function is recorded of Samuel,[38] Amos[39] and Jeremiah.[40] Ezekiel
actually describes God as lamenting the fact that He was unable to find
anyone to "stand in the breach" to protect the land from destruction

for its sins.[41] The Sodom and Gomorrah saga is, accordingly, the precursor of this biblical "doctrine of merit," a doctrine that has profound consequences for man, for it implies that the individual is of supreme importance and that from his actions may flow beneficial consequences for all society.

NOTES TO CHAPTER VIII

1. DEUT. 29:32; 32:32; ISA. 1:9; 3:9; 13:19; JER. 23:14; 49:18; 50:40; EZEK. 16:46ff.; HOS. 11:8; Amos 4:11; ZEPH. 2:9; LAM. 4:6.
2. See J. Penrose Harland, *BA*, V (1942), p. 22f.; VI (1943), pp. 44–47; Braslavsky, *HEH*, III, pp. 296–306.
3. GEN. 18:16–33; 19:1–29.
4. *Ibid.*, 19:23–26, 28f.
5. See N. Glueck, *River Jordan*, pp. 71–73; D. Baly, *The Geography of the Bible*, p. 205f.
6. GEN. 10:19.
7. On the location of the cities, see J. Penrose Harland, *BA*, V (1942), pp. 17–32.
8. See J. L. Kelso and R. A. Power, *BASOR*, 95 (1944), pp. 14–18.
9. For the association of salt with infertility and curse in Near Eastern literature, see F. Charles Fensham, *BA*, XXV (1962), pp. 48ff.
1 0. J. P. Harland, *op. cit.*; pp. 23–26; Braslavsky, *op. cit.*, pp. 95–98.
1 1. For a detailed description, see *ibid.*, pp. 88–108.
1 2. On Bab-edh-Dhraʿ, see Albright, *ARI*, pp. 42–66; *AP*, p. 77f.; *BASOR*, 14 (1924), pp. 5–9; 95 (1944), pp. 3–10.
1 3. See W. F. Albright, *BASOR*, 163 (1961), p. 51, n. 73.

1 4. See J. P. Harland, *op. cit.,* pp. 28ff.

1 5. *Idem, BA,* VI (1943), pp. 41–49; Braslavsky, *op. cit.,* pp. 316–320.

1 6. For earthquakes in Palestine in biblical times, see N. Shalem, *Jerusalem* [Hebrew], II (1949), pp. 22–34.

1 7. Baly, *op. cit.,* p. 25f.

1 8. E.g., DEUT. 29:22.

1 9. HOS. 11:8.

2 0. See M. Noth, *The History of Israel,* p. 120, n. 1. It is usual to assign chap. 18 to J and chap. 19 to a fusion of J and P.

2 1. GEN. 19:4–9.

2 2. EXOD. 3:7

2 3. JOB 34:28.

2 4. Cf., also, the use of the term in II KINGS 8:3, 5; JER. 20:8; HAB. 1:2; JOB 19:7, and note Isaiah's exhortation of those whose conduct had earned them the title "rulers of Sodom," "people of Gomorrah" (ISA. 1:10).

2 5. This is most likely a reflex of the tradition of GEN. 13:10.

2 6. Cf. the remarks of M. I. Finley, *The World of Odysseus,* p. 152, on the reason for the fall of Troy as portrayed in the Iliad.

2 7. See Kaufmann, *Toldot,* II, pp. 438–441.

2 8. Cf. LEV. 18:26ff.; 20:22; DEUT. 18:12.

2 9. Cf. Amos 1:3–2:3.

3 0. *ANET,* p. 435; cf. Lambert, *BWL,* p. 41, ll. 34ff.; cf., also, p. 22.

3 1. GEN. 18:26–32.

3 2. For this translation, see A. B. Ehrlich, *Randglossen,* p. 77.

3 3. On the law of hospitality and asylum, see de Vaux, *AI,* p. 10.

3 4. GEN. 19:8. See R. Patai, *Sex and Family,* p. 131.

3 5. On the "doctrine of merit," see G. F. Moore, *Judaism,* I, pp. 535–45; III, p. 164, n. 249; S. Schechter, *Aspects of Rabbinic Theology,* pp. 170–198; R. Gordis, *JNES,* IV (1945), p. 55.

3 6. GEN. 20:7.

3 7. EXOD. 33:14; cf. 34:8f.; NUM. 14:13–20.

3 8. I SAM. 7:8f.; 12:19, 23; 15:11.

3 9. AMOS 7:1–6.

4 0. JER. 5:1; 37:3; 42:2.

4 1. EZEK. 22:30.

CHAPTER IX

The Birth of Isaac
and the Akedah

GENESIS 21, 22

The Lord took note of Sarah as He had promised, and the
Lord did for Sarah as He had spoken. Sarah conceived and
bore a son to Abraham in his old age, at the set time of which
God had spoken. (21 : 1–2)

The repeated emphasis upon the birth of Isaac as being in accordance
with God's design, and the unusual aspect of the event, in that Abraham
was one hundred years old and Sarah ninety,[1] has already been explained
above as Scripture's medium for signifying the emergence of the people
of Israel as an extraordinary phenomenon, and its future and destiny
as being unique.[2] The idea of Isaac as the one and only true heir to the
Abrahamic tradition and covenant is reinforced by the notice of the
circumcision of the child eight days after birth[3] in fulfillment of the divine
command.[4]

The expulsion of Hagar and Ishmael

Unfortunately, the arrival of Isaac proved a cause of disharmony in Abraham's household. Sarah, the jealous mother, demanded the expulsion of Ishmael and Hagar:

> ". . . for the son of that slave shall not share in the inheritance with my son Isaac." (21 : 10)

Abraham was greatly distressed at the suggestion and was obviously reluctant to agree. It was only after the intervention of God in favor of Sarah that the issue was decided.[5]

This story raises several questions of a legal, sociological and theological nature. What was Ishmael's legal status and what rights did it confer upon him? How could the Bible conceive of God as acquiescing in what is an act of manifest inhumanity? Answering these questions is complicated by the fact that the Nuzi archives have not, thus far, proved to be of great help, except in so far as they show that Sarah would have had authority over Hagar.[6]

If we begin with the biblical material we may say with certainty that Ishmael was recognized as a legitimate son of Abraham. The text repeatedly emphasizes the fact of sonship.

> Abraham gave his son . . . the name Ishmael
> (16 : 15);
> Abraham took his son Ishmael . . . and his son Ishmael was thirteen years old when he was circumcised. . . . Thus Abraham and his son Ishmael were circumcised. . . .
> (17 : 23, 25, 26)

Abraham's reaction to Sarah's demand is one of sore displeasure,

> because it concerned a son of his.
> (21 : 11)

When Abraham died,

> His sons Isaac and Ishmael buried him in the cave of Machpelah. (25 : 9)

The genealogy of Ishmael is careful to point out that he is Abraham's son.[7]

Moreover, Sarah had actually undertaken in advance to recognize as her own male offspring sons born of the union with Hagar that she had herself initiated.[8] By her present action she was, in effect, repudiating her word. There cannot be any doubt as to the status of Ishmael. He was a legitimately recognized son of the patriarch.

Did this status assure automatic rights of inheritance for Ishmael? Sarah's justification of the proposed expulsion that

> the son of that slave shall not share in the inheritance with my
> son Isaac"   (21 : 10),

certainly suggests that it did. Otherwise, Ishmael's presence would not have been so threatening and the recourse to such extreme action would have been unnecessary.

According to the laws of Hammurabi, the sons of a slave-wife share the inheritance equally with the sons of the free woman, provided the father, at his own discretion, legitimates them. Should he not recognize them as his sons, the slave and her children are given their freedom.[9] We do not know whether legitimation would be required when the wife herself supplied the slave-girl to provide a son and heir,[10] but at any rate, the status and rights of such a son would certainly not have been inferior to those of an ordinary slave; and we have already seen that Abraham had undoubtedly recognized Ishmael as his son.

The laws of Lipit-Ishtar, about one hundred and fifty years earlier than Hammurabi, stipulate that the offspring of a slave-wife relinquish their inheritance rights in return for their freedom.[11]

In the light of the foregoing we may safely assume that Ishmael, as the legitimated son of Abraham, was entitled to his share of the inheritance. What Sarah demanded was that Hagar and her son be given their freedom, thereby renouncing all claim to a share of the family estate. This being the case, the entire episode can be seen as having taken place according to the social custom and legal procedure of the times. Abraham's distress would then not be over the legality of the act, which was not in question, but because of both fatherly love and moral considerations.

Viewed thus against the contemporary ancient Near Eastern background, our story projects the character of Abraham in much sharper relief. He is seen as a man torn between conflicting loves and rent by the rival claims of what society and law permitted and what righteousness seemed to demand. The narrative makes quite clear what Abraham's decision would have been. He would not have sent away Hagar and Ishmael, but would have resisted Sarah's prodding, were it not for God's intervention.

It is the injection of this latter element into the narrative that enables us to detect the sharpened moral sensibility of the narrator. It could be the only possible justification for the action that subsequently took place. Even more interesting is the fact that God has to justify his espousal of Sarah's cause, which He does for two reasons. First, because it is through Isaac that the Abrahamic line is to be continued, and second, because God will assuredly take care of the handmaid and her son. They will not be left to an uncertain fate in the desert of Beer-sheba, for a great future awaits Ishmael. Note the delicate shift from Sarah's motivation to God's. The matriarch was solely interested in safeguarding the material patrimony of her son. God is concerned with Abraham's posterity, with the fulfillment of the divine plan of history. A story that began as a reflection of ancient Near Eastern socio-legal convention has been transformed in the Bible into a situation involving moral dilemmas and God's long-range purposes.

The binding of Isaac

With the departure of Ishmael and Hagar, all obstacles were removed to the future of Isaac as the one and only heir, the recipient and transmitter of the divine promises. But suddenly, God commanded Abraham to take his son to "the land of Moriah," there to offer him up as a burnt offering on one of the heights.[12]

This soul-shattering event in the life of the patriarch comes as the climax of his career. It is frequently explained as registering a new era in the history of religion, marking the transition from one stage of religious development to another; namely, the rejection of human sacrifice and the substitution of an animal in its place.[13]

This interpretation is not without serious difficulties. We cannot evade the fact that the core of the narrative actually seems to assume the possibility that God could demand human sacrifice. It contains no categorical divine repudiation of the practice as such, and the replacement of Isaac by the ram is not the result of a command by God, but an exercise of Abraham's own initiative. The situation is far more complicated than appears on the surface.

Human sacrifice in the ancient Near East

Any discussion of the problems involved in the *Akedah* story, as it has come to be known (from the Hebrew, meaning, "binding" of Isaac), must begin with the extra-biblical material. Turning to the ancient Near Eastern world, we note that, if human sacrifice had ever, in fact, been widely and regularly practised, by the second millennium B.C.E., the age of the patriarchs, it had long been accepted that animal offering was, in normal circumstances, a perfectly satisfactory surrogate. In fact, according to the pagan world-view, animal offerings were vitally needed by the gods for their sustenance, dependent as they were upon material existence.[14] More frequently, the motivation of the votary was less altruistic, even when the gift was an expression of gratitude. He might bring his flocks to the gods on the basis of the utilitarian principle, *do ut des*, "I give that you may give." Man's gift would, it was hoped, stimulate the charitable instincts of his god and earn more material favors for the worshiper. Sometimes, the sacrifice would be meant to purge the donor of sin or rid him of his unclean state.[15]

Whatever the motivation, one thing is certain. Neither historically nor in biblical tradition is animal sacrifice an innovation of Abraham. The story of Cain and Abel indicates that the Bible regards the custom as belonging to the earliest forms of ritual.[16] The *Akedah* narrative cannot be intended to mark the transition from human to animal sacrifice. The latter had long predominated in Near Eastern religions. It was only an emergency of an extraordinary nature that called for a human in place of an animal victim.[17]

Canaan, however, seems to have been something of an exception in this respect, for there is much archaeological evidence to show that human sacrifice was more in vogue here than elsewhere, from very early times until far into the second millennium.[18]

The biblical sources furnish additional abundant testimony. The Torah legislation lists child-sacrifice among the abominations of the Canaanites,[19] and other texts consistently attribute its presence in Israel to the importation of foreign practice.[20] A concrete example of such a monstrous perversion of the religious idea among Israel's neighbors is provided by the story of the King of Moab who, in desperation, offered up his first-born son at a critical moment in battle.[21]

A belief in the efficacy of human sacrifice as a means of propitiating the deity was not unknown even in Israel. The mere fact that the armies of Israel and Judah desisted from further military engagement as a result of the rite just referred to, shows the impression it made upon the popular imagination. True, the story of Jephtah and his daughter is treated as exceptional[22] and cannot be taken as indicative of the norm, and kings Ahaz and Manasseh of Judah may well have been consciously aping alien cults.[23] But the prophets were certainly preaching against popular Israelite beliefs when they felt repeatedly called upon to dissociate God from this horrible aberration.[24]

In short, throughout the ancient Near East, though animal sacrifice was normal, official religions fostered the idea that there were occasions when the gods could be conciliated only by the offering of the fruit of the human womb, the most precious thing that this life affords. Even in Israel this monstrous idea was not entirely eradicated from the popular consciousness until the Babylonian Exile.[25]

The ancient nucleus

Attention was previously drawn to the fact that the story seems to assume the possibility of a divine demand on man to sacrifice his son. That Abraham responded to this call shows that such a notion was not irreconcilable with his concept of God. Most eloquent is Abraham's exceptional silence, quite out of keeping with his previous dialogues with God and in sharp contrast to his protestations about God's justice in the case of Sodom and Gomorrah. Further, one cannot gloss over the fact, previously mentioned, that God does not denounce human sacrifice as such in this story.[26]

All this is in such glaring contradiction to the Torah legislation and prophetic teaching that the conclusion is inescapable that the core of the *Akedah* narrative must belong to the earliest strata of Israelite traditions, containing echoes of a dim past and reflecting a popular, unofficial, notion of religion.[27]

This conclusion is reinforced by evidence of quite a different kind. The locale of the *Akedah* is described in the biblical account as "one of the heights" in the "land of Moriah" (22:2). Later tradition connected the place with the site of the Temple Mount in Jerusalem,[28] an association that lent itself readily to Midrashic embellishment. This identity cannot possibly be maintained, however. Jerusalem is not a three-days' journey from Beer-sheba and the hills of Judea would have amply sup-

plied the fuel requirements. It would not have been necessary to carry
along a supply of wood.[29] The unusual vagueness of the biblical specifications as to the location of Moriah is matched by the absence of any
further mention of the place in biblical literature—other than in the
Chronicler's Midrash, and even he does not refer to the *Akedah*. Most
remarkably, the site never became a shrine. In fact, the very name Moriah
is not to be found elsewhere in the ancient versions of the Bible,[30] nor
has it turned up, so far, in extra-biblical sources. It can only be that our
scriptural account has made use of a very ancient story about the patriarch, many of the details of which were either lost or purposely omitted
in the process of incorporation into the biblical narrative.[31]

The isolation of the kernel of the original tale is invaluable for an
understanding of the episode. It allows a better appreciation of the shifts
of emphasis and change in direction and focus that took place as the
Akedah story achieved its present literary form.

The Akedah *and the call at Haran*

The Torah presents the "binding of Isaac" as the climactic event in the
life of Abraham. Once it is over the process of fulfillment of the divine
promises gathers momentum and the great drama of history unfolds itself,
moving forward inexorably from scene to scene, leading to the formation
of the tribes and their consolidation into a great nation. Fittingly, it is
the last occasion on which God speaks to Abraham, so rounding out the
cycle of divine communications that began back in Haran.

This fact explains the external literary form of the *Akedah* story, for
there has been a deliberate attempt to cast the two fateful events—the
call at Haran and the *Akedah*—in a common literary mold.[32]

In Haran, God had introduced His call by the words, *"Go forth . . . to
the land that I will show you"* (12:1). At the *Akedah*, God employed similar language, *"Go forth . . . to the land* of Moriah . . . *on one of the heights
which I will point out to you"* (22:2). Just as previously the exact destination was withheld, so here the patriarch was not initially to know the
terminal point of his journey. As in the one case, the tension of the drama
about to be enacted is heightened by the accumulation of descriptive
epithets—"your land, your homeland, your father's house"—so in the
latter case, the same effect is created by the employment of the identical
device—"your son, your favored one, Isaac, whom you love." In Haran,
son took leave of father forever; at the *Akedah*, father and son were pre-

pared to see each other for the last time. Having obediently fulfilled his first mission, the patriarch found himself faced with a situation of grave danger to Sarah,[33] followed by defections from the family circle.[34] The identical pattern of events recurs this time, but prior to receiving the last mission. Sarah is in great peril[35] and Abraham's kith and kin are sent away.[36] The divine order to journey forth having been completed, Abraham built an altar at the "terebinth of Moreh."[37] So at the end of his final ordeal, the patriarch brought an offering on the altar he had built on one of the heights of Moriah.[38] Finally, the two narratives share in common divine blessings that are strikingly similar in content.[39]

The Torah, then, has used the ancient *Akedah* tale to encase the account of the spiritual odyssey of Abraham within a literary framework, opening and closing with divine communications that involve agonizing decisions carried to completion with unflinching loyalty, and culminating in promises of a glorious posterity.

The shift of emphasis

This literary recasting of the original story finds its parallel on the religious level. The primitive theme of human sacrifice, if not exorcised entirely, has been pushed into the background. The narrative as it now stands is almost impatiently insistent upon removing any possibility of misunderstanding that God had really intended Abraham to sacrifice his son. To make sure that the reader has advance knowledge of God's purposes, the story begins with a declaration that "God put Abraham to the test" (22:1).[40] If we point out that this is the only example of the use of this sentiment in connection with an incident in the life of the patriarch, we may gain some measure of the importance to be attached to this introduction. The emphasis on the underlying probative nature of the episode is once more made apparent at the conclusion of the trial when the outcome is beyond doubt.

> "For now I know that you fear God since you have not with-
> held your son." (22 : 12)

Most telling of all in this process of transformation is the atmosphere of singularity that pervades the entire narrative. The demand of God is presented as something extraordinary, something that a man would not dream of doing on his own initiative, and something that tries the believer to the utmost so that his response is by no means predictable. In other words, the *Akedah* in its final form is not an attempt to combat existing practice, but is itself a product of a religious attitude that recoils naturally from associating God with human sacrifice and which felt the need to explain the ancient tradition as an unprecedented and unrepeatable event, as a test of faith. The story, that is, has now evolved from its ancient primitive nucleus to become reflective of Israel's normative standpoint.

This development explains several unusual features of the *Akedah*. The absence of an explicit, unambiguous renunciation of child-sacrifice now falls into place. It is absent because it is unnecessary from the narrative viewpoint. That God rejected the practice as utterly abhorrent was taken for granted. The narrator's problem was to reconcile this obvious fact with the details of the ancient nucleus. This he did by shifting the focus from God to Abraham and by emphasizing the test of faith aspect.

The same explanation covers an unexpected omission from the epithets applied to Isaac.[41] It is well known that child-sacrifice was primarily conditioned by the concept of a special degree of sanctity attaching to the first-born male. Thus, it was his first born that the king of Moab sacrificed at a critical moment in battle.[42] The omission of the epithet "first-born" from the descriptions of Isaac, even though its addition would have made the magnitude of the sacrifice still more pronounced, underscores the desire to portray the divine command as *sui generis,* totally unrelated to the usual pagan rites.

The trial of faith

The transfer of the *Akedah* from the realm of ritual to the realm of faith, the shift from a story about tribute to the Deity to one about a trial of faith, involves certain biblical concepts dealing with the nature of God and the character of Abraham.

When "God put Abraham to the test" it was obviously not a trial, the outcome of which was meant to add to the sum of God's knowledge. Such an idea would obviously be incompatible with the biblical concept of the omniscience of God. If the story is included in biblical literature it is doubtless due to its didactic value for man.

The first lesson of the *Akedah* episode is to be sought in the definition of the relationship between man and God. Biblical faith is not a posture of passivity. It is not subscription to a doctrine and it bears no catechismic connotations. The existence of God is regarded in the Bible as being a self-evident proposition, not requiring affirmation. The Hebrew word *emunah* is best approximated by faithfulness, steadfast loyalty and, occasionally, trust. The important thing is that it finds its fullest expression in the realm of action. That is why in the Bible the term may be applied as well to God as to man. God is called *El Emunah*, "a faithful God," because

> "His deeds are perfect, all His ways are just . . . never false, true and upright." (D E U T . 32 : 4)

The essential quality of God's *emunah* is the non-capricious nature of His dealings with the world and the inviolability of His promises to man. The psalmist expresses it this way:

> For the word of the Lord is upright; and all His work is done in faithfulness. He loves righteousness and justice; The earth is full of the steadfast love of God. (P S . 33 : 4-5)

In the same way, man's *emunah*, his steadfast loyalty to God, has meaning only when it reveals itself as the well-spring of action, as being powerful enough to stand the test of suffering and trial.

The second lesson of the *Akedah* is to be found in the divine verdict,

> "For now I know that you fear God."
> (22 : 12)

That is to say, the value of an act may lie as much in the inward intention of the doer as in the final execution. God valued the readiness of Abraham to make the extreme sacrifice even though it was not completed.

Finally, the story reveals something more about the character of the patriarch. Attention was drawn previously to the intimate connection between the call at Haran, at the outset of the patriarch's career and the *Akedah*, the climax of his spiritual odyssey. The great difference between the two events is what constitutes the measure of Abraham's progress in his relationship to God. The first divine communication carried with it the promise of reward.[43] The final one held out no such expectation. On the contrary, by its very nature it could mean nothing less than the complete nullification of the covenant and the frustration forever of all hope of posterity. Ishmael had already departed. Now Isaac would be gone, too. Tradition has rightly seen in Abraham the exemplar of steadfast, disinterested loyalty to God.

1. GEN. 21:5; 17:17.
2. See above p. 83f.
3. GEN. 21:4.
4. *Ibid.,* 17:12. See above p. 131f.
5. *Ibid.,* 21:11f.
6. The text in question is to be found in *AASOR,* X (1930), p. 31, No. 2, l. 22; where it is uncertain whether the reading is ᶠ*Gi-li-im-ni-nu* [*la*] or [*-ma*]. The former is assumed by C. H. Gordon, *BA,* III (1940), p. 3; cf. *The Ancient Near East,* p. 123; R. de Vaux, *RB,* LVI (1949), p. 27; R. J. Tournay, in *DBS,* VI (1960), col. 664. However, if the correct reading be *-ma,* then the text simply confers authority on the mistress without giving any indication of its extent.
7. GEN. 25:12.
8. *Ibid.* 16:2.
9. See *ANET,* p. 173, § 171.
10. See Driver and Miles, I, p. 350, and n. 2.
11. See *ANET,* p. 160, § 25. See R. de Vaux, *RB,* LVI (1949), p. 27f. for an elucidation of the episode in the light of ancient Near Eastern legislation.
12. GEN. 22:1f.

1 3. Cf. J. H. Hertz, *The Pentateuch and Haftorahs*, p. 201; *SkG*, p. 332; *GuG*, p. 242.

1 4. See above p. 54.

1 5. See J. Pedersen, *Israel*, III–IV, pp. 299–375; cf. M. Eliade, *Cosmos and History*, pp. 109ff.

1 6. GEN. 4:6.

1 7. Cf. L. Woolley, *Abraham*, p. 160f.; S. N. Kramer, *ANET*, p. 50.

1 8. On human sacrifice in Canaan, see W. C. Graham and H. G. May, *Culture and Conscience*, pp. 77ff.; J. Finegan, *Light From the Ancient Past*, p. 148; E. Anati, *Palestine Before the Hebrews*, p. 427.

1 9. LEV. 18:21, 27; DEUT. 12:31; 18:9f.

2 0. II KINGS 16:3, 17:8, 17; 21:2, 6; PS. 106:37f.

2 1. II KINGS 3:27.

2 2. JUD. 11.

2 3. II KINGS 16:3; 21:6.

2 4. MICAH 6:7; JER. 7:31; 19:5; 32:35.

2 5. On human sacrifice in Israel, see de Vaux, *AI*, pp. 441–46; M. Sister, *Le-Toldot*, pp. 42–51.

2 6. See Kaufmann, *Toldot*, I, pp. 457, 666; II, p. 132; *idem, RI*, p. 137.

2 7. For the source analysis, see *GuG*, pp. 240ff.; M. Noth, *Überlieferungsgeschichte*, p. 125ff.

2 8. II CHRON. 3:1.

2 9. On the identity of Moriah see *SkG*, p. 328; N. Glueck, *Rivers in the Desert*, pp. 62ff.; see, however U. Cassuto in *Eretz-Israel*, III (1954), p. 16f.

3 0. See *SkG*, p. 328f.; Kittel, *BH*, to GEN. 22:2.

3 1. See the exhaustive study of S. Spiegel in *AMJV* [Hebrew], pp. 471–547, showing how the Midrashic literature has preserved remnants of many ancient popular traditions, often quite at variance with the biblical account.

3 2. See U. Cassuto, *Noah*, p. 202 and in *EBH*, I, col. 64.

3 3. GEN. 12:10–20.

3 4. *Ibid.* 13:11.

3 5. *Ibid.* chap. 20.

3 6. *Ibid.* 21:9ff.

3 7. *Ibid.* 12:6f.

3 8. *Ibid.* 22:13.

3 9. Cf., *ibid.* 12:2f., with 22:17f.

4 0. For the significance of the inversion of the Hebrew order, and the use of the definite article with God, see S. R. Driver, *Hebrew Tenses*, § 78 (3); *SpG*, p. 162.

4 1. GEN. 22:2.

4 2. II KINGS 3:27.

4 3. GEN. 12:2f.

CHAPTER X

Winding Up Affairs

GENESIS 23-25:1-18

With the climax of his career now behind him, Abraham's subsequent acts are concerned with winding up his affairs.

The death of Sarah is the occasion for acquiring a family sepulcher.[1] Then, Isaac has to be married to ensure the succession of the line.[2] That done, the patriarch could breathe his last "dying at a good ripe age, old and contented" (25:8).[3]

A resident alien

When Abraham first approached the citizens of Hebron to negotiate the purchase of a sepulcher for the interment of Sarah he described himself, in contrast to "the people of the land," as a "resident alien" (23:7, 4). This phrase indicates that the patriarch labored under a legal disadvantage. The alien could not normally acquire land, and he is usually classed in biblical literature, along with the orphan and the widow, among the oppressed of society.[4] When Scripture wishes to emphasize that land may not be sold in perpetuity, it compares the status of man in relation to God as that of a resident alien to the actual owner of real estate.

> But the land must not be sold beyond reclaim, for the land is
> Mine; you are but strangers resident with Me.
>
> (L E V . 25 : 23)

This restriction upon the rights of a resident alien to land-ownership explains why it was necessary for Abraham to petition the Hebronites for the favor of an exceptional privilege. It also determined the ensuing course of events and the ultimate nature of the transaction.

Abraham's immediate problem was to bury his dead wife. Obviously, there must have been for centuries some established procedure for burial among the semi-nomads who wandered up and down Canaan. What Abraham wanted, however, was to acquire in perpetuity a family vault that would be able to accommodate the mortal remains of future generations of his descendants.[5] The subsequent history of Machpelah[6] bears this out, for here were buried, in addition to Sarah, also Abraham himself,[7] Isaac and Rebekah, and Jacob and Leah.[8]

The Hittites

The citizens of Hebron whom Abraham encounters and with whom he negotiates are repeatedly identified as "the children of Heth."[9] To identify them as Hittites is to raise grave historical problems. The Hittites were originally a non-Indo-European people located in central Anatolia. About the beginning of the second millennium B.C.E., Indo-European elements invaded the area and apparently swamped the original inhabitants. A process of gradual expansion in Anatolia itself, as well as a southward movement towards Syria, led to the emergence of a Hittite empire which lasted from ca. 1600 B.C.E. until its final collapse about 1200 B.C.E. At no time, however, did the Hittite area of occupation reach as far south as Palestine. That Hebron should be in the hands of Hittites in Abraham's day is a historical riddle.[10]

On the other hand, the biblical sources reflect a consistent tradition listing the Hittites among the pre-Israelite peoples inhabiting Palestine.[11]

Esau took to himself Hittite wives,[12] something that was a source of bitterness to Isaac and Rebekah.[13] The spies Moses sent from the wilderness to scout the land of Canaan reported Hittites living in the hill country,[14] and the prophet Ezekiel also located them in southern Palestine in earliest times.[15]

It is true that the biblical Hittites in Palestine are fully Semitized; they have no trouble conversing with Abraham, and the names they bear are authentically Semitic.[16] Hence, it has been suggested that the epithet "Hittite" is a generalized loosely applied term for the peoples of greater Syria who originated in the far north. Yet the fact that Mamre is specified as an Amorite,[17] whereas Ephron and his fellow citizens of Hebron are called Hittites, shows that the Bible did distinguish ethnic elements in the pre-Israelite population.

Finally, the celebrated Table of Nations lists Heth, reputed ancestor of the Hittites, among the sons of Canaan, son of Ham.[18] It does not associate him with Japheth, which would have been more likely. This shows that Hittites must have been prominently connected with Canaan at some time or other, but that their northern, Indo-European origin had been forgotten.

Only future archaeological discoveries can hope to resolve the problem of the Canaanite Hittites in Abraham's time. In the meantime, we may point to a few pertinent facts from extra-biblical sources.

A treaty of alliance signed ca. 1280 B.C.E. between Ramses II of Egypt and Hattusilis, king of the Hittites, resulted in recognizing the suzerainty of Egypt over Palestine and southern Phoenicia.[19] From this one may learn that Palestine had previously been an arena of contention between the two powers. This conclusion is strengthened by mention of two earlier treaties between the Egyptian and Hittite empires. Perhaps the southern Palestinian Hittites were remnants of an earlier penetration, either military or commercial.[20]

The negotiations

The transaction took place at the city gate.[21] Throughout the Near East it was the practice to conduct the affairs of the community in the gateway, a popular meeting place for public gatherings.[22] Lot, it will be remembered, was sitting at the city-gate when the messengers came to him at evening-time.[23] It was there that Boaz went to redeem the estate of

Elimelech.[24] Amos the prophet called upon Israel to "establish justice in the gate" (Amos 5:15; cf. v. 12). Many a Nuzi legal document ends with the formula, "the tablet was written after the proclamation in the entrance of the gate."[25] The idea was to give the widest possible publicity to the settlement and to obtain the confirmation of the entire community, so that the likelihood of future litigation might be eliminated.

The haggling between the patriarch and Ephron seems, at first sight, to be a typical example of conventionalized oriental oratory. Yet a closer examination of the text reveals a rich use of legal terminology that is characteristic of Near Eastern court records. The description of the cave as being "at the edge of the field" (23:9) is a common and obvious means of property identification in land-sale documents.[26] Presumably, the vault was conveniently approachable from the road without the necessity of traversing the field in which it was situated.[27] Phrases like, "at the full price"[28] *(ibid.),* and "at the going merchants' rate"[29] (23:16); the use of the verb *ntn* in the sense of "to sell;"[30] the specific mention of the trees[31] are all reflective of an authentic judicial background. In fact, the final paragraph actually reads like a legal contract, even though no written document is mentioned.[32] It is to be noted that after the completion of the formalities of the sale have been recorded, we are told that Abraham buried Sarah, and then once again we are informed that the field with its cave was transferred from the children of Heth to Abraham as a burial site.[33] In other words, the act of burial, the use of the property, constituted the final stamp of transference of ownership.[34]

The purposes of the story

That the story of the purchase of Machpelah is in line generally with the narratives of the Book of Genesis in antiquity and authenticity of the background, is incontestable.

One might wonder, however, about the purposes of the Torah in including it in the patriarchal history. First, one may surmise that Machpelah became the recognized sepulcher of the fathers of the people of Israel and, as such, a national shrine throughout the biblical period.[35] It is indeed strange that no mention of the place is to be found in the Bible outside of the Book of Genesis; but post-biblical literature would seem to indicate an unbroken, popular, living tradition on the subject. The manner in which it was acquired and the details of the transaction would have been of perennial interest to the populace. It is also possible that the story was preserved because it reflected the great respect for the dead and the importance of proper interment characteristic of Israel. Perhaps, too, the whole episode was regarded as being of historic importance in that the patriarch actually acquired possession of land in Canaan, the first in Israel's history.

A wife for Isaac

Having made provision for a family sepulcher, Abraham proceeded further with the ordering of his earthly affairs. He commissioned the senior servant of his household to find a wife for Isaac. So strong still were his ties with his family back in Haran, and so tenuous his associations with the local inhabitants, that it was to his former homeland that Abraham directed his servant's steps. The idea of a Canaanite daughter-in-law was thoroughly obnoxious to him.[36] This attitude is reflected also in the reactions of Isaac and Rebekah to Esau's wives,[37] and in their anxiety lest Jacob, too, marry a Canaanite girl.[38] It is consonant with the Genesis picture of the patriarchs as strangers in Canaan, generally pursuing a policy of peaceful, yet detached, relationships with their neighbors, and repelled by the moral corruption about them.

The consciousness of his own advanced age led Abraham to extract an oath from his servant when a simple order would presumably have been adequate. We may sense here the nervousness at the possibility of not living to see the outcome of the mission.

The oath

The peculiar gesture accompanying the oath,

> "put your hand under my thigh"
> (24 : 2)

is unique to the Book of Genesis, occurring again only when Jacob adjured Joseph not to bury him in Egypt.[39] In both instances, it will be noted, the oath involves final testamentary instructions. Now the thigh in biblical usage is symbolic of the reproductive organs, the seat of the procreative powers. Thus, offspring may be described as "those who issue from the thigh."[40] The placing of the hand on the thigh when taking an oath in connection with the last wishes of a superior symbolizes, therefore, an involvement of posterity in the faithful implementation of the instructions and gives added weight to the solemnity and inviolability of the obligation incurred.

The aspect of faith

The quality of faith associated with Abraham at the covenant ceremony[41] shows itself once again in this situation. Answering the doubts of his servant, the patriarch is absolutely sure that the mission will be successfully accomplished.

> "The Lord, the God of heaven, who took me from my father's house and from the land of my birth, who promised me under oath, saying 'I will give this land to your offspring'— He will send his angel before you, and you will get a wife for my son from there."   (24 : 7)

These are the very last spoken words the Bible records of Abraham, and they are in striking contrast to the first utterance ascribed to him. At the outset of his career his very first words to God were expressions of doubt about each of the two elements of the divine promise—posterity and land.

> "O Lord God, what can you give me seeing that I die childless . . .,"   (15 : 2)

he had said despairingly of the former; and,

> "O Lord God, how shall I know that I am to possess it?"   (15 : 8)

was his response to the latter. Now he evokes both posterity and land, serenely confident that God's promises will work themselves out in history. Abram, the doubter, has become Abraham, the man of absolute faith.

The symbol of Isaac

The faith of Abraham, of course, derived from his personal experiences— the birth of Isaac and the *Akedah*. Without Isaac, all would again be confusion and despair. Hence, Abraham's insistence that his son must on no account leave the land.[42] Isaac in his person and by his very presence in Canaan symbolized the fulfillment of the bipartite blessing. That is why Isaac, alone of the patriarchs, never left Canaan and was, in fact, forbidden to do so by God Himself, even in days of famine.

> "Do not go down to Egypt; stay in the land which I point out to you. Reside in this land, and I will be with you and bless you; I will give all these lands to you and to your off-spring, fulfilling the oath that I swore to your father Abraham . . ."   (26 : 2f.)

This inextricable connection between Isaac and the land also found expression in the unique report, attributed neither to Abraham nor Jacob, nor even to the tribes, that he sowed the land, and that with great success.[43]

The role of providence

The modern reader of the Bible might well find strange the procedure adopted to find a wife for Isaac. It must be remembered, however, that the narrative reflects contemporary custom in which the father initiated the marriage transaction. Being too old to go himself, Abraham commissioned his trusted servant. But he gave him no precise instructions as to the kind of wife he was to look for, only that she was to be sought in the land of his birth. The patriarch was certain that the right wife would be found because Isaac's marriage was looked upon as the fulfillment of God's purposes.[44]

The Bible does not trouble us with the details of the long journey from Canaan to Haran. It picks up the story at the point where the servant made his way to the public wells. This was the natural thing for a stranger to do when first arriving in a foreign land, since the wells frequently served as meeting-places for townsfolk, shepherds and travelers, and often were assembly places for Bedouin rituals. It will be recalled that Jacob, too, arriving at Haran at the end of his flight from Beer-sheba, gravitated at once towards the well.[45] Moses did the same thing when he fled to Midian.[46]

The servant, we are told, made the camels kneel down by the well outside the city. The camel as a beast of burden in Abraham's time raises a historical problem which we have previously discussed.[47] From the available extra-biblical evidence it would appear that the camel was not effectively domesticated until the post-patriarchal period. From the point of view of the didactic purposes of Scripture, however, the camels play an indispensable role as the instrumentality of divine providence. They are going to be used to test the character of Isaac's bride-to-be.

One of the most characteristic qualities of biblical man was a profound and pervasive conviction about the role of divine providence in human affairs. Nowhere is this better demonstrated than in our narrative, and that all the more forcefully because it comes from the mouth of a simple, unnamed, servant. Be it coincidental or otherwise, one cannot fail to be impressed by the fact that it is this man who is the first person of whom it is expressly recorded in the Bible that he prayed for personal divine guidance at a critical moment of his life. We note that he did not ask for a miraculous intervention of God to designate the future bride of Isaac. On the contrary, he himself decided upon the criteria of suitability and choice. He prayed, rather, that his exercise of discretion might be in accordance with God's will.

> "... let the maiden to whom I say, 'Please lower your jar that
> I may drink,' and who replies, 'Drink, and I will also water
> your camels'—let her be the one whom you have decreed for
> your servant Isaac."   (24 : 14)

The first biblical prayer of this nature is of interest for several other reasons. It is an inaudible "prayer of the heart" uttered spontaneously and without formality. It implies a concept of the individual as a conscious personality, a religious unit in his own right as distinct from the community. Individual, direct contact with God, a feeling of constant nearness to the divine, an understanding of God as approachable—all these are prominent motifs in the religion of Israel, and they find expression in the simple pious prayer of Abraham's servant.

The wifely virtues

The image of an ideal wife, projected by the prayer of the servant and supplemented by the details of the narrative, is of considerable interest.[48]

Rebekah's beauty is not overlooked by the writer who, at the same time, stresses her chastity. The only criterion the servant lays down is that the girl must be generous and hospitable to strangers and kind to animals. This was apparently more important to him than family relationship, since he gave Rebekah the costly gifts he had brought with him even before discovering her identity.[49]

Laban

In the subsequent discussions between the servant and the girl's family we are struck by the prominence of Laban.

"Now Rebekah had a brother whose name was Laban."

(24 : 29)

His hospitality indeed matches that of his sister, except that the impression is unmistakably conveyed that it was not entirely disinterested, that it was, in fact, motivated by greed.[50] Scripture is here anticipating the character of Laban as it reveals itself later in his relations with Jacob. Otherwise, the conduct of the brother in our story is perfectly straightforward and honorable. But why should he have played such a dominant role?

When the servant has had his say, "Laban and Bethuel answered" (24:50), his name preceding that of his father. The latter, in fact, takes no more active part in the proceedings. It was only "Laban and his mother"—in that order—who received gifts, and it was they, too, who continued the negotiations.[51] When the young lady is about to depart, at last, for the journey to Canaan, the farewell blessing begins with, "O sister!" (24:60). Finally, when Rebekah is introduced into the Isaac narratives it is carefully noted that she is the "sister of Laban the Aramean" (25:20).

This conspicuous place accorded to Laban can now be explained in the light of the Nuzi archives. It is clear that the institution of fratriarchy, or authority of a brother, existed in Hurrian society. It gave one brother jurisdiction over his brothers and sisters. Since the Nuzi material has proved so fruitful in illuminating so many episodes of the patriarchal narratives, it is not unreasonable to assume that here, too, Hurrian custom lies behind the obvious prominence accorded to Laban in our story. He must have been the fratriarch and, as such, was simply exercising his proper functions.[52]

Marriage by consent

A surprisingly modern touch is added to our story by the response of Laban and his mother to the impatient request of the servant,

> "Give me leave to go to my master."
>
> (24 : 54)

They said,

> "Let us call the girl and ask for her reply."

Thereupon,

> They called Rebekah and said to her, "Will you go with this man?" And she said, "I will." (24 : 57f.).

Whether the girl's consent was required for the marriage itself, or because in this case the bride had to leave the paternal hearth for a foreign land, is not clear. But an interesting analogy to the degree of independence enjoyed by the woman is to be found in a Nuzi document which records that a man gives his sister in marriage to a certain Hurazzi. In the presence of witnesses the bride declared:

> "With my consent my brother Akkulenni gave me as wife to Hurazzi."

Notice how the declaration combines both elements of our biblical episode, the fratriarchal institution and the consent of the bride.[53]

The genealogical framework

The cycle of Abrahamic stories concludes with genealogical lists detailing the ramifications of the patriarch's numerous descendants.[54] These lists are interrupted by the notice of the death of Abraham "at a good ripe age, old and contented," with both Isaac and Ishmael attending to the burial.[55]

The genealogical data actually constitute a kind of literary and ideational consummation of the narrative that began with God's call at Haran. They are witness to a process of inner-biblical exegetical development.

The original blessing to Abraham promised simply to make his name great.[56] After the covenant established with him and the ensuing change of name, the promise is spelled out with greater precision. A "great name" means to be "the father of a multitude of nations." Abraham would be "exceedingly fertile," kings would issue from him.[57] Accordingly, the record of the demise of the patriarch is an appropriate place for the genealogical lists in that they demonstrate how the divine promise was fulfilled. That is to say, the entire Abrahamic biography is encased within a framework of promise and fulfillment.

1. G E N . Chap. 23.
2. *Ibid.* Chap. 24.
3. Actually, of course, he survived another 35 years after Isaac's marriage, dying when the twins were 15. This can be easily calculated from the data given in G E N . 21:5; 25:20, 26.
4. Cf. D E U T . 24:17; 27:19 *et al.* For the status of the alien in biblical times, see de Vaux, *AI,* pp. 74ff.; I. L. Seeligmann, in *EBH,* II, col. 546–49; M. Zer-Kabod, *OLD,* pp. 550–67, esp. pp. 555ff., 563.
5. For the development of the system of multiple burials in Canaan, see Wright, *Bib. Ar.,* p. 51; cf. A. Callaway, *BA,* XXV (1963), pp. 87–91.
6. The origin of the name is unclear. LXX, Vulg. and Targ. understood it adjectivally and translated it "double," referring either to the field or to the cave itself. Cf. B. Eruvin 53ᵃ. From Gen. 23:17, 19, it is clear that "Machpelah" has a more extensive connotation than the cave alone.
7. G E N . 25:9–10.
8. *Ibid.* 49:29–32; 50:13.
9. *Ibid.* 23:3, 5, 7, 10, 16, 18, 20. The gentillic form "Hittite" is used only of Ephron in v. 10 and in subsequent references to the purchase (G E N . 25:9; 49:29; 50:13).

However, the distinction between "children of Heth" and "Hittite" cannot be pushed too far; see *SpG*, p. 172f. Esau's wives are alternately described as "daughters of Heth" (G E N . 27:46) and "daughters of Hittites" (*ibid.* 26:34; 36:2). To add to the complication, they are also included in the broader category of "daughters of Canaan" (*ibid.* 28:1, 8; cf. 36:2). For the suggestion that Ephron may not be a personal name, see S. Yeivin, *Beth Mikra*, XVI (1963), p. 44; *Rivista degli Studi Orientali*, XXXVIII (1963), p. 298.

1 0. For a discussion of the problem of Hittites in Palestine, see F. F. Bruce, *The Hittites and the O. T.*, esp, pp. 15–23; O. F. Gurney, *The Hittites*, pp. 59–62. For the history and civilization of the Hittites, in addition to Gurney, *op. cit.*, see G. Contenau, *La Civilisation des Hittites;* A Goetze, *Kleinasien;* H. G. Güterbock in *EBH*, III, col. 320–58; E. A. Speiser in *WHJP*, I, pp. 156–61.

1 1. G E N . 15:20 *et al.*

1 2. *Ibid.* 26:34; 36:2.

1 3. *Ibid.* 26:35; 27:46; 28:1.

1 4. N U M . 13:29; cf. Josh. 11:3.

1 5. E Z E K . 16:3, 45.

1 6. Cf. the names of the Hittites in David's employ, I S A M . 26:6; I I S A M . 11:3.

1 7. G E N . 14:13.

1 8. G E N . 10:6.

1 9. See *ANET*, pp. 199–203. Not without interest is the mention of a revolt of Hittites in Ashdod in an inscription of Sargon II from 711 B.C.E., for which see *ANET*, p. 286.

2 0. This was suggested by A. E. Cowley, *The Hittites*, p. 9, on the basis of G E N . 23:16, "at the going merchants' rate." The same explanation has been put forward by C. H. Gordon, *JNES*, XVII (1958), p. 29, *Before the Bible*, p. 34, who pointed out that the Hittite enclave in Ugarit had a mercantile origin. On these enclaves, see Gordon in *SOL*, I, pp. 409–19, and A. F. Rainey, *IEJ*, XIII (1963), p. 314, See, also, n. 29 below.

2 1. G E N . 23:10, 18. This is so, irrespective of whether the phrase "all who went in, etc." means the elders who had a voice in the affairs of the community (E. A. Speiser, *BASOR*, 144 (1956), pp. 20–23), or simply all the citizens (G. Evans, *BASOR*, 150 (1958), pp. 28–33).

2 2. See L. Köhler, *Hebrew Man*, pp. 127–150, esp. pp. 130ff., 140f.; de Vaux *AI*, p. 152f.; and the description of the city-gate of Tell en-Nasbeh by W. F. Badè in *Werden u. Wesen*, p. 32f., and of Megiddo by Franken, *Primer*, p. 93.

2 3. G E N . 19:1.

2 4. R U T H 4:1ff.

2 5. See R. de Vaux, *RB*, LVI (1949), p. 25, n. 1.

2 6. Cf. E. Chiera, *JEIMN*, V, Nos, 483, ll. 4, 7f.; 487, l. 6; 530, l. 2. Ephron's insistence upon selling the entire field (v. 11), and the explicit mention of the field in the summary of the transaction (vv. 17, 20), as well as in each subsequent reference to Machpelah (G E N . 25:9–10; 49:29–32; 50:13), would certainly indicate a fact of some special significance. Most attractive is the suggestion of M. R. Lehmann, *BASOR*, 129 (1953), pp. 15–18, connecting it with the provisions of the Hittite Code, §§ 46, 47 (later version: see *ANET*, p. 190f.; J. Friedrich, *Die Hethitischen Gesetze*, pp. 31, 59). However, not only are the serious historical problems not

disposed of (R. de Vaux, *RB*, LXII (1955) p. 101), but the same rule about the payment of the feudal service seems to have been operative also in Ugarit and probably elsewhere; see L. R. Fisher, *JBL*, LXXXI (1962), p. 264; cf., also, Albright's careful wording in *BASOR*, 163 (1961) p. 48. Moreover, account has to be taken of the profound Mesopotamian influence upon Hittite culture, mediated via the Hurrians. This is evident in the fields of law, writing, religion and art; see Hawkes and Woolley, pp. 371–5, 389, 492, 498f., 650, 780f. There were also close legal relationships between Boghazköi and Ugarit; see E. A. Speiser, *JAOS*, LXXV (1955), p. 161. There would thus not need to be any direct link with the Hittite Code.

For other interpretations of Genesis 23, see the literature cited by Lehmann, *op. cit.*, p. 15, n. 1.

I should like to take the opportunity of expressing my thanks to Prof. Y. Muffs for drawing my attention to many important points and for sharing freely of his knowledge of Near Eastern law; see his forthcoming study of G E N . 23.

2 7. A. B. Ehrlich, *Randglossen*, I, p. 99.

2 8. See *SKG*, p. 335; E. A. Speiser, *JAOS*, LXXV (1955), p. 159, no. 37; Nougayrol, *PRU*, III, 15.109, l. 17; 16. 156, l. 10; 16. 174, l. 12; 16, 263, l. 18, for the Akkadian equivalent, *ana/ina šimti gamirti*.

2 9. This phrase is equivalent to the Akkadian *maḫirat illaku* in Old Babylonian contracts and is found already in the law code of Eshnunna § 41; see *SpG*, p. 171.

3 0. See G E N . 23:4, 9². Whether the same verb in the mouth of Ephron (v. 11³) means "to sell" or "to give as a gift" is problematical; see Lehmann, *op. cit.*, p. 15. The analysis of E. Z. Melamed, *Tarbiz*, XIV (1942), p. 13f. is difficult in the light of the clear meaning of *ntn* in G E N . 25:34; J O E L 4:3 with its remarkable parallel in the Kilamuwa inscription, l. 8; P R O V . 31:24; and the highly instructive variants between I I S A M . 24:21–24 and I C H R O N . 21:22–25. Furthermore, in the Akkadian economic tablets from Ugarit which contain considerable West Semitic linguistic substratum, the verb *nadânu* is frequently used in the sense of "to pay, sell;" see Nougayrol, *PRU*, III, 16.180 ll. 5–7; 16.140, l. 9; 15z, ll. 16–18; 16.135, l. 11; and repeatedly in 15.109 + 16.296.

3 1. G E N . 23:17 See *GuG*, p. 277, for similar mention of trees in Babylonian sale documents; cf. Nougayrol, *PRU*, III, 16.166 for an example from Ugarit. Lehmann, *op. cit.*, p. 17f., gives no source for "the consistent listing of the exact number of trees at each real estate sale" as a "well known," "characteristic trait in Hittite business documents." At any rate, the practice would not be specifically Hittite.

3 2. See *GuG*, p. 277; R. de Vaux, *RB*, LVI (1949), p. 24f.

3 3. G E N . 23:20.

3 4. See J. J. Rabinowitz in *EBH*, II, col. 296f. On the significance of *wa-yakŏm* (G E N . 23:17, 20), see *SkG*, p. 388, who connects with the usage of the same verb in L E V . 25:30; 27:14, 17, 19.

3 5. See, however, Kaufmann, *Toldot*, II, p. 550.

3 6. G E N . 24:1–9.

3 7. *Ibid.* 26:35; 27:46.

3 8. *Ibid.* 27:46; 28:1.

3 9. *Ibid.* 47:29.

4 0. *Ibid.* 46:27; E x o d . 1:5; J U D . 8:30.

4 1. *Ibid.* 50:6.

4 2. *Ibid.* 24:5, 8.

4 3. *Ibid.* 26:12.

4 4. *Ibid.* 24:7.

4 5. *Ibid.* 29:15.

4 6. EXOD. 2:15.

4 7. See above p. 105.

4 8. GEN. 24:12ff.

4 9. *Ibid.* v. 22.

5 0. *Ibid.* v. 30.

5 1. *Ibid.* vv. 53ff.

5 2. See C. H. Gordon, *RB*, XLIV (1935), p. 37; *JBL*, LIV (1935), pp. 223–231; E. A. Speiser, *BOS*, pp. 19ff.

5 3. For the text, see *AASOR*, X (1930), p. 61, No. 28, ll. 14ff. See R. de Vaux, *RB*, LVI (1949), p. 29.

5 4. GEN. 25:1–18.

5 5. *Ibid.* v. 8f.

5 6. *Ibid.* 12:2.

5 7. *Ibid.* 17:5f.

CHAPTER XI

Jacob and Esau

GENESIS 25 : 19 – 28 : 5

The birth of the twins

Having traced the lineage of Ishmael, the narrative now reverts to its central theme, the fortunes of those who are heirs to God's covenant. Like Abraham and Sarah before them, Isaac and Rebekah suffered from the curse of sterility. Isaac had been twice assured of posterity. Even before his birth, his father had been promised by God.

> "I will maintain My covenant with him as an everlasting covenant for his offspring to come." (17 : 19)

Again, after Isaac's birth, Abraham had been reassured that,

> ". . . it is through Isaac that offspring shall be continued. . . ." (21 : 12)

It must certainly have required a massive effort of faith to believe in those promises since for twenty long years they went unfulfilled. This time we are told nothing of any special measures taken to induce fertility, only of a desperate personal prayer that ultimately did not go unheeded.[1]

The events surrounding Rebekah's difficult pregnancy are rather enigmatic. We are told that,

> The children struggled in her womb, and she said, "If so, why do I exist?"   (25 : 22)

Whether these words are precisely what Rebekah meant it is hard to say, for the Hebrew original is not wholly clear. But that the mother-to-be was thoroughly distraught is not to be doubted, for

> . . . she went to inquire of the Lord. . . .
> *(ibid.)*

Unhappily, we cannot do more than surmise the reality behind this terse description. Did Rebekah go to a sanctuary to inquire of a priest or oracle? If so, what was its nature? What relationship did the matriarch have with the local cults? The text provides no answers to these intriguing questions, but the very brevity of narration is significant, no less than is the careful employment of the divine name YHWH, the particular name of the God of Israel, in both the inquiry and the response. Scripture wishes to dissociate Rebekah's action from any pagan cultic connections.

The divine response was promptly forthcoming:

> "Two nations are in your womb,
> Two peoples apart while still in your body;
> One people shall be mightier than the other,
> And the older shall serve the younger."
> (25 : 23)

Now this oracle must be understood in relation to the circumstances that elicited the original query, because it has a direct bearing upon the subsequent course of events. It seeks to interpret the "struggle in the womb" as a contest for priority of birth, as a pre-natal sibling rivalry over the possession of the birthright.[2] This idea is further emphasized by the picture of Jacob emerging from his mother's womb grasping the heel of Esau, as though making a final effort to supplant his brother.[3]

This competition is decisively settled by God.

"The older shall serve the younger,"

He declares, which means that Jacob was divinely designated to be the sole heir to the Abraham-Isaac covenanted heritage, even though Esau was victorious in the uterine struggle and was technically the first born. This is a presaging of the future, expressing the idea that Esau's history was to be bound up with the exhibition of physical power, while Jacob's destiny was to lie in a different direction. This interpretation is reinforced by the description of Esau as a "skillful hunter" in contrast to the "mild" Jacob (25:27), and by Isaac's last blessing to Esau depicting him as one who would "live by the sword" (27:40). At any rate, the oracle is intended to leave not a shadow of a doubt that Jacob was predestined by God to be the father of the Chosen People.

The moral issue

This fact is of vital importance to the understanding of the unfolding narrative. Jacob is portrayed as having acquired the birthright, first, by the heartless exploitation of the suffering of his own brother.[4] and then, by the crafty deception practised upon his blind old father.[5] Scripture, therefore, by means of the oracle story, wishes to disengage the fact of Jacob's election from the improper means the young man employed in his impatience to formalize his predestined, independent, right to the heirship. The Bible is not here condoning what has been obtained by trickery. On the contrary, the way the narrative is handled makes clear that Jacob has a claim on the birthright wholly and solely by virtue of God's predetermination. In other words, the presence of the oracle in the story constitutes, in effect, a moral judgment upon Jacob's behavior.

This implicit condemnation of the patriarch's unethical conduct is powerfully brought out through the cycle of biographic tales. Of Abraham, Scripture could relate that he died at "a good ripe age, old and contented" (25:8). Isaac could likewise be described as dying "in ripe old age" (35:29). But such notice is singularly lacking in respect of Jacob.[6] This patriarch could only report that the years of his life had been "few and hard" (47:9). The reference, of course, is to the unrelieved series of trials and tribulations that dogged his footsteps from the day he cheated his father until the last years of his life.[7]

The quiet, mild-mannered, home-loving Jacob, favorite of his mother, was forced into precipitate flight, abandoning home and hearth, exiled from his nearest and dearest, to be ruthlessly exploited for twenty years by his uncle Laban. It is not hard to see in the trickery Laban successfully practiced on Jacob in taking advantage of the darkness to substitute Leah for her sister,[8] the retributive counterpart, measure for measure, of Jacob's exploitation of his father's perpetual darkness by masquerading as his own brother.[9] The perpetrator of deception was now the victim, hoist with his own petard.

The biographical details of Jacob's life read like a catalogue of misfortunes. When he was finally able to make his escape and set out for home after two decades in the service of his scoundrelly uncle, he found his erstwhile employer in hot and hostile pursuit of him.[10] No sooner had this trouble passed than he felt his life to be in mortal danger from his brother Esau.[11] Arriving at last, at the threshold of Canaan, Jacob experienced the mysterious night encounter that left him with a dislocated hip.[12] His worst troubles awaited him in the land of Canaan. His only daughter, Dinah, was violated,[13] his beloved Rachel died in childbirth,[14] and the first son she had born him was kidnapped and sold into slavery, an event that itself initiated a further series of misfortunes.[15]

All the foregoing makes quite clear Scripture's condemnation of Jacob's moral lapse in his treatment of his brother and father. In fact, an explicit denunciation could hardly have been more effective or more scathing than this unhappy biography.

The importance of the birthright

The life situation behind the sibling rivalry for the birthright can be better understood in the light of the special status accorded the first-born in the biblical world.[16] Along with the first fruits of the soil and the male firstling of the herd and flock, the first-born son was considered to be sacred, the exclusive possession of God.[17] The abolition of human sacrifice meant, however, that the first issue of the human womb had to be redeemed from his sacral state.[18] This special sanctity attaching to the first-born son originally accorded him a privileged position in the cult, although at a later time the Levitical tribe displaced the first-born in Israel and appropriated his cultic prerogatives.[19] Being the primary guarantor of the future of the family line and, hence, of the preservation of the ancestral heritage, he naturally ranked second only to the head of the family whose successor he would automatically become. The status of first-born was thus bound up with responsibilities and obligations on the one hand, and rights, privileges and prerogatives on the other, including a double portion of the patrimony.[20] All these were formalized by the father's testamentary blessing. Finally, if it be remembered that the unique spiritual kinship between God and Israel is described in the Bible in terms of the father—first-born relationship,[21] we may understand the distinguished position of the latter in society.

The transference of the birthright

At this point an obvious question arises. Surely the validity of a claim on the birthright is decided by nature! Is not priority of birth the sole determining factor? How then could the birthright be transferred from one son to another?

It is a commonplace that legal prohibitions constitute sociological evidence of the most revealing kind. A practice suddenly proscribed by law may be safely assumed to have been previously both socially acceptable and legally valid. If, then, the Book of Deuteronomy expressly forbids the displacement of the first-born, it must reflect an earlier situation in which the father could exercise the right to disregard the laws of primogeniture.

> If a man has two wives, one loved and the other unloved, and both the loved and the unloved have borne him sons, but the first-born is the son of the unloved one—when he wills his property to his sons, he may not treat as first-born the son of the loved one in disregard of the son of the unloved one who is older. Instead, he must accept the first-born, the son of the unloved one, and allot to him a double portion of all he possesses; since he is the first fruits of his vigor, the birthright is his due. (DEUT. 21 : 15–17)

The social and legal situation behind this law is paralleled in documents from various parts of the ancient Near East.[22] A Nuzi tablet records the statement of a father,

"As regards my son Zirteshup, I at first annulled his relationship; but now I have restored him into sonship. He is the
elder son and a double share he shall receive. . . ."[23]

A marriage contract from the town of Alalakh in the extreme northwest
of Syria stipulates that the groom shall appoint a "first-born" from the
future sons of the present bride, even though another wife might give
birth to a son first.[24] This document is of considerable interest to the
student of the Bible, in that the first-born status is conferred pre-natally,
and in complete disregard of any possible natural claim to the contrary.
It at once calls to mind the oracular elevation of Jacob to first-born
status, displacing the elder Esau even before birth.

That the rules of primogeniture could be set aside by the father in
the patriarchal period is further demonstrated by two other incidents
that point in the same direction. Reuben, Jacob's own first-born, was
deprived of his birthright because he committed a crime against Bilhah,
his father's concubine. This event is commemorated in Jacob's farewell
address.

"Reuben, you are my first-born,
My might and first fruit of my vigor,
Exceeding in rank
And exceeding in honor.
Unstable as water, you shall excel no longer;
For when you mounted your father's bed,
You brought disgrace. . . ."   (49 : 3)

The Chronicler explicitly records, no doubt with this passage in mind,
that Reuben was the first-born of Israel,

but because he polluted his father's couch, his birthright was
given to the sons of Joseph, the son of Israel.

                                        (I CHRON. 5 : 1)

The other case involves Jacob's decision to pass over Manasseh in favor
of his younger brother Ephraim, much to the displeasure of Joseph.[25]

The actual sale of the birthright by one brother to another has a
remarkable parallel in one Nuzi document which provides for a certain
Kurpazah to part with his future inheritance share for three sheep
received immediately from his brother Tupkitilla. Doubtless, Kurpazah

would have been driven to such an agreement only by urgent need.[26] It should be noted that in the case of Jacob and Esau, the place of a written document is taken by an oath,[27] an equally binding form of agreement in antiquity.

The oral testament

The disregard of the rules of primogeniture in patriarchal times accurately reflects contemporary Hurrian-Canaanite custom and law. The same is true in respect of Isaac's final blessing. This oral benediction clearly had the same legal validity as a "last will and testament" document. A Nuzi court record deals with the case of Tarmiya who was involved in a lawsuit with his two older brothers who contested his right to possession of Sululi-Ishtar, a slave-girl. Tarmiya testified:

> "My father, Huya, was sick and lay on a couch; then my father seized my hand and spoke thus to me, 'My other sons, being older, have acquired a wife; so I give herewith Sululi-Ishtar as your wife.' " [28]

After examining the witnesses and the contestants, the court upheld the validity of the father's disposition of his property, even though delivered orally.

The biblical narrative has preserved this peculiarly Mesopotamian institution, even to the extent of incorporating into the text a phrase now recognized to be the Hebrew equivalent of a Nuzi legal formula. Isaac introduced the subject of his final blessing by saying,

> "I am, you see, so old that I do not know how soon I may die."   (27 : 2)

This is no mere oratory, for another Nuzi text detailing final disposition of property similarly opens with the statement, "Now that I am grown old." [29] Isaac's words thus had clear socio-juridical implications.

The striking, detailed correspondences between patriarchal practice and contemporary Near Eastern law and custom point up, once again,

the amazingly accurate historical memory reflected in the biblical narratives. They arouse renewed respect for the Bible as a source of history,
and help to illuminate the text to an extent not hitherto possible. But
they also help us to understand something of the way the narratives have
been transformed to serve a higher moral purpose. There is no doubt
that the way Jacob acquired his brother's birthright could not have
been considered either unusual or objectionable in the context of his
times. As a matter of fact, there is every reason to believe that Jacob's
dealings with Esau and his father represent a stage of morality in which
the successful application of shrewd opportunism was highly respected.[30]
It is all the more remarkable, therefore, that Scripture should have cast
the story in a mold of implicit reprobation, introducing the oracle element to make the transference of the birthright independent of subsequent events, and depicting the unbroken chain of Jacob's misfortunes
as the direct result of actions not regarded as reprehensible according
to the standards of his time.

1. GEN. 25:21.
2. Cf. HOS. 12:4 on which see H. L. Ginsberg, *JBL,* LXXX, (1961), p. 342, n. i.
3. GEN. 25:26.
4. *Ibid.* 25:29–34.
5. *Ibid.* 27:1–29.
6. Cf. *ibid.* 47:28; 49:33.
7. See U. Cassuto in *EBH,* III, col. 718f.
8. GEN. 29:21ff.
9. *Ibid.* 27:1ff.
1 0. *Ibid.* chap. 31.
1 1. *Ibid.* 32:4–33:16.
1 2. *Ibid.* 32:25–33.
1 3. *Ibid.* chap. 34.
1 4. *Ibid.* 35:16–20.
1 5. *Ibid.* 37:39ff.
1 6. See de Vaux, *AI,* pp. 41f., 53.
1 7. Cf. EXOD. 13:2, 22–28; Deut. 15:19.
1 8. Cf. EXOD. 13:12–15; 34:20; Num. 18:15.

1 9. Cf. N U M . 3:5–13; 8:5–19.

2 0. I. Mendelsohn, *BASOR*, 156 (1959), p. 39f., shows that the preferential status of the first-born prevailed in Nuzi, Assyria, Syria, and Palestine, as well as in Babylonia between the fall of Ur III and the rise of Hammurabi's empire. It is not to be found in the codes of Lipit-Ishtar or Hammurabi. Mendelsohn believes that the institution had its origin and *raison d'être* in the religious, social and economic needs of semi-nomadic and predominantly agricultural societies.

2 1. Cf. E X O D . 4:22; J E R . 31:8.

2 2. See R. de Vaux, *RB*, LVI (1949), p. 30; I. Mendelsohn, in J. L. Blau, ed., *Essays on Jewish Life*, p. 356f.; E. A. Speiser, *IEJ*, VII (1957), p. 212f.

2 3. See E. A. Speiser, *AASOR*, X (1930), No. 8, p. 39.

2 4. See I. Mendelsohn, *BASOR*, 156 (1959), pp. 38–40.

2 5. G E N . 48:13–20.

2 6. See C. H. Gordon, *BA*, III (1940), p. 5.

2 7. G E N . 25:33.

2 8. *ANET*, p. 220. See E. A. Speiser, *AASOR*, XVI (1936), No. 56, p. 107; Gordon, *op. cit.*, p. 8.

2 9. See E. A. Speiser, *JBL*, LXXIV (1955), pp. 252–56.

3 0. See C. H. Gordon, *The Ancient Near East*, p. 127.

CHAPTER XII

Jacob and Laban

GENESIS 28-32

The vision at Bethel

Ostensibly to find himself a wife from among his own kinsmen, but actually to escape the wrath of his brother Esau, Jacob set out for the land whence his mother had come.

Travel after sunset being out of the question, the fugitive lay down to spend the night under the open sky, his head resting on a stone. Here, on the road from Beer-sheba to Haran, he experienced an extraordinary dream-vision that was to prove a turning-point in his life.[1]

Angels were climbing up and down a stairway that spanned heaven and earth. God, who was standing by him, introduced Himself to Jacob as "the God of your father Abraham and the God of Isaac," acknowledging thereby his spiritual succession. He then repeated the traditional promise of posterity and land and added, because of Jacob's special situation, an assurance of personal protection in exile and a guarantee of safe return to the land of his birth.

Jacob awoke from his dream with startled shock. He exclaimed,

"Surely the Lord is present in this place,[2] and I did not know
it! How awesome is this place! This is none other than the
abode of God, and that is the gateway to heaven."

(28 : 16f.)

Thereupon, he turned the stone that he had put under his head into a
cultic pillar, sanctified it with oil, and renamed the site Bethel, or "house
of God" in place of its current name Luz. Jacob made a vow to God,
conditional upon his safe return.[3]

This narrative contains some very unusual features and seems to be
an amalgam of several individual traditions, all of great antiquity.[4]

In the first place, it is evident that the coinage of the name Bethel is
ascribed to Jacob himself,[5] and the sanctity of the site is understood as
deriving solely from the patriarch's theophanic experience. Now this, in
itself, is a very interesting tradition in the light of subsequent developments, for the Bethel sanctuary became thoroughly illegitimate to the
later biblical writers. Once King Jeroboam exploited the place for his
own political purposes to create a rival to the Jerusalem Temple,[6] the
worship at Bethel was regarded as unqualifiedly sinful to the Judeans.[7]
In the eighth century B.C.E., when the temple there was at the height of
its prestige as the royal and national sanctuary of the Kingdom of Israel,[8]
the Bethel cult earned the outright condemnation of the prophet Amos,[9]
while Hosea, the only northern Israelite literary prophet, was even more
severe in his castigations, actually designating Bethel by Beth-Aven, the
"house of God" as the "house of delusion."[10] Despite all this, the story
connecting Jacob with Bethel and its consecration was neither expunged
from the text, nor re-edited in conformity with later events. Clearly, the
association of Bethel with Jacob must have belonged to the earliest and
most hallowed traditions of Israel.

Historically, however, the ascription of the origins of Bethel to this
patriarch presents grave difficulties, for Abraham is twice recorded as
having worshiped at an altar he himself had built in the vicinity of
Bethel.[11] It might be assumed, that the mention of the city as Bethel is
there an anachronism and that Abraham's altar was not necessarily at the
same site as Jacob's. But the very fact that Abraham built an altar in the
area, although no theophany is recorded to account for the choice of site,
means that the Bethel region either had already a sacred history in Abraham's time, or that it acquired one as a result of Abraham's cultic activities. Either way, its holiness would have preceded Jacob's experience.

As a matter of fact, all the evidence points in the direction of a Canaanite origin for "Bethel" and the sanctuary situated at the place bearing that name. The second component of the name, El, betrays its pre-Israelite connections. It can refer to none other than El, a well-known Semitic deity and the name of the head of the Canaanite pantheon. Bethel derived its name from being the cultic center of this god. Originally a designation of just the temple of El, it gradually encompassed the entire surrounding urban area. Ultimately it even became the name of the god himself, so that a god Bethel is known to us from several extra-biblical sources.[12]

This contrast between historic reality and the biblical story of Jacob is of monumental importance for the understanding of the nature of biblical religion and its development. It serves to map out the spiritual boundary lines that divided Israel from its neighbors. The details of the scriptural narrative reveal a subtle and deliberate rejection of pagan notions even as they employ their idiom.[13]

The dream imagery reflects a decidedly Mesopotamian background already familiar to us from the "Tower of Babel" episode. The stairway that Jacob saw connecting heaven and earth recalls at once the picture of the ziqqurat with its external ramp linking each stage of the tower to the other.[14] The note that "its top reached the sky" (28:12) and the identification of the site of the dream as "the gateway to heaven" (28:17), is reminiscent of the stereotyped phraseology used in connection with the Babylonian temple-towers.[15] But it differs from pagan mythology in that the stairway of Jacob's dream is not a channel of communication between man and God. The deity does not descend by it to the human realm and man does not ascend to the divine sphere. The chasm between the two is unbridgeable by physical means. Indeed, the background presence of the angels serves to highlight this fact, for the stairway is obviously for them alone. They are merely ornamental, playing no role in the theophany.

Next, we note the emphatic expressions of wonderment that the dream-vision occasions, the only such example in all of the patriarchal narratives. It is true that this is God's first self-manifestation to Jacob; but neither Abraham nor Isaac showed any surprise in their time of initial confrontation with the divine voice. The text is most emphatic about Jacob's ignorance of the holiness of the place.[16] In fact, there was nothing there at all, only stones. Jacob set up a stone pillar to commemorate the revelation he had experienced and vowed[17] that when he would at some future date return in peace, he would build a sanctuary on the bare site.[18]

Indeed, twenty years later Jacob erected there an altar in fulfillment of
his promise and the place was henceforth known as Bethel.[19] All this
serves but one purpose—to dissociate, absolutely and unmistakably,
the pagan cult of Bethel from the sanctity the place held in Israelite consciousness. Hence the emphasis on the divine name YHWH. It is He
who is standing by Jacob. It is as YHWH that He introduces Himself.[20]
"Surely YHWH is in this place," exclaims Jacob on awakening (28:16).
So exclusively devoted to the worship of the God of Jacob is the sanctuary at Bethel, that when the patriarch finally returns from Mesopotamia
and is about to visit Bethel once again, he orders his household and all
who accompanied him to rid themselves of the alien gods in their midst,
to purify themselves and to change their garments before approaching
the site.[21]

The radical departure from Near Eastern religious ideas is further
evident in three other aspects or inferences of our story. Sanctuaries were
generally regarded as having been built by the gods themselves, or at
least with their active participation, and usually at the creation of the
world.[22] In the case of Bethel, there is no doubt that it is a strictly human
production, even if executed at divine behest,[23] and that it had no hallowed antecedents. Moreover, in erecting the stone pillar,[24] Jacob is
actually reversing accepted religious notions. Normally, a stone was holy
and an object of worship because it was thought to be the abode of a
numen. In this case, however, the stone pillar is simply memorializing
the scene of the theophany and is accorded no inherent sanctity. Finally,
and perhaps the most radical departure of all from the ideas of the times,
is the ascription of the sanctuary of Bethel to an event in the life of the
patriarch. Pagan temples usually resulted from events in the lives of the
gods. In our story the mythological elements are completely lacking.

In sum: the biblical narrative ignores the non-Israelite sacred history
of Bethel, inferentially dissociates itself from all pagan connections, and
recasts events and motifs in the light of Israelite concepts. The wide gap
between history and the biblical account constitutes, in fact, the measure
of the chasm separating the religion of the Bible from that of the world
out of which it grew.

Jacob in Laban's household

Buoyed up by the profound spiritual experience he had undergone at
Bethel, Jacob continued his journey to the home of his mother's family.

The biblical narrator is careful to expose the hand of divine providence at work in the unfolding drama, fulfilling the promise of the nocturnal revelation that God would not abandon the patriarch in the land of his exile.

Like Abraham's servant many years before, Jacob arrived at the well of Haran just as his own kith and kin appeared on the scene. But the glaring contrast between the well-laden entourage that Abraham had sent and Jacob's precipitate, lonely flight, on foot and empty-handed, emphasizes the reprehensible nature of Jacob's actions which had led to his present plight. Jacob was welcomed into the home of his uncle Laban and before long found himself to be a working member of the family, husband to Laban's two daughters, and shepherd of his sheep.[25]

We have previously called attention to the evidence of historic antiquity embodied in the contrast between Jacob's experience, and the legislation of the priestly code which forbids the simultaneous or even successive marriage to two living sisters.[26] We also observed nemesis at work in the way Jacob's own masquerading as his brother meets its counter-stroke in the substitution of Leah for her sister Rachel.[27] But retributive justice is not the only motif here. Just as Jacob's succession to the birthright was divinely ordained irrespective of human machinations, so it must be assumed that Jacob's unwanted marriage to Leah was understood by the narrator as part of God's scheme of things. For from this union issued the tribes of Levi and Judah which shared between them the spiritual and temporal hegemony of Israel, providing the two great and dominating institutions of the biblical period, the priesthood and the Davidic monarchy.

Jacob's position in Laban's household has long been puzzling and even now it cannot be truly said that all the problems have been cleared up. However, it is widely agreed, on the basis of the Nuzi documents, that the assumption of Laban's adoption of Jacob provides the most plausible explanation at the present time.[28]

When Jacob first arrived at his uncle's home we hear only of two daughters who tended the sheep. The first mention of sons does not come until twenty years later.[29] It may be presumed that Jacob's position as principal heir by virtue of adoption had, in the meantime, yielded to the prior rights of natural-born sons who became increasingly jealous of their prerogatives and more and more sensitive to Jacob's growing wealth.

This kind of situation is well illustrated in the Nuzi archives. Adoption records frequently specify that a natural-born son would displace the adopted son as principal heir. One such involves a transaction in which

Nashwi, son of Ar-Shenni, adopted Wullu under these conditions, but also gave him his daughter in marriage.[30] A closer parallel to the Laban-Jacob relationship would be hard to find. Still further evidence of the authentic social background are other tablets that show that it was not uncommon for a father to give his daughter a wedding gift of a maid,[31] just as did Laban to Leah and Rachel,[32] although it ought to be noted that the incidental intrusion of Zilpah and Bilhah into the narrative is really introductory to their future role as mothers of tribes.

The theme of feminine sterility, common to Sarah and Rebekah, is encountered once again in the cycle of Jacob stories. Rachel was barren, and, like Sarah, resorted to the device of concubinage as provided by the custom of the time.[33] The issue, however, is handled here a little differently, giving the opportunity for an inferential observation about the compassionate nature of God.

> The Lord saw that Leah was unloved and he opened her
> womb.   (29 : 31)

The tribes

The biblical narratives tell of the birth of twelve sons to Jacob through his wives and concubines, eleven of them in North Mesopotamia and one in Canaan.[34] These sons, in turn, fathered tribes, the confederation of which constituted the people of Israel.[35] This picture seems simple enough, except that its very simplicity raises many questions.

In the first place, this is hardly the way nations historically come into being, developing by natural increase from a single individual. Secondly, if this account be accepted as factual the contingent problems are insuperable. Levi was born in Mesopotamia and his great-grandsons, Moses and Aaron, led the Exodus from Egypt. Only two generations, that is, intervened between Levi and Moses.[36] Yet the tribe of Levi numbered no less than 22,000 males not long after the Exodus.[37] Joseph lived to see the birth of sons to Machir, son of Manasseh.[38] These sons of Machir took part in military expedition in the lifetime of Moses.[39] Most remarkably, the census taken one year after the Exodus shows that in three generations Manasseh had grown from a single individual to a tribe that could count 32,200 males over the age of twenty.[40]

For our present purposes it is of no importance that these statistics in themselves involve critical problems of their own. What is of interest is that their mere presence betrays a far more complex understanding of the tribal situation than the Book of Genesis narratives would imply at first sight. The picture there sketched cannot be isolated from the evidence provided by other sources.

It should not be overlooked that even the Genesis narratives often convey the impression that the patriarchs themselves were not simply individuals accompanied by small family units, but actually heads of clans. The quarrel and subsequent separation of Abraham and Lot over the limited resources of the land sounds far more like clan rivalry than a dispute between two tiny family units.[41] Abraham's ability to muster at short notice a small army of 318 retainers "born into his household,"[42] suggests that he headed a large establishment of many hundred souls. The same impression is gained from the reports of Jacob's return to Canaan.[43] Moreover, when dealing with Jacob's sons, Scripture specifically designates Reuben and Simeon, at least, as "heads of their respective clans,"[44] and the obscuring of the differentiation between the ancestor and the tribe bearing his name is obvious from the concluding formula of the blessings of the dying Jacob to his sons gathered around his bed:

All these were the tribes of Israel, twelve in number.

(49 : 28)

The individual has imperceptibly become blended with the group.[45]

The phenomenon we are here discussing is unique to the Bible in the literature of the ancient world. No other people, as far as is known, had a genealogical concept of history. Clan, tribal and national relationships are expressed through the ascription of common ancestry to a single individual, the eponymous ancestor.[46]

This notion is not to be confused with that of the Romans and the Greeks, who recognized eponymous founders. The legendary Romulus was the accepted founder of Rome who gave his name to the city and its inhabitants; but he was not regarded as having literally fathered the Roman people, nor did the Romans reconstruct a chain of family descent from him.[47] In biblical historiography, on the other hand, a pedigree became the literary form through which ethnic origins and groupings are described.

The "Table of Nations"[48] represents an excellent example of this system. Seventy peoples who came within the geographic purview of the ancient Hebrews are traced back to the three sons of Noah. Cush (Ethiopia), Mizraim (Egypt), Put (in Africa) and Canaan, for example, are listed as four brothers, all sons of Ham, which means that these four peoples had, in remote antiquity, cultural and political, if not other, affiliations.[49] The same applies to the other geographic and ethnic listings. Nahor, brother of Abraham, is designated father of twelve sons,[50] several of whose names are known to us from elsewhere as those of places, tribes and peoples.[51]

That the biblical writer often himself viewed the genealogical system as nothing more than a convenient schematization may be shown from the merging of the individual with the tribe, as illustrated above. Other examples are to be found in the "Table of Nations." Japheth, son of Noah, is credited with seven sons. Elishah and Tarshish are the names of the first two, but the others are given as gentilics, "the Kittim and the Dodanim" (10:4). In the case of Mizraim, all the names of the seven sons are given in the form of gentilics, not as proper names, viz., the Ludim, the Anamim, the Lehabim, etc. The same personification of the group is to be found in respect to the line of Ishmael. He was prenatally destined to be "the father of twelve chieftains" (17:20). When the names are later listed "in the order of their birth," they turn out to be those of a confederation of Arab tribes.

> These are the sons of Ishmael and these are their names by
> their villages and by their encampments: twelve chieftains of
> as many tribes.   (25 : 16)

In other words, tribal relationships are treated as family relationships and are expressed in terms of such, by being reconstructed into genealogies.

Regarded in this light, it is clear that the narratives of the Book of Genesis recounting the birth of Jacob's sons, actually constitute an important historic document. Just as these stories accurately reflect the legal and social customs of the times about which they purport to deal, so they may yield authentic information about the early union and fortunes of the tribes of Israel. This is not to say that the patriarchs were fictitious characters or that the Hebrew tribes were not ultimately related by ties of consanguinity. On the contrary, one of the unique features of the patriarchal narratives is that the fathers were not, as among other peoples, mythological personages, super-human heroes or idealized saints. They are vividly portrayed as human beings, vitally involved in the struggle for existence, subject to temptation like all other men and like them, too, possessed of human frailties and strength of character, and experiencing the joys and sorrows of life. But it must not be forgotten that the narratives and genealogies provide the outward literary form by which a very complex state of affairs is reduced to simple terms. The "sons of Jacob" were doubtless chieftains of tribes that existed already in the patriarchal period, a situation exactly analogous to the previously cited "sons of Ishmael."

The Hebrew tribes, all except Benjamin, arose and confederated in Mesopotamia. Since they are grouped according to the wives of Jacob, we may trace some of the stages of federal evolution. The six Leah tribes must have originally constituted a distinct fraternity. The handmaid tribes must have enjoyed a subordinate status. Benjamin must have joined Joseph and the confederacy after the migration to Canaan.

That the inter-tribal relationships portrayed in the Book of Genesis are not in conformity with the historic reality of the Joshua-Judges period has previously been shown. It was stressed that this very disharmony is a sure sign that the narratives accurately respond to the true situation in pre-conquest times, otherwise their invention would be inexplicable. Consequently, the primogeniture of Reuben and Manasseh indeed records the early, but lost, supremacy of these tribes. The national tribal groupings are also very early, for after the conquest of Canaan those subsumed under one mother did not possess geographical unity or propinquity. Of the Leah tribes, Reuben was in East Jordan, Simeon and Judah in the south of Canaan, Issachar and Zebulun in the North, and Levi had no territory. Of the Rachel tribes, Benjamin was adjacent to, and its fortunes politically bound up with, Judah, rather than with his fraternal Joseph tribes.

In conclusion it ought to be added that the tribal organization of early Israel corresponds to what is known of many peoples in the ancient world. It was, in fact, characteristic of semi-nomadic peoples in the Near East. Edom was a conglomerate of clans,[52] as were Midian,[53] the Arabs[54] and the Arameans.[55] The tribal organization of the latter, as well as of the Amorites, is now abundantly illuminated from the Mari archives.[56] All this is far different from the Canaanite monarchic city-state structure.

Jacob's escape

Resuming once again the story of Jacob in Laban's household, we find him completing twenty years of service. His material success aroused the envy of Laban's sons and he made up his mind to return home. Prompted by a divine call, and with the backing of his wives, Jacob assembled the members of his family, gathered together his possessions, and awaited a suitable opportunity to slip away.[57]

The reaction of Rachel and Leah to Jacob's suggestion of flight can now be understood through the Nuzi material. The women declared,

> "Have we still a share in the inheritance of our father's house?
> Are we not reckoned by him as outsiders? For he has sold us
> and then used up our purchase price."   (31 : 14–15)

The first part of this complaint fits in well with what is known of the inferior status of foreign slaves in Nuzi.[58] An outsider, deprived of local relatives who could supply protection or demand redress, would be a likely object of exploitation. As to the second sentence, the reference is most probably to the marriage arrangements which Laban had made with Jacob, exacting from him fourteen years of service in payment of the bridal price for his two wives. Normally, the groom deposited with the bride's father or guardian a sum of money to be settled on the bride. In this case, the service substituted for the money. The regular term for the bridal-price payment in biblical Hebrew is *mohar*.[59] In our text the word *kesef* is used. In Nuzi documents this same word is sometimes employed instead of the usual technical term. Moreover, the Akkadian idiom expressing utilization of the bridal purchase money is the very one used by Rachel and Leah.[60] It is uncertain, though, whether Laban is being accused of improvident disposition of the monetary equivalent of Jacob's years of service, or of downright larceny.

At any rate, Jacob made good his escape while Laban was away on a sheep-shearing mission. A curious detail of this flight is Rachel's appropriation of her father's *terafim*.[61] That this can be none other than the images of gods is apparent from Laban's angry accusation when he finally caught up with this son-in-law,

> "Why did you steal my gods?"
> (31 : 30)

That these particular figurines were small and portable is obvious from the way Rachel quickly managed to conceal them in the camel cushion.[62] We must therefore be dealing here with the private household gods. Once again the archives of Nuzi throw a little light on the matter. The oft-cited adoption contract of Nashwi and Wullu stipulates as follows:

> If Nashwi has a son of his own, he shall divide (the estate) equally with Wullu, but the son of Nashwi shall take the gods of Nashwi. However, if Nashwi does not have a son of his own, then Wullu shall take the gods of Nashwi.[63]

We do not yet know the exact interpretation of this clause, nor the precise significance attaching to the possession of these household gods. They certainly had great religious significance, and this and other texts indicate that they would normally belong to the paterfamilias. But why Rachel stole them it is impossible to say. The Nuzi tablet provides only North Mesopotamian and hence, local, coloration for the incident.[64]

From Laban's actions and Jacob's fearful imprecation[65] we may gather that the theft of the gods was a grievous offence.[66] This impression is reinforced by the importance attached to their disposition in the kind of legal document just cited. For this reason, the way the biblical narrator handles the story is highly significant. In direct speech the objects are called "my gods" by Laban, and "your gods" by Jacob in response.[67] This dissociation of the patriarch from the terms of religious expression accepted by Laban is further emphasized by Jacob's contemptuous reference to the figurines as "household objects."[68] Even more derisive is the descriptive epithet *terafim* in the narration, as distinct from the direct speech. While the etymology of the word is obscure, it undoubtedly has ignominious connotations.[69] Finally, it is not at all improbable that to the narrator the culminating absurdity in the religious situation was reached when Rachel hid the idols in the camel cushion and sat upon them in a state of menstrual impurity.[70] In the light of the Israelite notions of the clean and unclean,[71] the description of Rachel's act implies an attitude of wilful defilement and scornful rejection of their religious significance.

Laban's futile search for his gods provoked Jacob to an impassioned outpouring of righteous indignation and protestations of injured innocence. We are treated to a revealing picture of the hard life and the trials and tribulations of the shepherd in ancient times. Jacob asserts that Laban had exacted recompense whenever an animal entrusted to his care had been lost by accident or force majeur.[72] If Hammurabi's laws be any guide in this situation, Jacob is accusing his uncle of having far exceeded his legal rights, for a shepherd who could prove lack of negligence was not liable in such circumstances.[73]

Laban made no detailed reply to Jacob's allegations. Instead, he suggested that the two conclude a pact of mutual non-aggression and peaceful coexistence. Jacob must have been most happy to rid himself of Laban at last and he readily agreed. Anxious to provide his daughters with legal protection under divine sanction in a strange, far-off land, Laban inserted a clause in the pact restricting Jacob's right to take additional wives in the future.[74]

Such stipulations are unknown elsewhere in the Bible, but in recent years legal documents from Nuzi and the town of Alalakh in northern Syria have shown that impositions of this kind upon the son-in-law were not infrequent in that part of the world.[75] The Nashwi-Wullu contract provided that,

> . . . if Wullu takes another wife he shall forfeit the lands and buildings of Nashwi.[76]

Another tablet, a marriage document, stipulates that,

> Zilikkushu shall not take another wife in addition to Naluya.[77]

Jacob and Laban sealed the pact they had made between them by erecting stone monuments and partaking of a sacrificial meal.

Jacob across Jabbok[78]

Having concluded the pact, Laban departed for his own land, and the kindred ties between the Hebrews and Mesopotamia were forever severed. A new era was about to open in the career of Jacob and the development of the people of Israel. Two incidents, each mysterious, mark the transition.

> Jacob went on his way and angels of God encountered him.
>
> (32 : 2)

It is most likely that this bare mention of a meeting with "God's camp" was once part of a fuller story preserved in popular tradition.[79] It is now so truncated, however, as to be beyond all possibility of reconstruction. But if we remember that Jacob's departure from the land of promise was marked by a vision of "angels of God" (28 : 12), and that neither then nor now is there any explanation for the phenomenon, nor any role for the angels in the narrative, we may presume that our report here serves no other purpose than to provide a literary framework for the Jacob and Laban cycle of stories, which constitute a distinct unit within the larger biography of the patriarch.

The second incident, more detailed and even more perplexing, signifies the impending shift of emphasis from the individual to the people of Israel. Jacob had arrived at a point on the meandering river Jabbok. His wives and company had already crossed over, and Jacob was left alone. Suddenly, a man wrestled with him until daybreak when, seeing that the combat was indecisive, he wrenched Jacob's hip. But Jacob hung on to his adversary, refusing to allow him to depart until he would bless him. Thereupon, the man changed Jacob's name to Israel. He refused, however, to give his own name and vanished as the sun's rays shed their first light upon a limping Jacob. In commemoration of the night's events, the site of the encounter was named Peniel.[80]

Moreover,

> That is why the children of Israel to this day do not eat the
> thigh muscle that is on the socket of the hip.   (31 : 23-33)

This story, unparalleled in biblical literature, is thoroughly bewildering. What is the identity of the nameless assailant? Why did he beg for disengagement just as the sun was coming up? Why was this so urgent that Jacob was able to extort a blessing from the "man" as the price of release? One wonders, too, how the change of name is an adequate response to the appeal for a blessing and why the adversary struck the patriarch on the hip. What logical connection can there be between this occasion and a dietary restriction? Finally, one may well ask if there is any special significance to be read into the fact that the location of this singular spectacle was the river Jabbok, and that its timing was nocturnal.

We shall probably never be able to provide complete and certain answers to all these questions. At best, we can hope to relieve somewhat the harsh obscurity of the story by analyzing the various motifs in the

light of parallels, noting at the same time the transformations that have
taken place in the process of appropriation into biblical literature.[81]

The first detail to arrest our attention is the river as the scene of the
struggle. This immediately calls to mind the innumerable tales in world
literature of river-spirits who fight with humans seeking to cross their
abodes. Insofar as rivers frequently prove unexpectedly treacherous, they
were believed to possess some malevolent power dangerous to life. From
this notion of the personification of the river is but a brief step, so that
travelers would take good care to propitiate the river-god through sacrifice, libation or other ceremony before attempting to ford. Bearing this in
mind, it is clear that in the original story, the spirit of the swift-flowing
Jabbok must have tried to prevent Jacob from crossing the river. The
bare bones of this ancient saga betray an unmistakably folkloristic flavor
in the use of this motif and in the obvious word-play involving the name
of the river (in Hebrew: *yabbok*) and the word for, "he wrestled" (in
Hebrew: *va-ye'abek*).

Equally well known is the second motif of a demonic being whose
power is restricted to the duration of the night and who is unable to
abide the breaking of the dawn. An evident corollary is the opportunity
afforded a brave soul to derive personal profit from the situation. He who
can hold on to the demon long enough can bend him to his will. This
temporal limitation upon demonic power explains the desperate crip-
pling blow the adversary inflicted upon Jacob.

How have these primitive motifs been treated in our biblical account?
If the mysterious assailant was originally a river-spirit, there is nothing
in the text to reveal it as such. He is described simply as a "man." He
refuses to give a name when asked, even discouraging the very questioning. Yet clearly it is no ordinary human that appears suddenly out of the
stillness of the night to engage the patriarch in desperate combat. For in
changing Jacob's name to Israel he says,

"You have striven with beings divine and human."
(32 : 29)
In naming the site of the encounter Peniel, Jacob explains,

"I have seen a divine being face to face."
(32 : 31)
Centuries later the prophet Hosea refers to this incident and describes
Jacob as having striven with "divine beings," "an angel" (Hos. 12:4–5).
"The man," thus has become a "divine being," an *elohim*—a generic

term in biblical Hebrew for supernatural beings.[82] Jacob's assailant was an angel in the guise of man. He is never, significantly, identified with YHWH.

Two other instances of a similar nature may be cited in which "man" and "angel" are used interchangeably. Abraham saw three "men," human enough to have their feet bathed and to eat and drink. When they depart for Sodom and when they arrive there, they are still called "men." But as the story unfolds they are described as "angels."[83]

Similarly, an "angel of the Lord" appeared to Manoah's wife.[84] She described him to her husband as "a man of God." Manoah went out to "the man" and asked him if he were "the man" who had spoken to his wife. He then offered him a meal "not knowing that he was the angel of God." When the angel had finally disappeared, Manoah fearfully told his wife,

"We shall surely die for we have seen *elohim*."

(J U D . 13 : 22)

This statement strongly resembles that of Jacob,

"I have seen *elohim* face to face, yet my life has been preserved," (32 : 31)

and the analogy may be pressed still further in that in both instances the *elohim* is asked for his name and vanishes in anonymity.

In sum: the demonic river-spirit of the original tale has been transformed in the scriptural narrative. All those features characteristic of river-crossing combats have been omitted from our narrative. There is no mention of any of the usual ceremonies designed to propitiate the spirit.

Vagueness of the description of the adversary contrasts strongly with the usual pattern in which the spirit assumes the form of animals, serpents and monsters, constantly shifting from one guise to another in the course of its attacks. That Jacob knew nothing at all about a river-spirit of Jabbok is evident from the total unexpectedness of the attack and the request for a name. The nocturnal assailant has become a member of the divine retinue conforming to the monotheistic pattern of biblical angelogy.[85]

Of course, the idea of a divine retinue is folkloristic and very early; but it has nothing in common with the pagan pantheon. The angels have no definable personalities and pursue no independent existence.

They are both nameless and characterless, vanishing as suddenly as they appear. The use of angelic imagery is not allowed to violate the non-mythological nature of the religion of Israel.

The same rejection of pagan ideas is to be found in the dietary proscription of the thigh muscle. This is obviously a very ancient and well-known Israelite practice which has been connected etiologically with our Jacob story. Now this connection, historical or not, is very revealing. From all over the pagan world there are innumerable examples of taboos on parts of the body of animals because these were the sacred food of the gods and spirits, or because they were potentially noxious to humans.[86] The thigh, being regarded as the seat of the reproductive powers, would acquire an especially sacral character.[87] But none of these reasons is given in the biblical account. Instead, an "historic" explanation is produced, so that the practice commemorates an event of epochal importance in the life of the patriarch. Whatever origins or associations it may once have had are all discarded or forgotten.[88]

The major significance of the episode derives, of course, from the change of name that resulted. This, as was explained in relation to Abraham and Sarah,[89] portends a new destiny, effectuates a decisive break with the past and inaugurates a fresh role, all symbolized here by the substitution of Israel for Jacob.

As usual with the biblical onomasticon, the popular etymologizing is more expressive than scientific origins. The scriptural understanding of the name, "Jacob," is evocative of disapprobation and is suggestive of ethical standards that, at best, are hardly edifying.[90] The struggle with the angel may, therefore, imply the final purging of those unsavory qualities of character that marked his past career.[91]

It now remains to discuss the significance of the geographical locale. The river Jabbok is mentioned several times in the Bible but always in the same context, as a boundary at the time of Israelite occupation of East Jordan. It constituted the limit of Israel's first victory against the kings of the promised land after it emerged from the desert wanderings.[92] For reasons of strategy, logistics and morale, this success was of incalculable importance to Israel. It was the harbinger of the fulfillment of the divine blessing to the patriarchs. Is it not remarkable that Jacob's nocturnal encounter with the angel and the change of name to Israel should occur precisely at the moment he crosses the boundary into the first territory of the promised land to be occupied in the future by the people of Israel?

1. GEN. 28:10ff.
2. Note the frequent repetition of "place" (Hebrew: *māqōm*) in this section: 28:11, 16, 17, 19. *GuG*, pp. 166, 317, understands as "a cultic site." Cf. de Vaux, *AI*, p. 291.
3. GEN. 28:18–22. The vow was fulfilled as reported in 35:1–15.
4. GEN. 28:10–22 is usually taken as a fusion of the J and E sources, whereas in chap. 35, vv. 1–8, 14 are assigned to E and vv. 9–13, 15 to P.
5. GEN. 28:18; 35:15.
6. I KINGS 12:26–33.
7. Cf. *ibid.* 13:1–5.
8. AMOS. 7:13.
9. *Ibid.* 3:14; 4:4; 5:5.
10. HOSEA 4:15; 5:8; 10:5, cf. v. 8; AMOS 5:5. H. L. Ginsberg, *JBL*, LXXX (1961), p. 343, n. 0, has happily translated "delusionville."
11. GEN. 12:8; 13:3f.
12. See O. Eissfeldt, *AR*, XXVIII (1930), pp. 1–30; J. Philip Hyatt, *JAOS*, LIX (1939), pp. 81–98; Albright, *ARI*, pp. 168–75.
13. See Kaufmann, *RI*, p. 259.
14. The word *sullām* occurs only here. On its connection with the ziqqurat, see Jastrow, *RBBA*, p. 290, n. 1.

1 5. See above, p. 70.
1 6. G E N . 28:10f.
1 7. It is worth considering whether Jacob's vow does not conform to the *šalmu balṭu* type, on which see R. Harris, *JCS*, XIV (1960), p. 134ff.
1 8. G E N . 28:21f.
1 9. *Ibid.* 35:7
2 0. *Ibid.* 28:13
2 1. *Ibid.* 35:2f.
2 2. Cf. above, p. 69f.
2 3. G E N . 35:1.
2 4. *Ibid.* 28:18.
2 5. *Ibid.* 29:1ff. Cf. the laws of Eshnunna, *ANET*, p. 162, §25.
2 6. See above, p. 87.
2 7. G E N . 29:23–25. See above, p. 184.
2 8. On adoption, see above, p. 122f. On Laban's relationships with Jacob, see C. H. Gordon, *BA*, III (1940), pp. 5ff.; R. de Vaux, *RB*, LVI (1949), p. 33f.
2 9. G E N . 31:1; cf. v. 41.
3 0. Gordon, *op. cit.*, p. 5; *ANET*, p. 219f.
3 1. See *ANET*, p. 220.
3 2. G E N . 29:26, 29.
3 3. See above, p. 127ff.
3 4. G E N . chaps. 29–30; 35:16–18.
3 5. It has become widely accepted that the twelve tribes of Israel constituted an amphictiony, or tribal league centered upon a central shrine, after the manner of the Greeks; see M. Noth, *Das System; The History of Israel*, pp. 85ff. See, however, the searching criticisms of H. M. Orlinsky, *OA*, I (1962), pp. 11–20; cf., also, Y. Kaufmann, *Joshua*, p. 55f.
3 6. E X O D . 6:16–20.
3 7. N U M . 3:39.
3 8. G E N . 50:23.
3 9. N U M . 32:39.
4 0. *Ibid.* 1:36f.
4 1. G E N . 13:5f.
4 2. *Ibid.* 14:14; cf. 17:23.
4 3. *Ibid.* 32:8, 14ff.
4 4. E X O D . 6:14.
4 5. On this characteristic of biblical thinking, see J. Pedersen, *Israel*, I–II, p. 277f.; cf. H. Wheeler Robinson in *Werden u. Wesen*, pp. 49–62.
4 6. See de Vaux, *AI*, pp. 4ff., who points out that the construction of genealogies also characterized the early days of Islam.
4 7. Pointed out to me by Professor H. L. Ginsberg.
4 8. G E N . 10.
4 9. Cf. Pedersen, *op. cit.*, I–II, p. 257f.
5 0. G E N . 22:20–24.
5 1. See *SpG*, p. 167f.
5 2. G E N . 36:9ff., 40ff.
5 3. N U M . 25:15.

5 4. GEN. 17:20; 25:13-15.
5 5. *Ibid.* 22:20-24.
5 6. See A. Malamat in *EBH,* IV, col. 573f.; *JAOS,* LXXXII (1962), pp. 143-150.
5 7. GEN. 31.
5 8. On foreign slaves in Nuzi, see J. Lewy, *HUCA,* XIV (1939), pp. 611ff.; *ibid.,* XV (1940), pp. 47ff.; Gordon, *op. cit.,* p. 7.
5 9. GEN. 34:12; EXOD. 22:15; I SAM. 18:25.
6 0. Cf. *AASOR,* X (1930), p. 64, no. 31, ll. 14f. See M. Burrows, *JAOS,* LVII (1937), pp. 259-76.
6 1. GEN. 31:19.
6 2. *Ibid.* 31:6.
6 3. *ANET,* p. 219f.
6 4. The idea that possession of the household gods was in some way connected with the legality of title to the inheritance has found widespread acceptance; see the sources cited by M. Greenberg, *JBL,* LXXXI (1962), p. 240f. However, Greenberg has cast serious doubt on the validity of this interpretation *(ibid.* pp. 239-248). Note the cautious view of C. H. Gordon, *BA,* III (1940), p. 6; *The Ancient Near East,* p. 129. See, also H. M. Gevaryahu, *Beth Mikra,* XV-XVI (1962), pp. 81-86.
6 5. GEN. 31:32.
6 6. See D. Daube, *Studies in Biblical Law,* pp. 205, 207.
6 7. GEN. 21:30, 32.
6 8. *Ibid.* v. 37.
6 9. Albright, *ARI,* p. 207, n. 63, suggests a meaning "old rags;" cf. *FSAC,* p. 311, "vile things." L. Koehler and W. Baumgartner, *Lexicon in Veteris Testamenti Libros,* p. 1041, suppose a root *trf,* meaning "to perish," "act ignominiously." See, however, E. Ben Yehuda, *Thesaurus,* pp. 7918-7922, esp. p. 7921, n. 4. For the obviously odious connotation, cf. II KINGS 23:24.
7 0. GEN. 31:34f. See *VRG, ad loc.*
7 1. LEV. 15:19-24.
7 2. GEN. 31:39.
7 3. See *ANET,* p. 177, §§ 264-7; Driver and Miles, I, pp. 453-66; II, p. 91; R. de Vaux, *RB,* LVI (1949), p. 33. cf., however, *ANET,* p. 218ᶜ.
7 4. GEN. 31:50.
7 5. See I. Mendelsohn, in J. L. Blau, ed., *Essays on Jewish Life,* pp. 351-57.
7 6. *ANET,* p. 220.
7 7. *AASOR,* XVI (1936), p. 105, No. 55, ll. 29-30.
7 8. See F. Van Trigt, *OS,* XII (1958), pp. 280-309, J. L. McKenzie, *CBQ,* XXV (1963), pp. 71-76.
7 9. See *SkG,* p. 405; F. Van Trigt, *op. cit.*
8 0. GEN. 32:1-33.
8 1. For the parallels, see Frazer, *Folklore,* II, pp. 410-425; *GuG,* pp. 364ff.
8 2. Cf. PSS. 8:6; 97:7.
8 3. GEN. 18:2, 16, 22; 19:5, 8, 10, 12, 15.
8 4. JUD. 13:3-22.
8 5. For a comprehensive review, see J. S. Licht, in *EBH,* IV, col. 975-990; T. H. Gaster in *IDB,* I, pp. 128-134; Kaufmann, *Toldot,* II, pp. 423-429.
8 6. See Frazer, *op. cit.,* p. 423.

8 7. See W. Robertson Smith, *The Religion of the Semites,* p. 380, n. 1.

8 8. See Kaufmann, *Toldot,* I, p. 545; *RI,* p. 105f.

8 9. See above, p. 129f.

9 0. Cf. G E N . 27:36; J E R . 9:3; H O S . 12:4.

9 1. On the name Israel, See G. A. Dannel, *Studies in the Name Israel;* B.-Z. Dinur, *OLD,* pp. 114–41.

9 2. N U M . 21:24.

CHAPTER XIII

Joseph

GENESIS 37–50

Apart from the Judah and Tamar episode,[1] and Jacob's farewell blessing,[2] the rest of the Book of Genesis is devoted to the story of Joseph.
In numerous ways this section differs markedly from the preceding
patriarchal biographies.[3] It is by far the longest and most complete
account, and although an interweaving of traditions is discernible,[4] it is
not a collection of isolated incidents. There is an unparalleled continuity of narrative set forth with the consummate skill of a master
story-teller who employs to the full the novelistic techniques of character
delineation, psychological treatment, the play upon the emotions and
the cultivation of suspense.

Unique, too, is the somewhat secular mold in which the biography
is cast. The miraculous or supernatural element is conspicuously absent.
With the apparent exception of a single incident which involves Jacob,[5]
not Joseph, there are no divine revelations, no altars, no cultic associations. God never intervenes openly and directly in Joseph's life as He
does with Abraham, Isaac and Jacob.

On the one hand, there is an unusual lack of specifics. Other than the vague "land of Goshen," there are no place names, and nowhere do we learn the name of the pharaoh. On the other hand, the Joseph biography is distinguished by a wealth of background material, detailing the customs, practices and conditions of a non-Israelite people—matters outside the scope of interest of Scripture in the preceding patriarchal stories. This phenomenon may probably be accounted for by the fact that the descent of the children of Israel to Egypt was an event heavy with destiny, for it was the indispensable prelude to the drama of oppression and redemption which is the over-riding motif of biblical theology.

Yet this experience, which the Bible presents as having been fraught with eternal spiritual significance, was the culmination of a chain of events set in motion by initial causes which were temporal, petty, sordid and mundane in the extreme. A father's favoritism, tittle-tattle, sibling jealousies, egotistic boyish dreams—all the unlovely elements of a family situation containing the infallible ingredients of explosive tragedy —such was the raw material which Providence was to shape to its own purposes.

"A coat of many colors"

The narrative opens with a picture of the seventeen-year-old Joseph who commands none of our sympathies. The "bad reports" of his brothers which Joseph brings to his father were certainly not calculated to endear him to them;[6] nor was the garment which Jacob presented him likely to ameliorate the brothers' antipathy. Its precise nature eludes us, it being variously but uncertainly explained as "a coat of many colors," "a long-sleeved robe," "an ornamented tunic"; there is no doubt, however, that it was a token of special favor and perhaps, too, of luxury and lordship.[7] In a later age it was the distinctive dress of the virgin daughters of royalty.[8] At any rate, to the brothers the coat was a hated symbol of favoritism and a cause of discord.

The dreams

Even more potent a source of disharmony were Joseph's dreams. The strong feelings they aroused must be understood against the background of the times. Throughout the biblical world, dreams were recognized as vehicles of divine communication. Several instances of this have already been encountered. God revealed His will in dreams to Abimelech, King of Gerar,[9] to Jacob[10] and to Laban.[11] In each experience the theophany is straightforward and the message perfectly clear. This is not the case with Joseph's dreams,[12] nor with those of the butler and the baker[13] and Pharaoh.[14] Here, the symbol, not the words, is the language of intelligence, and the dream is therefore enigmatic.[15]

Against this background, it is not to be wondered at that dreams are frequently productive of anxiety. To be ignorant of the true meaning is to be deprived of knowledge that might well be vital to one's welfare. Notice how in each of the cryptic dreams God does not figure explicitly in the content. Yet it is tacitly accepted that He is the ultimate source of the message being conveyed. This does not mean that the ancients did not recognize such a thing as an idle dream. They did; and that is why dreams in the Joseph biography always come in pairs, to prove their seriousness.[16]

In the two great centers of Near Eastern civilization, Egypt and Mesopotamia, at either extremity of the Fertile Crescent, the science of dream interpretation was highly developed as a specialized skill, and a vast literature devoted to the subject came into being.[17] One extant Egyptian papyrus, inscribed about 1300 B.C.E. and claiming to be a copy of an archetype at least five hundred years older, is actually a reference book of dream interpretations arranged systematically according to symbol and meaning.[18] We are told, for example, that seeing a large cat in a dream is good, for it portends a large harvest. Looking into a deep well, on the other hand, is bad, for it is premonitory of incarceration.

The accepted predictive aspect of dreams was cause enough for the brothers to take Joseph seriously. But insofar as a dream was recognized to be inseparable from personality, it meant also that the dreamer somehow bore a measure of responsibility for his dreams. Joseph's visions of lordship, therefore, betrayed his true aspirations and contained, at the same time, the potentiality of fulfillment. That is why they could arouse hostility so intense as to culminate in a conspiracy to murder.[19]

The sale into slavery

The opportunity for mischief arose when Joseph was sent by his father to visit his brothers who had driven the sheep far from home in search of pasture. The road led from Hebron to Shechem and on to Dothan, where Joseph finally caught up with his brothers. This route corresponds exactly to the ancient north-south road west of the Jordan which traversed the central hill country the entire length of the Palestinian watershed.[20] Each of the cities mentioned was an important town along this road. Dothan, in the Valley of Jezreel, has been excavated since 1953 and is known to have existed as early as 3000 B.C.E[21]

It was here at Dothan that the brothers stripped Joseph of his tunic, threw him into a pit and then sold him into slavery[22] to wandering caravan traders,[23] alternately called Ishmaelites[24] and Midianites.[25] The variation may well be due to an interweaving of different traditions. It is also possible that "Ishmaelite" is here not used as an ethnic designation, but simply as an appellative for nomadic merchants. Support for this may be found elsewhere in the Bible where, in a parenthetic note explaining why Midianites possessed golden earrings, we are told that it was "because they were Ishmaelites" (J U D . 8:24). The traders, whoever they were, brought Joseph down to Egypt and sold him in the slave market.

The chief source for the supply of slaves in Egypt was war with foreign countries. Peaceful slave-trafficking was also well established and both Syria and Palestine fed the market.[26] Two documents from Egyptian sources well illustrate this particular type of commerce in human misery. One is the last will and testament of King Amen-em-het III (end of the nineteenth century B.C.E.) in which he disposes of four Asiatic slaves, received as a gift from his brother.[27] Far more interesting is a papyrus from ca. 1740 B.C.E., a section of which is an inventory of servants on an estate.[28] Of the 95 slaves listed by name, 37 are Semitic. In each case, the name is preceded by a note "male/female Asiatic." The women are employed as weavers, the men and children work as domestics, cooks, brewers and warehouse-keepers. Whereas the adults have retained their Semitic names, those of the children are already Egyptianized. These slaves are not prisoners-of-war, for the inventory derives from an age of no military activity in Palestine and Syria, and when commercial intercourse between these two countries and Egypt is well attested. The sale of Joseph into Egyptian slavery thus accords well with what is known about the importation of slaves from Palestine.

In Potiphar's house

The caravan traders disposed of Joseph to a certain Potiphar, a courtier and chief steward of Pharaoh himself.[29] The name of Joseph's master is all but identical with that of his future father-in-law Potiphera,[30] and has possibly been deliberately abbreviated in order to distinguish the one from the other. The name itself has now been duplicated in Egyptian sources in the form of *Pa-di-pa-re* meaning, "He whom Re (the sun-god) has given." Personal names compounded of *Pa-di* and a divine appellation are very common in the Egyptian onomasticon.[31]

The description "chief steward," literally "chief cook," appended to Potiphar would correspond to the Egyptian title *wdpw* which originally also meant "cook," but which came to be a general designation for people attached to the services of nobles, princes and kings.[32]

Unfortunately, the name of the pharaoh for whom Potiphar worked is not given, an omission that greatly complicates the chronological problem. The title "Pharaoh" originally was a composite of two words, *per-aa,* meaning, "the great house," and referring to the royal palace. It was not until the fifteenth century B.C.E. that it came into use as signifying the king.[33] This extension of usage, a typical instance of metonymy, has its parallel in the English reference to the king as "the Crown."

Joseph won the confidence of his master by his diligence and administrative abilities and soon found himself promoted to be Potiphar's personal attendant and overseer of the entire estate.[34] This function conforms to that frequently encountered in Egyptian texts as *mer-per,* or comptroller.[35]

The authentic Egyptian coloration of the Joseph biography, apparent in a variety of numerous details, finds its strongest expression in the story of the unsuccessful attempt by Potiphar's wife to seduce Joseph.[36] The motif of a married woman making improper proposals to one who rejects her, and then protecting herself by accusing the man of having attempted her dishonor, is not uncommon in world literature.[37] One is reminded of the Greek tales of Bellerophon and Antcia, and of Hippolytus and Phaedra, as well as of similar stories in the Arabian Nights and the Decameron. But since the "Tale of Two Brothers" is easily the oldest version of all, and since it originated on Egyptian soil, it is clearly of special interest to the study of the Joseph narrative. The earliest manuscript is dated 1225 B.C.E., but it is evident to Egyptologists that the story had a long history antedating by far the particular papyrus that has been preserved.[38]

The Egyptian story tells of two brothers, Anubis and Bata, who lived together. Anubis was married, Bata was a bachelor. One day, when the former was not at home, his wife tried to seduce Bata who virtuously

rejected her advances. Knowing well her fate should her husband discover the truth, the guilty wife anticipated events by slandering the
hapless Bata who was forced to make a hasty flight from the murderous
intentions of Anubis who followed in hot pursuit. Bata succeeded,
finally, in convincing his brother of his innocence, and Anubis returned
home, slew his wife and threw her body into the river.

It is very unlikely that this particular story was the direct source of the
tale about Joseph and Potiphar's wife. However, as an Egyptian literary
theme, it may well have influenced the artistic form in which the biblical
story has been recorded. A contrasting analysis of the two stories will
help clarify the distinctive biblical presentation and make manifest the
spirit which animated it.

The "Tale of Two Brothers" is a genre of literature intended for
purely idle entertainment. It is adorned with several mythological elements such as talking cows, the miraculous appearance of a river, the
resurrection of the dead, and many others. A particularly repulsive item
is the self-mutilation of Bata who casts his dismembered limb into the
river where it is swallowed by a fish.[39] All these aspects of the Egyptian
story find no echo in the biblical narrative.

Another basic difference is the scriptural silence about the fate of
the temptress, usually a prominent element in this type of literature.
The reason for this disinterest is that our story was not intended for
entertainment purposes and was not told for its own sake. The focus of
attention is upon Joseph's reaction and upon the incident as a causative
link in the chain of events leading to Joseph's subsequent rise to power,
his reconciliation with his brothers and their settlement in Egypt. The
picture of Joseph as it emerges from the pages of this biblical narrative
is far different from that of Joseph back in his father's home. So skill-
fully has our story been set forth, that in our sympathy and admiration
for the hero's nobility of character we have forgotten those displeasing
traits that alienated us at the outset. Joseph is now the unconscious
instrument of God's providence and his behavior in the face of temptation demonstrated his worthiness for the role. The moral excellence
of the young man can be appreciated all the more if it can be remembered
that he was a slave and that sexual promiscuity was a perennial feature
of all slave societies. Moreover, the ambitious Joseph might well have
considered that the importuning wife of his master had presented him
with a rare opportunity, worth exploiting, to advance his personal and
selfish interests.

Probably nothing is more indicative of the wide chasm separating Israel from its neighbors than the line of argument used by Joseph in rejecting the repeated entreaties of the would-be adultress. Speaking to a pagan woman, he says that his submission would be both a violation of the confidence placed in him by his master, and a sin against God.[40] This conforms to the general biblical view, noted already many times, that the moral law has universal application, equally binding upon all humanity. At the same time, this plea of Joseph expresses another distinctive biblical concept of morality. Adultery is a sin against God. It is not a matter of social impropriety or breach of convention, not just an indignity to the husband or an outrage upon society. It is a religious offense in which God is vitally involved. In other words, the sanction of morality is divine, not social, and for this reason morality is absolute and not relative.

It will doubtless be remembered that the same idea was expressed by Abraham when he feared the violation of his wife at the hands of the men of Gerar.

"I thought," said Abraham, "surely there is no fear of God in this place, and they will kill me because of my wife."
(20 : 11)

This concept of morality as God-given, rather than utilitarian, suffuses the Torah legislation and explains a fundamental difference in its treatment of adultery from that of the ancient law codes of the Near East. In the latter, the guilty parties are regarded as having committed an affront to the husband who, for that reason, is accorded the power to determine the punishment. The Torah,[41] however, regarding the breach of morality as a sin against God, departs radically from Near Eastern custom and makes no such provision for the husband to exercise his discretion.[42]

The interpretation of dreams

Why Potiphar chose to incarcerate Joseph instead of executing him, as might have been expected, we can never know. Being an officer of the court, Potiphar put Joseph among the royal prisoners in what is eight times referred to in our Hebrew text as the *bet ha-Sohar*. This term is nowhere else to be found in the Bible and may well be of Egyptian origin.

If it be Hebrew, then since the basic root may possibly carry with it the idea of roundness, it may well refer to a house of detention within a fortress in which royal prisoners were confined. We do know from Egyptian texts that such, indeed, was the practice.[43]

In prison, Joseph's winsome personality and transparent integrity soon won him the confidence and favor of the chief jailer. This allowed Joseph to come into contact with royal prisoners, the chief cupbearer and the chief baker. The former held an important office in the court of Pharaoh, and was actually a trusted advisor of the king. In a document from the time of Rameses III (12th century) we even find butlers sitting as judges. The office of chief baker is interesting in the light of what is known of Egyptian gastronomy. No less than fifty-seven varieties of bread and thirty-eight different types of cake are attested in the texts. The baker is reflecting native epicurean propensity when he dreams of baskets containing "all kinds of food that a baker prepares" (40:17).[44]

The same careful attention to local background is revealed in the narration of Pharaoh's dreams. The river Nile, from which emerged the contrasting types of cows, is called in the Hebrew *ye'or*,[45] a word corresponding to the Egyptian word for river and applied especially to the Nile. It is of some interest to note that this form of the word was in use only from the eighteenth dynasty on (1546–1085). Another Egyptian loanword in our text is *aḥu*,[46] the reed-grass in which the cows were grazing in Pharaoh's dream. The cows, themselves, provide yet another local touch, for they were abundant and important in the Egyptian economy in contrast to sheep which played a very minor role. This is the exact reverse of the situation in Palestine.[47]

Turning now to a different aspect of the dreams, it will doubtless have been observed that whereas the cupbearer, baker and Pharaoh all needed the services of an interpreter to extract meaning from the imagery,[48] Joseph's dreams, although falling into the same symbolic category, were at once comprehensible to the narrator and his brothers. This distinction is more than incidental. Despite the fact that Israel shared with its pagan neighbors a belief in the reality of dreams as a medium of divine communication, it never developed, as in Egypt and Mesopotamia, a class of professional interpreters or a dream literature. In the entire Bible, only two Israelites engage in the interpretation of dreams—Joseph and Daniel—and significantly enough, each serves a pagan monarch, the one in Egypt, the other in Mesopotamia, precisely the lands in which oneiromancy flourished. Moreover, in each case, the Israelite is careful to disclaim any innate ability, attributing all to God.[49] Nor does skill at dream interpretation play any part in the definition of biblical wisdom or the equipment of prophet and sage.[50]

The seven year famine

A very common motif in ancient Near Eastern literature is the seven year cycle during which nature is dormant and unproductive and famine stalks the land.[51] In unraveling the symbolism of Pharaoh's dreams, Joseph finds a premonition of just such a seven year famine.[52] A late Egyptian text dealing with the reign of King Djoser (ca. twenty-eighth century B.C.E.) well illustrates the setting. It reads:

> I was in distress on the Great Throne, and those who are in the palace were in heart's affliction from a very great evil, since the Nile had not come in my time for a space of seven years. Grain was scant, fruits were dried up, and everything which they eat was short.[53]

Joseph, who twice had demonstrated successfully his administrative talents,[54] realized that the heaven-sent opportunity of a lifetime had come knocking at his prison gates. This was a situation he exploited to the full, immediately producing a plan of action for the timely storage of surplus grain in anticipation of the lean years ahead. So impressed was Pharaoh with Joseph's discernment and wisdom that he at once adopted the proposals and appointed Joseph to administer them.

Joseph's elevation

The biblical narrative describes Joseph's elevation to high office, his duties and his titles, with an unusual wealth of detail. Scholars are thus in the fortunate and rare position of being enabled to examine this story in the light of the considerable body of accumulated knowledge about the government and court of the Pharaohs.[55]

It is clear at once that Scripture exhibits an extraordinary degree of familiarity with Egyptian customs. The multiplicity of titles and functions assigned to Joseph corresponds fully to the known Egyptian

penchant for the generous distribution of honors and titles to officials
of the great bureaucracy. Some might boast of a dozen or more titles,
some real, some purely ornamental and prestigious. This curiosity has
to be borne in mind together with the fact that the duties and titles assumed by Joseph were not exclusive to the Egyptian Vizierate. We do
not know beyond the shadow of a doubt that Joseph was actually appointed Grand Vizier of Egypt, although he certainly penetrated the
ranks of the highest nobility of the land and was one of the most important officials in the government.[56]

Joseph was placed in charge of the palace,[57] which probably means
that he was given control over the king's personal estates. This would
correspond to the titles "Great Steward of the Lord of the Two Lands,"
"The Great Chief in the Palace." When Pharaoh told Joseph,

> "only with respect to the throne shall I be superior to you,"
>
> (41 : 40)

it meant that he was to report directly to the king. This was a prerogative
shared by several officials, some of whom had such colorful titles as
"Great Favorite of the Lord of the Two Lands," "Foremost among his
courtiers," "Great One in the Palace." Joseph was further placed in
charge of all the land of Egypt,[58] a function that accords with the appellation "Chief of the Entire Land." As a symbol of the delegation of authority, Pharaoh handed Joseph the royal seal.[59] The reference is
certainly to the title "Royal Seal-Bearer," borne by Viziers as well as
other high officials. As to His Majesty putting "the chain of gold" around
his neck, this is a well-known Egyptian symbol of investiture, one of
the highest distinctions the king could bestow.[60] One other title held by
Joseph is also known to us from Egyptian sources. When Joseph dis-
closes his true identity to his brothers, he describes himself, among other
things, as "father to Pharaoh."[61] This is the equivalent of an Egyptian
title "God's Father," in which "God" refers to the living king.[62]

Joseph's chief task was to lay up an adequate store of food during
the years of plenty and to be responsible for its distribution during the
years of famine. It is one of those strange quirks of history that the shepherd boy, a member of a semi-nomadic clan, should become Secretary
of Agriculture, and perhaps Joseph's first dream, dealing with binding
sheaves in the field,[63] contained a hint of his future vocation. At any
rate, it is certain that he assumed one of the well-known Egyptian titles,
"Overseer of the Granaries of the Upper and Lower Egypt." The holder

of this office was also responsible for the collection of tax payments on field produce, which is precisely one of the functions that Joseph performed.[64]

Not so simple is the change of Joseph's name to Zaphenath-paneah.[65] This is indeed in conformity with the tendency of Asiatics in Egypt to adopt Egyptian names. The inventory of Semitic slaves referred to above clearly illustrates this process.[66] Further, Joseph's new name is good Egyptian and means, "the god has spoken and he (the bearer of the name) shall live." The difficulty is, however, that this type of name does not appear in Egyptian sources before the twelfth century B.C.E., long after the Exodus period.[67] The same problem exists in relation to the name Asenath, borne by Joseph's wife.[68] It means, "she belongs to (the goddess) Neith." The name itself has not yet been found, but the type was current from the eighth century B.C.E.[69] Here, again, we shall have to await further evidence before deciding finally upon the critical implications of this data.

Joseph married into the elite of the nobility. His father-in-law was none other than Poti-phera, High Priest of On.[70] This city was the great cultic center of the sun-god, Re. Hence, it was variously known as "the House of Re," "Beth Shemesh" in Hebrew[71] and Heliopolis in Greek. The word On is a Hebraized form of an Egyptian word *Iwnw*, which means "a column," the name of the city deriving from its most outstanding architectural features, columns and colonnades.[72] The High Priest of On held the exalted title, "Greatest of Seers," and it is quite appropriate that he should have been called Potiphera meaning, as previously explained, "He whom Re has given."

The question might well be raised as to whether a foreigner could really have risen to such high office in the Egyptian government. This problem can be answered with an emphatic affirmative. From the time of the famous king Akhnaton (ca. 1370–1353 B.C.E.) we know of a Semite named Yanhamu who was Egyptian commissioner for Palestine and Syria. Under Merneptah (ca. 1224–1214 B.C.E.) a certain Ben-Ozen, who came from a place situated east of Lake Tiberius, rose to become the royal herald or marshal at the court, and received two Egyptian names from the king, while a brother of Merneptah had been given in marriage by his father Ramses II (ca. 1290–1224) to the daughter of a Syrian sea-captain named Ben-Anath. It was not at all extraordinary for foreigners, and Semites in particular, to be welcomed by the court and to rise to positions of responsibility and power in the government.[73]

Attention must now be drawn to two tendencies that our narrative has very delicately opposed one against the other.[74] On the one hand, the foreign origins of Joseph are constantly emphasized. The Egyptians with whom he comes in contact are always aware of them. Potiphar's wife sneeringly calls him "a Hebrew,"[75] Joseph tells the cupbearer that he was kidnapped "from the land of the Hebrews" (40:15),[76] the cup-bearer describes Joseph to Pharaoh as "a Hebrew youth" (41:12); the Egyptians did not eat with Joseph because their particularistic religion forbade them to dine with Hebrews. Against this external counter-pressure to assimilation is opposed an inner drive towards Egyptianiza-tion on the part of Joseph. His outer garb, his changed name, his marriage to a daughter of the High Priest of Re, and his mastery of the Egyptian language[77] were all calculated to make him outwardly indistinguishable from his fellow Egyptians, and although they could not accept Joseph whole-heartedly as their equal, he was yet, apparently, so thoroughly satisfied with his situation that he preferred not to be reminded of his past. He expresses this most clearly in the names he gives to his two sons.

> Joseph named the first-born Manasseh, meaning, "God has made me forget completely my hardship and my parental home." And the second he named Ephraim, meaning, "God has made me fertile in the land of my affliction." (41 : 51f.)

It is just when this point has been reached that Joseph's brothers appear once again on the scene.

The reconciliation

The biblical spotlight, focused so far almost exclusively upon Joseph, now shifts, or rather widens, its beam to encompass the rest of the family as well. The custom of the semi-nomads of Canaan and East Jordan to descend to Egypt in search of food and pasture has previously been noted in connection with the peregrinations of Abraham. We cited there a report of an Egyptian frontier official recording the passage of Edomite shepherds into the Delta pasturage.[78] The fact that the official was em-powered to grant permission in such cases without having to consult

higher authority shows that the expedition of Joseph's brothers to Egypt
was nothing extraordinary.[79]

The main interest of the narrative is now in the complex human situation, the fulfillment in life of Joseph's boyhood dreams, the interplay
of emotions, the testing of the brothers' honesty and sense of fraternal
love and responsibility. Joseph forces his brothers into a position in
which they have no option but to appear once again before him together
with his own dear Benjamin. The climax of the drama is at hand. Joseph
carefully contrives a desperate situation in which the brothers are com-
pelled to show, once and for all, whether they have reformed since the
day they so brutally sold him into slavery. Benjamin is accused of stealing
Joseph's divining-goblet,[80] the sacredness of which object makes the
crime all the more heinous.[81] Divination by means of pouring liquid
into a cup was widely practiced all over the ancient world;[82] it is interesting that it should appear in the Bible specifically in a story in which the
setting is pagan and in which the practitioner passes himself off as an
Egyptian.[83]

Needless to say, the brothers measure up to the highest ideal of integrity. Judah's eloquence, full of pathos and passion, leads to the denoue-
ment, and Joseph reveals his true identity to his dumbfounded brothers.[84] From then on the action moves swiftly. The brothers return to
Canaan to bring their father the incredible news and to make prepa-
rations for the entire clan to settle in Egypt, at least while the famine still
lasts.[85]

The settlement in Goshen

The temporary nature of the Egyptian settlement is repeatedly emphasized in the biblical sources. Jacob's initial reaction to the suggestion
of visiting his son makes this perfectly clear.

> "My son Joseph is still alive! I must go and see him before
> I die."   (45 : 28)

Passing through Beer-sheba, Jacob receives a vision in which God seeks
to dispel the patriarch's hesitation and fears, and assures him that Israel
would return.

> "Fear not to go down to Egypt, for there I will make you a
> great nation. I Myself will go down with you to Egypt, and
> I Myself will also bring you back."   (46 : 3–4)

This divine communication serves the purpose of transforming the descent to Egypt from a family visit into an event of national significance,
which has its preordained place in God's scheme of things. The promise
to "bring you back" obviously does not apply to Jacob personally. The
"you" here is the people of Israel of which the patriarch is the personification.

The area of Israelite settlement in Egypt is known by the name of
Goshen in the biblical texts. Joseph suggested the district because of its
proximity to his own residence[86] and its excellent grazing facilities.[87]
It must have been located in the northeastern part of the Delta, because it
was to Goshen that Joseph went to meet his father coming from
Canaan.[88] This is the same general area in which those Edomite
shepherds were given permission to pasture their sheep on Egyptian
soil.[89] Since Goshen was easily accessible from the royal palace,[90] it
means that the capital of Egypt at that time must have been in the Delta
region. Of all the known capitals of Egypt, Avaris, alone, fits this description. Now Avaris is the same as Tanis, called in Hebrew, Zoan. It was
founded about the year 1725 B.C.E. by the Hyksos invaders who made
it their capital. In the time of Ramses II (ca. 1290–1224) it was known
as Per-Ramses. It is interesting that Goshen is described as the "Land
of Ramses,"[91] and while the name must here be an anachronism it helps
to identify Avaris (or Tanis) as the capital in the time of Joseph. This
identification is clinched by a tradition mentioned in the Book of
Psalms,[92] designating the area of Israelite settlement in Egypt as "the
plain of Zoan (Tanis)."[93]

This fact makes it highly likely that the descent of Jacob and his clan
to Egypt was connected in some way with the period of the Hyksos
domination. This term means, literally, "foreign rulers" and applies to
that ethnic amalgam, of which northwestern Semites constituted the
predominant element, that migrated to Egypt via Canaan in the second
half of the eighteenth century. By the year 1700 B.C.E. they had succeeded
in consolidating their hold over lower Egypt, and for the next one
hundred and fifty years until their expulsion ca. 1550, they presided
over an empire that covered the entire western half of the Fertile Crescent.

It was the Hyksos who first introduced the horse and chariot into Egypt. Joseph could not, therefore, have ridden around the country "in the chariot of the second-in-command" (41:43) before the Hyksos invasion. Nor could his capital city have been situated in the Nile Delta before this time.

The data given in the Book of Exodus confirm that the land of Goshen was quite near the frontier, and that "a mixed multitude" of non-Egyptians also resided there.[94] At the same time, since sheep-rearing was an unpopular occupation few Egyptians apparently occupied the region.[95] In other words, throughout the Israelite sojourn in Egypt, two factors were at work which tended to minimize the impact of Egyptian life, culture and religion upon the people. The first was ideological, the belief that the Egyptian episode was to be of limited duration and that the occupation of the promised land was the fulfillment of Israel's aspirations. The second was geographical, the actual physical isolation from the mainstream of Egyptian life. These factors go a long way towards explaining why, of all the cultures that left their impress upon the Bible, that of Egypt was the least prominent.[96] They also help to elucidate how Israel was able to maintain its national cohesion, its language and traditions throughout the years of Egyptian bondage.

The nationalization of land

The reconciliation of Joseph with his family having been effected, and the settlement of the tribes in the land of Goshen completed, the narrative turns its attention, once again, to the doings of Joseph.

One of the aspects of the Egyptian economy that struck the Hebrew writer as being most remarkable, apparently, was the concentration of landownership and other property in the hands of the state.[97] This, in fact, is the situation that prevailed after the expulsion of the Hyksos in the middle of the sixteenth century B.C.E. But it must have taken place quite gradually and over the life times of more than one pharaoh. Its attribution to Joseph is probably intended to emphasize the great benefits his administration bestowed upon the regime and to point up the base ingratitude, therefore, of the later pharaohs "who did not know Joseph" (E X O D . 1:8). At any rate, the story betrays, once again, an intimate knowledge of Egyptian affairs.[98]

The same is true of the report that the priests were exempted from the nationalization laws.[99] The temples, alone, after the reorganization of the country attendant upon the successful anti-Hyksos revolution, possessed free landed property.[100]

The death of Jacob and Joseph

Apart from these meager details about Joseph's career, nothing more is known about the lives of Jacob and his family in the land of Egypt. The seventeen years that Jacob sojourned there[101] are shrouded in silence, as are the fifty-four years by which Joseph outlived his father.[102] Only the patriarch's farewell blessings to his sons are quoted at length, and the funerary arrangements given in detail.

A touch of local color is added by the mention of the embalming of Jacob, as well as of Joseph after him,[103] the only instances in the Bible of such a peculiarly Egyptian practice. It is well-known that mummification, with all its elaborate ritual, played an important role in the cult of the dead. It had a distinctly religious connotation and was connected with the belief in survival after death, a belief in immortality which the Egyptians were incapable of dissociating from the notion of the physical survival of the body.[104] This being the case, it is all the more worthy of note that the embalming of Jacob and Joseph has no religious setting, but seems to have been a purely practical measure. Since Jacob was to be buried far from the place of his death,[105] and Joseph hundreds of years later,[106] the preservation of the corpse was desirable.

Another item of interest to Egyptologists is the age of Joseph at his death, for one hundred and ten years was considered to be the ideal life-span in ancient Egypt. This notion is exemplified by the words of one vizier who writes:

> What I have done on earth is not inconsiderable. I attained
> one hundred and ten years of life.[107]

So far, no less than twenty-seven such references to this ideal age limit have been noted in Egyptian texts.[108]

The contrast between Jacob's state funeral and his burial in the ancestral vault at Machpelah, and the quiet burial of Joseph in Egypt is most striking. One can sense the deterioration in the situation of the

Israelites that had taken place in the intervening fifty-four years. Both Jacob and Joseph die with the divine promise of redemption on their lips.[109] The patriarchal period thus opens[110] and closes on the same note. The formative period in Israel's history is over and the great national drama is about to unfold.

> "God will surely take notice of you and bring you up from this land to the land which he promised on oath to Abraham, to Isaac and to Jacob." (50 : 24)

1. GEN. 38.
2. *Ibid.* 49.
3. See G. von Rad, *VT,* (Supplement), Vol. I (1953), pp. 120ff.
4. Assigned mainly to J and E, with an admixture of P.
5. GEN. 46:1ff.
6. *Ibid.* 37:2f.
7. On this, see *SpG,* p. 289f.
8. II SAM. 13:18.
9. GEN. 20:3.
1 0. *Ibid.* 28:12ff.; 31:11.
1 1. *Ibid.* 31:24.
1 2. *Ibid.* 37:5-10.
1 3. *Ibid.* 40:5ff.
1 4. *Ibid.* 41:1ff.
1 5. On the subject of dreams in the Bible and Near East, see J. Pedersen, *Israel,* I-II, pp. 134-140; E. L. Ehrlich, *Der Traum im A. T.;* A. Leo Oppenheim, *The Interpretation of Dreams in the ANE;* W. Richter, *BZ,* VII (1963), pp. 202-220.
1 6. C. H. Gordon, *Before the Bible,* p. 64, compares the way Gilgamesh is informed of Enkidu's arrival *(ANET,* p. 76, cf. p. 83).

1 7. See above n. 15. On Egyptian dream literature, see J. M. Janssen, *JEOL*, V (14), (1959), pp. 63–66; Vergote, pp. 48–52; Montet, pp. 75ff.

1 8. *ANET*, p. 495.

1 9. GEN. 37:5–20.

2 0. See D. Baly, *The Geography of the Bible*, p. 112; S. Yeivin, *MTYA*, p. 19.

2 1. See J. Finegan, *Light From the Ancient Past*, p. 147f.

2 2. On the price of 20 shekels obtained for Joseph (GEN. 37:28), see I. Mendelsohn, *Slavery in the ANE*, p. 117.

2 3. On the caravan traders, see Vergote, pp. 10ff.; Janssen, *op. cit.*, pp. 63–72. For the important role that the products mentioned in GEN. 37:25 played in the economy of Egypt, see Vergote, *loc. cit.*

2 4. *Ibid.* 37:25, 27f.; 39:1.

2 5. *Ibid.* 37:28, 36.

2 6. See Vergote, pp. 16–20; Janssen, *op. cit.*, p. 64.

2 7. *ANET*, p. 229.

2 8. See W. K. Simpson, *JAOS*, LXXIII (1953), p. 87; W. F. Albright, *JAOS*, LXXIV (1954), pp. 222–33; Hayes, *Papyrus*; G. Posener, *Syria*, XXXIV (1957), pp. 145–63; Montet, p. 18f.

2 9. GEN. 37:36; 39:1.

3 0. *Ibid.* 41:45.

3 1. On the name, see Vergote, pp. 146ff.; Montet, p. 22. It has been found on a stela which cannot be dated before the XXIst dynasty (1085–945); see Janssen, *op. cit.*, p. 67f.

3 2. See Vergote, pp. 31ff.

3 3. See T. O. Lambdin, *JAOS*, LXXIII (1953), p. 153; Wilson, *CAE*, p. 102, Vergote, pp. 45ff.

3 4. GEN. 39:4.

3 5. Vergote, p. 24f.

3 6. GEN. 39:7–20.

3 7. See Vergote, pp. 22–25.

3 8. See *ANET*, pp. 23ff.; J. H. Breasted, *The Development of Religion*, pp. 358ff.

3 9. See Albright, *FSAC*, p. 67 and n. 41.

4 0. GEN. 39:8f.

4 1. Cf. LEV. 20:10; DEUT. 22:22.

4 2. See M. Greenberg in *YKJV*, pp. [11]–[13].

4 3. See Vergote, pp. 25ff.

4 4. On the butler and baker, see Vergote, pp. 35–37.

4 5. GEN. 41:1. On *Ye'ōr*, See Lambdin, *op. cit.*, p. 151; Janssen *op. cit.*, p. 68; Montet, p. 51; M. Beroshi in *EBH*, III, col. 413; Ch. Rabin in *EBH*, IV, col. 1076.

4 6. GEN. 41:2. On *Aḥu*, see Lambdin, *op. cit.*, p. 146; Y. Braslavsky and M. Zohari in *EBH*, I, col. 205; Janssen and Rabin. *loci cit.*; Vergote pp. 59ff.

4 7. For the seven cows motif in Egypt, see E. A. Wallis Budge, *The Book of the Dead*, pp. 327, 644f.; Janssen, *op. cit.*, p. 66; Vergote, p. 56f.

4 8. On the Ḥartumim (GEN. 41:8, 24), see Lambdin, *op. cit.*, p. 150f.; M. Beroshi in *EBH*, III, col. 287; Vergote, pp. 67ff., 80–94; Janssen, *op. cit.*, p. 65.

4 9. GEN. 40:8, 16; DAN. 2:19–23, 27f., 30.

5 0. See Kaufmann, *Toldot*, I, pp. 507ff.; *RI*, p. 93f.

5 1. See C. H. Gordon, *Orientalia,* XXII (1953), pp. 79–81; *Before the Bible,* p. 69f.

5 2. G E N . 41:27, 30f.

5 3. *ANET,* p. 31. On this text and its history, see Janssen, *op. cit.,* p. 69. On famine in Egypt, see J. Vandier, *La Famine dans l'Égypte Ancienne;* Montet, pp. 83–39.

5 4. G E N . 39:2f., 22f.

5 5. See *ANET,* pp. 212ff., for a selection of documents relating to the office of Vizier in the fifteenth cent. B.C.E.

5 6. On the Egyptian bureaucracy and Joseph's titles and functions, see W. A. Ward, *JSS,* V (1960), pp. 144–50; Vergote, pp. 98ff.; Janssen, *op. cit.,* p. 66f. It should be noted that Joseph has to seek permission to bury his father in Canaan, and he turns not directly to the king, but to "Pharaoh's court" to lay his appeal before the monarch (G E N . 50:4f.).

5 7. G E N . 41:40; 45:8.

5 8. *Ibid.* 41:41; cf. v. 43; 42:6; 45:8.

5 9. *Ibid.* 41:42. It is not unlikely that the Hebrew *ṭabba'at* has an Egyptian origin; see Lambdin, *op. cit.,* p. 151; Vergote, pp. 116ff.; Ch. Rabin in *EBH,* IV, col. 1077.

6 0. G E N . 41:42. See Vergote, pp. 121–35; T. A. Thompson, *The Bible and Archaeology,* p. 45. No certain etymology has yet been determined for *Abrekh* (G E N . 41:43). For a summary of the principal theories, see Vergote, pp. 135ff., 151.

6 1. G E N . 45:8.

6 2. See Vergote, p. 114f.

6 3. G E N . 37:7.

6 4. *Ibid.* 47:24.

6 5. *Ibid.* 41:45.

6 6. See W. F. Albright, *JAOS,* LXXIV (1954), p. 223.

6 7. For the principal theories as to the origin of the name and its history, see Vergote, pp. 141–146; Janssen, *op. cit.,* p. 67; Montet, p. 22. On the Greek form, see Janssen, *loc. cit.;* W. F. Albright, *BASOR,* 140 (1955), p. 31.

6 8. G E N . 41:45.

6 9. See Vergote, pp. 148ff.; Janssen, *op. cit.,* p. 68.

7 0. G E N . 41:45, 50.

7 1. J E R . 43:13.

7 2. See A. Rowe, *PEQ,* XCIV (1962), pp. 133–142.

7 3. On this subject, see J. H. Breasted, *A History of the Ancient Egyptians,* p. 318; Wilson, *CAE,* p. 258; Montet, p. 21f.; J.M.A. Janssen, *Chronique d'Égypte* XXVI, No. 51 (1951), pp. 50–62. On Yanḥamu, see *ANET,* p. 486; W. F. Albright, *BASOR,* 89 (1943), pp. 7–15; E. F. Campbell, *BA,* XXIII (1960), 16ff.

7 4. See *VRG,* p. 374.

7 5. G E N . 39:14, 17. On this term, see above, p. 115 and the notes thereto.

7 6. On this phrase, see J. M. Grintz, *OLD,* pp. 92–102, in which he maintains that "Hebrew" here is but a translation of the Egyptian term *Sutu.* See, also, above, Chap. VI, n. 21.

7 7. G E N . 42:33.

7 8. See above, p. 102.

7 9. G E N . 42:1–3. For a bas-relief representation of starving foreigners who found

succor from famine in Egypt, see *ANEP*, No. 102, on which see J. M. A. Janssen, *JEOL*, V (14) (1959), p. 69f.

8 0. On this, see L. Y. Rahmani in *EBH*, II, col. 401f.

8 1. See D. Daube, *Studies in Biblical Law*, p. 207.

8 2. See Vergote, pp. 172–76.

8 3. G E N . 44:1–12.

8 4. *Ibid.* v. 13–45:3.

8 5. *Ibid.* 45:9–11.

8 6. *Ibid.* 45:10.

8 7. *Ibid.* 45:10; 46:31–34; 47:6–11. On 46:34, see R. de Vaux, *RB*, LXII (1955), p. 103.

8 8. *Ibid.* 46:29.

8 9. See above, p. 102.

9 0. G E N . 45:10; 47:1f., 5.

9 1. *Ibid.* 47:11.

9 2. P S . 78:12, 43.

9 3. On the identification of Goshen, see Vergote, pp. 183–87; Montet, pp. 15ff.; 53f., 57ff.

9 4. E X O D . 13:17f.; 12:38.

9 5. G E N . 43:34; 47:6. On sheep rearing in Egypt, see Vergote, pp. 188f.

9 6. See Kaufmann, *Toldot*, II, pp. 22f.; *RI*, pp. 220f. For the impact of Egypt on Israel, see W. St. Smith, *JBR*, XIX (1951), pp. 12–15; J. M. A. Janssen, *ATO*, pp. 29–63; Montet; J. A. Wilson, *WHJP*, I, pp. 338–41.

9 7. G E N . 47:13–26.

9 8. See G. Steindorff and K. C. Seele, *When Egypt Ruled the East*, p. 88; Vergote, pp. 190ff.; cf. de Vaux, *AI*, p. 140.

9 9. G E N . 47:22.

1 0 0. Steindorff, *op. cit.*, p. 88; cf. Herodotus, *Histories*, II, § 168.

1 0 1. G E N . 47:28.

1 0 2. This can be simply calculated from the fact that Joseph was 30 when he rose to power (G E N . 41:46), and had lived through 7 years of plenty and 2 years of famine by the time his father arrived in Egypt (*ibid.* 45:6). He was thus 39 at that time, and, hence, 56 when his father died 17 years later (*ibid.* 47:28).

1 0 3. G E N . 50:2, 26.

1 0 4. On embalming and its religious significance, see H. Frankfort, *Ancient Egyptian Religion*, pp. 92f.; Kaufmann, *Toldot*, I, pp. 209f.; Vergote, pp. 197ff.

1 0 5. G E N . 50:13.

1 0 6. *Ibid.* v. 25; E X O D . 13:19; J O S H . 24:32.

1 0 7. *ANET*, p. 414; cf. esp. n. 33.

1 0 8. See J. M. A. Janssen, *OMRO*, XXXI (1950), pp. 33–44; Vergote, pp. 200f.

1 0 9. G E N . 48:3–4, 21; 50:24f.

1 1 0. *Ibid.* 12:2f.

KEY TO ABBREVIATIONS

A A S O R *Annual of the American Schools of Oriental Research*
Adam Cassuto, U., *MeAdam ad Noaḥ*
A I de Vaux, R., *Ancient Israel*
A M B L Bodenheimer, F. S., *Animal and Man in Biblical Lands.*
A M J V *Alexander Marx Jubilee Volume*
A N E P Pritchard, J., ed., *The Ancient Near East in Pictures*
A N E T Pritchard, J., ed., *Ancient Near Eastern Texts Relating to the Old Testament*
A P Albright, W. F., *The Archaeology of Palestine*
A R *Archiv für Religionswissenschaft*
A R I Albright, W. F., *Archaeology and the Religion of Israel*
A T O *L'Ancien Testament et L'Orient*
B A *Biblical Archaeologist*
B A N E Wright, G. E., ed., *The Bible and the Ancient Near East*
B A R Campbell, E. F., ed., *The Biblical Archaeologist Reader*
B A S O R *Bulletin of the American Schools of Oriental Research*
Before Philosophy Frankfort, H., *et al., Before Philosophy*
B G Heidel, A., *The Babylonian Genesis*
B H Kittel, R., *Biblia Hebraica*

Bib. Ar.   Wright, G. E., *Biblical Archaeology*
B J R L   *Bulletin of the John Rylands Library*
B O S   Altmann, A., ed., *Biblical and Other Studies*
Building Inscriptions   Langdon, S., *Building Inscriptions of the Neo-Babylonian Empire*
B W L   Lambert, M., *Babylonian Wisdom Literature*
B Z   *Biblische Zeitschrift*
C A E   Wilson, J. A., *The Culture of Ancient Egypt*
C B Q   *Catholic Biblical Quarterly*
C N I   *Christian News from Israel*
D B S   Pirot, L., et al., *Dictionnaire de la Bible, Supplément*
E B H   *Encyclopaedia Biblica*, [Hebrew]
E Y B H   Aharoni, Y., *Eretz Yisrael Bitqufat HaMiqra*
F A O   Moscati, S., *The Face of the Ancient Orient*
F S A C   Albright, W. F., *From the Stone Age to Christianity*
G S L   Garelli, P., ed., *Gilgamesh et sa Légende*
GuG   Gunkel, H., *Genesis*
H B S   Kramer, S. N., *History Begins at Sumer*
H E H   Braslavsky, J., *HaYada'ta et Ha'Aretz?*
H U C A   *Hebrew Union College Annual*
I D B   *Interpreter's Dictionary of the Bible*
I E J   *Israel Exploration Journal*
J A O S   *Journal of the American Oriental Society*
J B L   *Journal of Biblical Literature*
J B R   *Journal of Bible and Religion*
J C S   *Journal of Cuneiform Studies*
J E I M N   Chiera, E., *Joint Expedition with the Iraq Museum at Nuzi*
J E O L   *Jaarbericht . . . Ex Oriente Lux*
J I A S   *Journal of the Institute of Asiatic Studies*
J N E S   *Journal of Near Eastern Studies*
J Q R   *Jewish Quarterly Review*
J S S   *Journal of Semitic Studies*
L G J V   *Louis Ginzberg Jubilee Volume*
L S   Tur-Sinai, *HaLashon veHaSefer*
M T Y A   Yeivin, S., *Meḥqarim BeToldot Yisrael VeArṣo*
Noah   Cassuto, U., *MeNoaḥ ad Avraham*
O L D   *Oz LeDavid*
O M R O   *Oudheidkundige Mededeelingen uit het Rijksmuseum van Oudheden te Leiden*
O S   *Oudtestamentische Studien*
O T A E   Wright, G. E., *The Old Testament Against its Environment*
O Y S   *Oṣar Yehudei Sepharad*
P E Q   *Palestine Exploration Quarterly*
P R U   Nougayrol, J., *Le Palais Royal D'Ugarit III*
R B   *Revue Biblique*
R B B A   Jastrow, M., *Religious Belief in Babylonia and Assyria*
R I   Kaufmann, Y., *The Religion of Israel*
R I S A   Barton, G.A., *Royal Inscriptions of Sumer and Akkad*

S A T   Forbes, R, J., *Studies in Ancient Technology*
S B O   *Studia Biblica et Orientia*
Schorr   Ginzberg, L., ed., *Studies in Memory of Moses Schorr*
S O L   *Studi Orientalistici in Onore di Giorgio Levi Della Vida*
S J A   *Southwestern Journal of Anthropology*
S K G   Skinner, J., *Critical and Exegetical Commentary on Genesis*
S M   Kramer, S. N., *Sumerian Mythology*
SpG   Speiser, E. A., *Genesis*
S R H   Baron, S., *Social and Religious History of the Jews*
Thesaurus   Ben Yehuda, E., *Thesaurus Totius Hebraitatis*
Toldot   Kaufmann, Y., *Toldot Ha'Emunah HaYisre'elit*
V R G   Von Rad, G., *Genesis*
V T   *Vetus Testamentum*
W H J P   Speiser, E. A., ed., *World History of the Jewish People*
Y K J V   Haran, M., ed., *Yehezkel Kaufmann Jubilee Volume*
Z A W   *Zeitschrift für die Alttestamentliche Wissenschaft*
Z D M G   *Zeitschrift der Deutschen Morgenländischen Gesellschaft*
Z S   *Zeitschrift für Semitistik und verwandte Gebiete*

BIBLIOGRAPHY

Abramsky, S., "Melchizedek King of Salem" [Hebrew], *Beth Mikra*, XIII (1962), pp. 105–109.

Abramsky, S., "Whence came the Philistines?" [Hebrew], *Beth Mikra*, XIV (1962), pp. 100–103.

Abramsky, S., "Melchizedek King of Salem" [Hebrew], OLD, Jerusalem, 1964, pp. 142–164.

Aharoni, Y., "The Land of Gerar," IEJ, VI (1956), pp. 26–32.

Aharoni, Y., *Eretz-Yisrael Bitqufat HaMiqra*, Jerusalem, 1962.

Aharoni, Y., "Tamar and the Roads to Elath" IEJ, XIII (1963), pp. 30–42.

Albright, W. F., "The Archaeological Results of an Expedition to Moab and the Dead Sea," BASOR, 14 (1924), pp. 2–12.

Albright, W. F., "Bronze Age Mounds of Northern Palestine and the Hauran," BASOR, 19 (1925), pp. 5–19.

Albright, W. F., "New Israelite and pre-Israelite Sites," *BASOR*, 35 (1929), pp. 1–14.

Albright, W. F., "Archaeology and the Date of the Hebrew Conquest of Palestine," BASOR, 58 (1935), pp. 10–18.

Albright, W. F., "The Babylonian Matter in the Pre-deuteronomic Primeval History (JE) in GEN. 1–11." JBL, LVIII (1939), pp. 91–103.

Albright, W. F., *Archaeology and the Religion of Israel*. Baltimore, 1942.

Albright, W. F., "Two Little Understood Amarna Letters from the Middle Jordan Valley," BASOR, 89 (1943), pp. 7–17.

Albright, W. F., "A Prince of Taanach in the Fifteenth Century B.C.," BASOR, 94 (1944), pp. 12–27.

Albright, W. F., "Early-Bronze Pottery from Bab ed-Dra' in Moab," BASOR, 95 (1944), pp. 3–11.

Albright, W. F., [Review of HUCA (v. 16–18)], JBL LXIV (1945), pp. 285–296.

Albright, W. F., "Cuneiform Material for Egyptian Prosopography, 1500–1200 B.C.," JNES, V (1946), pp. 7–25.

Albright, W. F., "The Hebrew Expression for 'Making a Covenant' in Pre-Israelite Documents," BASOR 121 (1951), pp. 21–22.

Albright, W. F., "Northwest Semitic Names in a List of Egyptian Slaves from the Eighteenth Century B.C.," JAOS, LXXIV (1954), pp. 222–233.

Albright, W. F., *Archaeology of Palestine*. London, 1954.

Albright, W. F., "New Light on Early Recensions of the Hebrew Bible," BASOR, 140 (1955), pp. 27–33.

Albright, W. F., *From the Stone Age to Christianity*, Garden City, New York, 1957.

Albright, W. F., "Abram the Hebrew: A New Archaeological Interpretation," BASOR, 163 (1961), pp. 36–54.

Albright, W. F., "Some Remarks on the meaning of the Verb *SHR* in Genesis," BASOR, 164 (1961), p. 28.

Albright, W. F., *The Biblical Period from Abraham to Ezra*. New York, 1963.

Anati, E., *Palestine Before the Hebrews*, New York, 1963.

Artzi, P., "Ur Kasdim," OLD, Jerusalem, 1964, pp. 71–85.

Avigad, N., and Yadin, Y., *The Genesis Apocryphon*, Jerusalem, 1956.

Badé, W. F., "New Discoveries at Tell en-Nasbeh," in P. Volz, *et al.*, eds., *Werden und Wesen des Alten Testaments*, Berlin, 1936, pp. 30–36.

Baly, D. *The Geography of the Bible*. New York, 1957.

Baly, D. *Geographical Companion to the Bible*. New York 1964.

Bar-Deroma, H., "Kadesh-Barne'a" PEQ, 96 (1964), pp. 101–134.

Baron, S., *Social and Religious History of the Jews*, Philadelphia, 1952–.

Barton, G. A., *Archaeology and the Bible*, Philadelphia, 1917.

Barton, G. A., *Royal Inscriptions of Sumer and Akkad*, New Haven, 1929.

Beek, M. A., *Atlas of Mesopotamia*, New York, 1962.

Begrich, J., "Mabbul: Eine exegetisch-lexikalische Studie," ZS, VI (1928), pp. 135–153.

Ben-Shem, I., "The Location of Ur of the Chaldees" [Hebrew] OLD, Jerusalem, 1964, pp. 86–91.

Bentzen, A., *Introduction to the Old Testament*, Copenhagen, 1959.

Ben-Yashar, M., "GEN. 4:7," [Hebrew], Beth Mikra, XVI (1963), pp. 116–119.

Ben Yehuda, E., *Thesaurus Totius Hebraitatis* [Hebrew], New York, 1959.

Beroshi, M., "Hartumim," EBH, III, col. 287.

Bodenheimer, F. S., *Animal and Man in Biblical Lands*, Leiden, 1960.

Bottéro, J., *Le Problème des Ḫabiru à la 4e Rencontre Assyriologique Internationale*. (Cahiers de la Société Asiatique, XII.) Paris, 1954.

Braslavsky, J., *Hayada'ta et Ha'Aretz?* Tel-Aviv, 1947–.

Breasted, J. H., *A History of the Ancient Egyptians*, New York, 1908.
Breasted, J. H., *The Development of Religion and Thought in Ancient Egypt*, New York, 1959.
Bright, J., *A History of Israel*. Philadelphia, 1959.
Brown, N. O., *Hesiod's Theogony*, Indianapolis, 1953.
Bruce, F. F., *The Hittites and the Old Testament*, London, 1947.
Budge, E. A. W., *The Book of the Dead*, New York, 1960.
Burrows, M., "The Complaint of Laban's Daughters," JAOS, LVII (1937), pp. 259–276.
Buttrick, G. A., Ed., *The Interpreter's Dictionary of the Bible*, 4 vols., New York, 1962.

Callaway, J. A., "Burials in Ancient Palestine from the Stone Age to Abraham," BA, XXVI (1963), pp. 74–91.
Campbell, E. F., "The Amarna Letters and the Amarna Period," BA, XXIII (1960), pp. 2–22.
Campbell, E. F., and D. N. Freedman, eds. *The Biblical Archaeologist Reader*, 2, Garden City, New York, 1964.
Campbell, J., *The Masks of God*, 3 vols., New York, 1959–1962.
Cassuto, U., "Epic Poetry in Israel," [Hebrew], *Knesseth*, VIII, (1943–44), pp. 121–142.
Cassuto, U., "Eden the Garden of God," [Hebrew], *Studies in Memory of Moses Schorr*, New York, 1944, pp. 248–258.
Cassuto, U., *Me'Adam ad Noaḥ*, Jerusalem, 1953.
Cassuto, U., *MiNoaḥ ad Avraham*, Jerusalem, 1953.
Cassuto, U., *Commentary on the Book of Exodus* [Hebrew], 2nd. ed., Jerusalem, 1953.
Cassuto, U., "Abraham" EBH, I, col. 61–67.
Cassuto, U., "Dammeseq Eliezer" EBH, II, Col. 675–677.
Cassuto, U., "Jerusalem in the Pentateuch," *Eretz-Israel*, III (1954), pp. 15–17.
Cassuto, U., "Jacob" EBH, III, col. 715–722.
Cassuto, U., "Chronology in the Pentateuch," EBH, IV, col. 247–249.
Castellino, G. R., "Genesis IV 7," VT, X (1960), pp. 442–45.
Cazelles, A., "Connexions et Structure de Gen. XV," LXIX, (1962), pp. 321–349.
Chiera, E., *Joint Expedition with the Iraq Museum at Nuzi*, Vol. V, Mixed Texts, Philadelphia, 1934.
Childe, G., *Man Makes Himself*, New York, 1962.
Childes, B. S., *Myth and Reality in the Old Testament*, Naperville, Ill., 1960.
Contenau, G., *La Civilisation des Hittites et de Hourrites du Mitanni*, Paris, 1948.
Cowley, A. E., *The Hittites*, London, 1920.

Dannel, G. A., *Studies in the Name Israel*, Uppsala, 1946.
Daube, D., *Studies in Biblical Law*, Cambridge, 1947.
Della Vida, G. L., "El 'Elyon in Genesis 14:18–20," JBL, LXIII (1944), pp. 1–9.
van Dijk, A. M., "La Découverte de la Culture Littéraire Sumérienne et la Signification pour l'Histoire de l'Antiquité Orientale" *Journées Bibliques de Louvain, 6, 1954: L'Ancien Testament et l'Orient*. (Orientalia et Biblica Lovaniensia, 1), Louvain, 1957, pp. 5–28.
Dinur, B-Z., "The Narratives Concerning the Name 'Israel' and the Biblical Tradition Thereon" [Hebrew], OLD, Jerusalem, 1964, pp. 114–141.

Dossin, G., "Les Archives Economiques du Palais de Mari," *Syria*, XX (1939), pp. 97–113.
Drachman, A. B., *Atheism in Pagan Antiquity*, Copenhagen, 1922.
Driver, G. R., and Miles, J. C., *The Babylonian Laws*, 2 vols., Oxford, 1952.
Driver, G. R., *Canaanite Myths and Legends*, Edinburgh, 1956.

Ehrlich, E. L., *Der Traum im Alten Testament*, Berlin, 1953. (BZAW 73).
Eichrodt, N., *Theology of the Old Testament*, London, 1961.
Eissfeldt, O., "The Alphabetical Cuneiform Texts from Ras Shamra Published in 'Le Palais Royal d'Ugarit,' v. II, 1957," JSS, V (1960), pp. 1–49.
Eissfeldt, O., "Der Gott Bethel," AR, XXVIII (1930), pp. 1–30.
Eliade, M., *Cosmos and History*, New York, 1959.
Eliade, M., *The Forge and the Crucible*, New York, 1962.
Encyclopaedia Biblica, [Hebrew], Jerusalem, 1950–.
Evans, G., " 'Coming' and 'Going' at the City Gate—A discussion of Professor Speiser's Paper," BASOR, 150 (1958), pp. 28–33.

Fensham, F. C., "Salt as Curse in the Old Testament and Ancient Near East," BA, XXV (1962), pp. 48–50.
Finegan, J., *Light From the Ancient Past*, Princeton, N.J., 1959.
Finkelstein, J. J., "Bible and Babel," *Commentary*, v. 26, (1958), pp. 431–444.
Finley, M. I., *The World of Odysseus*, New York, 1959.
Fisher, L. R., "Abraham and his Priest-King" JBL, LXXXI (1962), pp. 264–270.
Forbes, R. J., *Studies in Ancient Technology*, 8 vols., Leiden, 1955–1964.
Franken, H. J., *et al.*, *A Primer of Old Testament Archaeology*, Leiden, 1963.
Frankfort, H., *Cylinder Seals*, London, 1939.
Frankfort, H., *Ancient Egyptian Religion*, New York, 1948.
Frankfort, H., *Kingship and the Gods*, Chicago, 1948.
Frankfort, H., *The Problem of Similarity in Ancient Near Eastern Religions*, (The Frazer Lecture, 1950), Oxford, 1951.
Frankfort, H., *The Birth of Civilization in the Ancient Near East*, New York, 1956.
Frankfort, H., et al., *Before Philosophy*, Baltimore, 1961.
Frazer, J., *Folklore in the Old Testament*, 3 vols., London, 1919.
Free, J. P., "Abraham's Camels," JNES, III (1944), pp. 187–193.
Freedman, D. N., "The Original Name of Jacob," IEJ, 13 (1963), pp. 125–126.
Friedrich, J., *Die Hethitischen Gesetze*, Leiden, 1959.

Garelli, P., ed., *Gilgamesh et sa Légende*, Paris, 1960.
Gaster, T. H., "Cosmogony," IDB, I, pp. 702–709.
Gaster, T. H., *Thespis*, New York, 1961.
Gevaryahu, H. M., "In Clarification of the Nature of the *Terafim* in the Bible," [Hebrew], *Beth Mikra*, XV (1962), pp. 81–86.
Gibson, J. C. L., "Light from Mari on the Patriarchs," JSS, VII (1962), pp. 44–62.
Ginsberg, H. L., "Hosea's Ephraim, More Fool than Knave," JBL, LXXX (1961), pp. 339–347.
Ginzberg, L., *Legends of the Jews*, 7 vols., Philadelphia, 1909–1938.
Ginzberg, L., and A. Weiss, eds., *Studies in Memory of Moses Schorr*, New York, 1944.
Glueck, N., *The River Jordan*, Philadelphia, 1946.

Glueck, N., "The Age of Abraham in the Negeb," BA, XVIII (1955), pp. 2-9.

Glueck, N., "The Negev," BA, XXII (1959), pp. 82-97.

Glueck, N., *Rivers in the Desert*, New York, 1959.

Goetze, A., and Levy, S., "A fragment of the Gilgamesh Epic from Megiddo," [Hebrew], *Atiqot*, II (1957-58), pp. 108-115, [English] (1959), pp. 121-128.

Goetz, A., *Kleinasien*, 2nd ed., Munich, 1957.

Goetz, A., "Remarks on the Ration Lists from Alalakh VII," JCS, XIII (1959), pp. 34-38.

Gordis, R., "Corporate Personality in Job: A Note on 22:29-30," JNES, IV, (1945), pp. 54-55.

Gordis, R., "The Knowledge of Good and Evil in the Old Testament and the Qumran Scrolls," JBL, LXXVI (1957), pp. 123-138.

Gordon, C. H., "Fratriarchy in the Old Testament," JBL, LIV (1935), pp. 223-231.

Gordon, C. H., "Parallèles Nouziens aux Lois et Coutumes de l'Ancien Testament," RB, XLIV (1935), pp. 34-41.

Gordon, C. H., "The Story of Jacob and Laban in the Light of the Nuzi Tablets," BASOR, 66 (1937), pp. 25-27.

Gordon, C. H., "Biblical Customs and the Nuzi Tablets," BA, III (1940), 1-12.

Gordon, C. H., *Ugaritic Literature*, Rome, 1949.

Gordon, C. H., *Ugaritic Manual*, Rome, 1955.

Gordon, C. H., "Colonies and Enclaves," *Studi Orientalistici in Onore di Giorgio Levi della Vida*, Instituto per l'Oriente, I, pp. 409-419, Rome, 1956.

Gordon, C. H., "Abraham of Ur" in *Hebrew and Semitic Studies Presented to G. R. Driver*, Oxford, 1963, pp. 77-84.

Gordon, C. H., "Abraham and the Merchants of Ura," JNES, XVII (1958), pp. 28-31.

Gordon, C. H., *Before the Bible*, London, 1962.

Gordon, C. H., *The Ancient Near East*, New York, 1965.

Graham, W. C., and H. G. May, *Culture and Conscience*, Chicago, 1936.

Graves, R., *The Greek Myths*, 2 vols, New York, 1955.

Gray, M. P., "The Ḥâbirū-Hebrew Problem in the Light of the Source Material Available at Present," HUCA, XXIX (1958), pp. 135-202.

Greenberg, M., *The Ḥab/piru*, New Haven, 1955.

Greenberg, M., "Another Look at Rachel's Theft of the Teraphim," JBL, LXXXI (1962), pp. 239-248.

Gressman, H., *The Tower of Babel*, New York, 1928.

Grintz, J. M., "The Philistines in Gerar and the Philistines on the Sea Coast," [Hebrew], *Studies in Memory of Moses Schorr*, New York, 1944, pp. 96-112.

Grintz, J. M., "The Immigration of the First Philistines in the Inscriptions" [Hebrew], *Tarbiz*, 17 (1945-46), pp. 32-42; 19 (1947-48), p. 64.

Grintz, J. M., "The Land of the Hebrews," [Hebrew], OLD, Jerusalem, 1964, pp. 92-102.

Gunkel, H., *Schöpfung und Chaos in Urzeit und Endzeit*, Göttingen, 1921.

Gunkel, H., *Genesis*, 5th ed., Göttingen, 1922.

Gunkel, H., *The Legends of Genesis*, New York, 1964.

Gurney, O. R., *The Hittites*, London, 1952.

Güterbock, H. G., "Het, Hittites," EBH, III, col. 320-355.

Guttmann, J., "The Story of the 'Generation of the Dispersal' in Greek Literature," [Hebrew], in OLD, Jerusalem, 1964, pp. 585-594.

Halkin, A. S. "The Medieval Jewish Attitude Toward Hebrew," in: Altmann, ·A., ed. *Biblical and Other Studies,* Cambridge, Mass., 1963, pp. 233-248.

Haran, M., "Descriptive Outline of the Religion of the Patriarchs," [Hebrew] OLD, Jerusalem, 1964, pp. 40-70.

Haran, M., ed., *Yehezkel Kaufmann Jubilee Volume,* Jerusalem, 1960.

Harland, J. P., "Sodom and Gomorrah," BA, V (1942), pp. 17-32; VI (1943), pp. 41-54.

Harris, R., "Old Babylonian Temple Loans," JCS, XIV, (1960), pp. 126-137.

Hawkes, J., and L. Woolley, *Prehistory and the Beginnings of Civilization* (History of Mankind, I), London, 1963.

Hayes, W. C., *A Papyrus of the Late Middle Kingdom in the Brooklyn Museum,* New York, 1955.

Heidel, A., *The Babylonian Genesis,* Chicago, 1963.

Heidel, A., *The Gigamesh Epic and Old Testament Parallels,* Chicago, 1963.

Henninger, P. J., "Was bedeutet die rituelle Teilung eines Tieres in zwei Hälften? Zur Deutung von Gen. 15, 9ff.," *Biblica,* XXXIV (1953), pp. 344-353.

Hertz, J. H., *The Pentateuch and Haftorahs,* London, 1938.

Holt, J. M., *The Patriarchs of Israel,* Nashville, 1964.

Hooke, S. H., *Babylonian and Assyrian Religion,* Oxford, 1962.

Hyatt, J. P., "The Deity Bethel and the Old Testament," JAOS, LIX (1939), pp. 81-98.

Isserlin, B. S. L., "On Some Possible Early Occurrences of the Camel in Palestine," PEQ, LXXXII (1950), pp. 50-53.

Jacobsen, Th., *The Sumerian King List,* Chicago, 1939.

James, E. O., *The Ancient Gods,* London, 1960.

Janssen, J. M. A., "On the Ideal Lifetime of the Egyptian," OMRO, XXXI (1950), pp. 33-44.

Janssen, J. M. A., "Fonctionnaires Sémites au Service de l'Égypte," *Chronique d'Égypte,* XXVI, No. 51 (1951), pp. 50-62.

Janssen, J. M. A., "À Travers les Publications Égyptologiques Récentes Concernant l'Ancien Testament" *Journées Bibliques de Louvain, 6, 1954: L'Ancien Testament et l'Orient.* (Orientalia et Biblica Lovaniensia, I), pp. 29-63.

Janssen, J. M. A., "Egyptological Remarks on the Story of Joseph in Genesis," JEOL, V (1959), pp. 63-72.

Jastrow, M., *Religious Belief in Babylon and Assyria,* New York, 1911.

Kadushin, M., *Worship and Ethics,* Chicago, 1964.

Kapelrud, A. S., "Temple Building, a Task for Gods and Kings," *Orientalia,* XXXII (1963), pp. 56-62.

Kardimon, S., "Adoption as a Remedy for Infertility in the Period of the Patriarchs," JSS, III (1958), pp. 123-126.

Kaufmann, Y., "The Bible and Mythological Polytheism," JBL, LXX (1951), pp. 179-197.

Kaufmann, Y., "The Genesis and Nature of the Religion of Israel," [Hebrew] *Molad,* 17 (1959), pp. 331-338.

Kaufmann, Y., *Toldot Ha'Emunah HaYisre'elit,* [Hebrew], Tel-Aviv, 1942-1956.

Kaufmann, Y., *Joshua,* [Hebrew], Jerusalem, 1959.

Kaufmann, Y. *The Religion of Israel,* Chicago, 1960.

Kaufmann, Y., "The Hebrews in Biblical Literature," [Hebrew], OLD, Jerusalem, 1964, pp. 103-113.

Kelso, J. L., and A. R. Power, "Glance Pitch from Tell Beit Mirsim" BASOR, 95 (1944), pp. 14-18.

Kittel, R., *Biblica Hebraica*, 3rd ed., Stuttgart, 1945.

Koehler, L. and Baumgartner, W., *Lexicon in Veteris Testamenti Libros*, Leiden, 1948-1953.

Köhler, L., *Hebrew Man*, New York, 1956.

Kraeling, E. G., "The Earliest Hebrew Flood Story," JBL, LXVI (1947), pp. 279-293.

Kraeling, E. G., "The Tower of Babel," JAOS, 40 (1920), pp. 276-281.

Kraeling, E. G., "Xisouthros, Deucalion and the Flood Traditions," JAOS, 67 (1947), pp. 177-183.

Kramer, S. N., "The Epic of Gilgamesh and its Sumerian Sources," JAOS, LXIV (1944), pp. 7-23, 83.

Kramer, S. N., *History Begins at Sumer*, New York, 1959.

Kramer, S. N., "Man's Golden Age: A Sumerian Parallel to Genesis XI.1," JAOS, LXIII (1943), pp. 191-194.

Kramer, S. N., "Sumerian Literature and the Bible," SBO, III (1959), pp. 185-204.

Kramer, S. N., *Sumerian Mythology*, New York, 1961.

Lambdin, T. O., "Egyptian Loan Words in the Old Testament," JAOS, LXXIII (1953), pp. 145-155.

Lambert, W. G., *Babylonian Wisdom Literature*, Oxford, 1960.

Lambert, W. G., "The Domesticated Camel in the Second Millennium—Evidence from Alalakh and Ugarit," BASOR, 160 (1960), pp. 42-43.

Lambert, W. G., "New Light on the Babylonian Flood," JSS, V (1960), pp. 113-23.

Langdon, S., *Building Inscriptions of the Neo-Babylonian Empire*, Paris, 1905.

Lehmann, M. R., "Abraham's Purchase of Machpelah and Hittite Law," BASOR, 129 (1953), pp. 15-18.

Lewy, J., "Ḫabirū and Hebrews," HUCA, XIV (1939), pp. 587-623.

Lewy, H., "Nāḫ et Rušpān," *Mélanges Syriens offert à M. René Dussaud*, Paris, 1939, I, pp. 273-275.

Lewy, J., "A New Parallel Between ḪĀBIRŪ and Hebrews," HUCA, XV (1940), pp. 47-58.

Lewy, H. & J., "The Origin of the Week and the Oldest West Asiatic Calendar," HUCA, XVII, (1942-43), pp. 1-152.ᶜ

Lewy, J., "The Old West Semitic Sun-God Ḥammu," HUCA, XVIII (1943-44), pp. 429-488.

Licht, J. S., "Angel of the Lord, Angels," EBH, IV., col. 975-990.

Lindblom, J., "Theophanies in Holy Places in Hebrew Religion," HUCA, XXXII (1961), pp. 91-106.

Liver, J., "Melchizedek" [Hebrew], in EBH, IV, col. 1154-57.

Lods, A., *Israël des origines au milieu du VIIIᵉ siècle*, Paris, 1930.

McKenzie, J. L., "Jacob at Peniel: Gn. 32, 24-32," CBQ, XXV (1963), pp. 71-76.

Malamat, A., "Mari," EBH, IV, col. 559-579.

Malamat, A., "Man and the Bible: Some Patterns of Tribal Organization and Distribution," JAOS, LXXXII (1962), pp. 143-150.

Malinowsky, B., *Magic, Science and Religion,* New York, 1954.

Marcus, R., "The Tree of Life in Proverbs," JBL, LXII (1943), pp. 117–120.

May, H. G., "The Patriarchal Idea of God," JBL, LX (1941), pp. 113–128.

Mazar, B., "The Aramean Empire and its Relations with Israel," BA, XXV (1962), pp. 98–120.

Meek, T. J., *Hebrew Origins,* New York, 1960.

Melamed, E. Z., "The Purchase of the Cave of Machpelah," [Hebrew], *Tarbiz* XIV (1942), pp. 11–18.

Medenhall, G. E. "Mari," BA, XI (1948), pp. 1–19.

Mendenhall, G. E., "Law and Covenant in Israel and the Ancient Near East," BA, XVII (1954), pp. 26–46, 49–76.

Mendenhall, G. E., "Poppy and Lettuce in Northwest-Semitic Covenant Making" BASOR, 133 (1954), pp. 26–30.

Mendelsohn, I., *Slavery in the Ancient Near East,* New York, 1949.

Mendelsohn, I., "On the Preferential Status of the Eldest Son," BASOR, 156 (1959), pp. 38–40.

Mendelsohn, I., "On Marriage in Alalakh," in Blau, J. L., *et al.,* eds. *Essays on Jewish Life and Thought,* presented in honor of Salo Wittmayer Baron, New York, 1959, pp. 351–357.

Mendelsohn, I., "A Ugaritic Parallel to the Adoption of Ephraim and Manasseh" IEJ, 9 (1959), pp. 180–183.

Moore, G. F., *Judaism,* 3 vols., Cambridge, 1950.

Moscati, S., *The Semites in Ancient History,* Cardiff, Wales, 1959.

Moscati, S., *The Face of the Ancient Orient,* Garden City, New York, 1962.

Montet, P., *L'Égypt et la Bible,* Neuchâtel, 1959.

Noth, M., *Die Israelitischen Personennamen im Rahmen der Gemeinsemitischen Namengebung,* Stuttgart, 1928.

Noth, M., *Das System der Zwölf Stämme Israels,* Stuttgart, 1930.

Noth, M., *Überlieferungsgeschichte des Pentateuch,* Stuttgart, 1948.

Noth, M., "Noah Daniel and Hiob in Ezechiel XIV", VT, 1 (1951), pp. 251–260.

Noth, M., *Gesammelte Schriften zum Alten Testament,* Munich, 1957.

Noth, M., *The History of Israel,* New York, 1958.

Nougayrol, J., *Le Palais Royal D'Ugarit III,* Paris, 1955.

Oppenheim, A. L., "The Mesopotamian Temple," BA, VII (1944), pp. 54–63.

Oppenheim. A. L., *The Interpretation of Dreams in the Ancient Near East,* Philadelphia, 1956.

Orlinsky, H. M., *Ancient Israel,* Ithaca, 1956.

Orlinsky, H. M., "The Plain Meaning of Ruaḥ in Gen. 1.2," JQR, XLVIII (1957), pp. 174–182.

Orlinsky, H. M., "The Tribal System of Israel and Related Groups in the Period of the Judges," OA, I (1962), pp. 11–20.

Oz LeDavid, Biblical Essays in Honor of David Ben Gurion [Hebrew], Jerusalem, 1964.

Pallis, S. A., *The Babylonian Akitu Festival,* Copenhagen, 1926.

Parrot, A., *The Tower of Babel,* New York, 1955.

Parrot, A., *The Flood and Noah's Ark,* New York, 1955.

Parrot, A., *Sumer,* London, 1960.

Parrot, A., *Abraham et son Temps,* Neuchâtel, 1962.

Patai, R., *Sex and Family in the Bible and the Middle East,* Garden City, New York, 1959.

Pedersen, J., *Israel: Its Life and Culture,* 4 vols., London, 1959.

Pirot, L., *et al., Dictionnaire de la Bible, Supplément,* Paris, 1928.

Pope, M., *EL in the Ugaritic Texts,* Leiden, 1955.

Posener, G., "Les Asiatiques en Egypte sous les XIIe et XIIIe Dynasties" *Syria,* XXXIV (1957), pp. 145–163.

Priest, J. F., "*Orkia* in the Iliad and Consideration of a Recent Theory," JNES, XXIII (1964), pp. 48–56.

Pritchard, James, ed., *Ancient Near Eastern Texts Relating to the Old Testament,* 2nd. ed., Princeton, 1955.

Rabinowitz, J. J., "Ownership," EBH, II, col. 295–298.

Rad, G. von, "Josephsgeschichte und altere Chokma," VT Supplement 1, Congress Volume, 1953, pp. 120–127.

Rad, G. von, *Genesis,* London, 1961.

Rainey, A. F., "Business Agents at Ugarit," IEJ, XIII (1963), pp. 313–321.

Ravn, O. E., "Der Turm zu Babel," ZDMG, 91 (1937), pp. 352–372.

Ravn, O. E., *Herodotus' Description of Babylon,* Copenhagen, 1942.

Richter, W., "Traum und Traumdeutung im AT: Ihre Form und Verwendung," BZ, VII (1963), pp. 202–220.

Roscher, W. H., *Die Zahl 40 in Glauben, Brauch und Schriften der Semiten,* Leipzig, 1909.

Roscher, W. H., *Der Omphalosgedanke bei Verschiedenen Völkern besonders den semitischen,* Leipzig, 1918.

Rowe, A., "The Famous Solar-City of On," PEQ, 94 (1962), pp. 133–142.

Rowley, H. H., "Recent Discovery and the Patriarchal Age," BJRL, XXXII (1949), pp. 44–79.

Rowley, H. H., *From Joseph to Joshua,* London, 1950.

Rowley, H. H., *The Unity of the Bible,* Cleveland, 1961.

Saggs, H. W. F., "Ur of the Chaldees," *Iraq,* XXII (1960), pp. 200–209.

Sanders, N. K., *The Epic of Gilgamesh,* Baltimore, 1960.

Sarna, N. M , "The Psalm for the Sabbath Day," JBL, LXXXI (1962), pp. 155–168.

Schechter, S., *Aspects of Rabbinic Theology,* New York, 1901.

Schnabel, P., *Berossos u. die Babylonisch–Hellenistiche Literatur,* Leipzig, 1923.

Schunck, K. D., *Benjamin: Untersuchungen zur Entstehung u. Geschichte eines israelitischen Stammes,* Berlin, 1963.

Seeligmann, I. L., "Stranger," EBH, II, col. 546–549.

Segal, M. H., "The Religion of Israel before Sinai" JQR, LII, (1961), pp. 41–68.

Shalem, N., "Earthquakes in Jerusalem," [Hebrew], *Jerusalem,* II (1949), pp. 22–54.

Simpson, W. K., "New Light on the God Reshef" JAOS, LXXIII (1953), pp. 86–89.

Singer, C., *et al., A History of Technology,* 2 vols., Oxford, 1954.

Sister, M., *LeToldot HaHevrah VehaSifrut BiTequfat HaMiqra,* Tel-Aviv, 1962.

Skinner, J., *Critical and Exegetical Commentary on Genesis.* (International Critical Commentary), Edinburgh, 1930.

Smith, W. R., *The Religion of the Semites*, New York, 1956.
Smith, W. S., "The Relationship between Egyptian Ideas and Old Testament Thought," JBR XIX (1951), pp. 12–15.
Speiser, E. A., "New Kirkuk Documents Relating to Family Laws," AASOR, X (1930), pp. 1–73.
Speiser, E. A., "Ethnic Movements in the Near East in the Second Millennium B.C.," AASOR, XIII (1933), pp. 13–54.
Speiser, E. A., "One Hundred New Selected Nuzi Texts," transliterated by R. H. Pfeiffer, with translations and commentary by E. A. Speiser, AASOR, XVI, (1935–36).
Speiser, E. A., " 'I know Not the Day of My Death'," JBL, LXXIV, (1955), pp. 252–256.
Speiser, E. A., "Akkadian Documents from Ras Shamra," JAOS, LXXV (1955), pp. 154–165.
Speiser, E. A., " 'Ed in the Story of Creation," BASOR, 140 (1955), pp. 9–11.
Speiser, E. A., " 'Coming' and 'Going' at the City Gate," BASOR, 144 (1956), pp. 20–23.
Speiser, E. A., "Word Plays in the Creation Epic's Version of the Founding of Babylon," *Orientalia*, XXV (1956), pp. 317–323.
Speiser, E. A., "The Biblical Idea of History in its Common Near Eastern Setting," IEJ, VII (1957), pp. 201–216.
Speiser, E. A., "Hori, Horites," EBH, III, col. 57–61.
Speiser, E. A., "The Rivers of Paradise," in: *Festschrift Johannes Friedrich*, Heidelberg, 1959, pp. 473–485.
Speiser, E. A., "Three Thousand Years of Biblical Study," *Centennial Review* IV (1960), pp. 206–222.
Speiser, E. A., "The Verb *SHR* in Genesis and Early Hebrew Movements," BASOR, 164 (1961), pp. 23–28.
Speiser, E. A., "The Wife-Sister Motif in the Patriarchal Narratives," in Altmann, A., ed., *Biblical and Other Studies*, Cambridge, Mass., 1963.
Speiser, E. A., *Genesis* (Anchor Bible), Garden City, New York, 1964.
Spiegel, S., "Noah, Daniel and Job . . ." *Louis Ginzberg Jubilee Volume*, New York, [English Section], pp. 305–355.
Spiegel, S., "Concerning the Legends of the *Akedah*. . . ," in *Alexander Marx Jubilee Volume*, New York, 1950, [Hebrew Section], pp. 471–547.
Steindorff, G., and Seele, K. C., *When Egypt Ruled the East*, Chicago, 1963.

Tadmor, H., "Historical Implications of the Correct Rendering of Akkadian *dâku*," JNES, XVII (1958), pp. 129–141.
Thompson, J. A., *The Bible and Archaeology*, Grand Rapids, Michigan, 1962.
Thompson, R., *The Epic of Gilgamesh*, London, 1928.
Tournay, R. J., "Nouzi," DBS, VI (1960), col. 646–674.
Tur-Sinai, N. H., *Halashon vehaSefer*, 3 vols., Jerusalem, 1948–57.

Ullendorff, E., "The Knowledge of Languages in the Old Testament" BJRL, XLIV (1961–2), pp. 455–465.

Vandier, J., *La Famine dans l'Égypte Ancienne*, Cairo, 1936.
Van Trigt, F., "La Signification de la Lutte de Jacob près du Yabboq, Gen. xxxii 23–33," OS, XII (1958), pp. 280–309.

Vaux, R. de, "Les Patriarchs Hébreux et les Découvertes Modernes," RB, LIII (1946), pp. 321–348; LV (1948), 321–347; LVI (1949), 5–36.

Vaux, R. de, *Ancient Israel*, New York, 1961.

Vergote, J., *Joseph en Égypte*, Louvaine, 1959.

Vincent, L. H., "De la Tour de Babel au Temple," RB, LIII (1946), pp. 403–440.

Voegelin, E., *Order and History*, Louisiana, 1956.

Wallis, G., "Eine Parallele zu Richter 19 29ff und I Sam 11 5ff aus dem Briefarchiv von Mari," ZAW, LXIV (1952), p. 57–61.

Walz, R., "Zum Problem des Zeitpunkts der Domestikation der altweltlichen Cameliten," ZDMG, CI (1951), pp. 29–51.

Walz, R., "Neue Untersuchungen zum Domestikationsproblem der altweltlichen Cameliten," ZDMG, CIV (1954), pp. 45–87.

Ward, W. A., "The Egyptian Office of Joseph," JSS, V (1960), pp. 144–50.

Wellhausen, J., *Prolegomena to the History of Ancient Israel*, New York, 1957.

Wensinck, A. J., *The Ideas of Western Semites Concerning the Navel of the Earth*, Amsterdam, 1916.

Widengren, G., *The King and the Tree of Life in Ancient Near Eastern Religion*, Uppsala, 1951.

Wilson, J. A., *The Culture of Ancient Egypt*, Chicago, 1951.

Woolley, L., *Ur of the Chaldees*, New York, 1930.

Woolley, L., *Abraham*, London, 1936.

Woolley, L., "Stories of the Creation and the Flood," PEQ, 88 (1956), pp. 14–21.

Wright, G. E., *The Old Testament Against its Environment*, London, 1950.

Wright, G. E., ed., *The Bible and the Ancient Near East:* Essays in honor of W. F. Albright, Garden City, New York, 1961.

Wright, G. E., *Biblical Archaeology*, Philadelphia, 1962.

Yeivin, S., *Meḥqarim BeToldot Yisrael VeArso*, Tel-Aviv, 1960.

Yeivin, S., "Studies in the Patriarchal Period," [Hebrew], *Beth Mikra*, XVI (1963), pp. 13–47.

Yeivin, S., "The Age of the Patriarchs," *Rivista degli Studi Orientali*, XXXVIII (1963), pp. 277–302.

INDEX OF SUBJECTS

The Seattle School
2510 Elliott Ave.
Seattle, WA 98121
theseattleschool.edu